Fotos | photos EDUARD HUEBER

Liesbeth Waechter-Böhm

BAUMSCHLAGER & EBERLE

BAUTEN UND PROJEKTE | BUILDINGS AND PROJECTS 1996 – 2002

HANS ULLRICH GRASSMANN | ELMAR HASLER | JOST KUTTER | PETER RAAB | CHRISTIAN TABERNIGG

Das Werk ist urheberrechtlich geschützt.
Die dadurch begründeten Rechte, insbesondere die der Übersetzung, des Nachdrucks,
der Entnahme von Abbildungen, der Funksendung, der Wiedergabe auf photomechanischem
oder ähnlichem Wege und der Speicherung in Datenverarbeitungsanlagen bleiben,
auch bei nur auszugsweiser Verwertung, vorbehalten.
© 2003 Springer-Verlag/Wien
Printed in Austria

Graphik | Graphic design A | H Haller
Cover Bürogebäude Flughafen Wien-Schwechat | Office Building Vienna-Schwechat Airport
Reproduktion und Offsetdruck | Printed by
A. Holzhausens NfG., A-1140 Wien
Gedruckt auf säurefreiem, chlorfrei gebleichtem Papier – TCF

Übersetzung | Translation
Pedro M. López into English, Norma Keßler into German (Frampton Essay)
SPIN: 10875635

Bibliografische Information Der Deutschen Bibliothek
Die Deutsche Bibliothek verzeichnet diese Publikation in der
Deutschen Nationalbibliografie; detaillierte bibliografische Daten
sind im Internet über <http://dnb.ddb.de> abrufbar.

Mit zahlreichen farbigen Abbildungen

ISBN 3-211-83822-8
Springer-Verlag Wien New York

INHALT | CONTENTS

8 Kenneth Frampton

Bauten und Projekte
Buildings and Projects

20 VIE Skylink in Wien-Schwechat, A
VIE Skylink in Wien-Schwechat, Austria

32 Verwaltungsgebäude Saeco in Lustenau, A
Saeco Administration Building in Lustenau, Austria

38 Bürohaus und LKW-Werkstätte Ospelt in Vaduz, FL
Ospelt Office Building and Auto Repair Shop in Vaduz,
Duchy of Liechtenstein

44 Bürogebäude IT Data Center Zumtobel AG in
Dornbirn, A
Office Building IT Data Centre Zumtobel AG in
Dornbirn, Austria

54 Verwaltungsgebäude für WHO/UNAIDS in Genf, CH
WHO/UNAIDS Administration Building in Geneva,
Switzerland

60 Bürogebäude Münchener Rückversicherung, D
Münchener Rück Office Building, Germany

76 Werbeagentur Baschnegger, Sanierung und Zubau
in Dornbirn, A
Baschnegger Advertising Agency, Refurbishment and
Expansion in Dornbirn, Austria

82 Hafengebäude Rohner in Fussach, A
Rohner Port Building in Fussach, Austria

90 Betriebsgebäude Sirch in Böhen, D
Sirch Industrial Building in Böhen, Germany

96 Einfamilienhaus Flatz in Vaduz, FL
One-Family House in Flatz, Vaduz, Duchy of Liechtenstein

102 Einfamilienhaus in H, D
One-Family House in H, Germany

108 Öko-Hauptschule in Mäder, A
Ecological School in Mäder, Austria

118 Sanierung und Erweiterung der HTL in Bregenz, A
Refurbishment and Expansion of the Technical School
in Bregenz, Austria

130 Erweiterung der ETH in Zürich, CH
Expansion of the ETH in Zurich, Switzerland

134 Wohnen am Lohbach in Innsbruck, A
Lohbach Residential Project in Innsbruck, Austria

144 Wohnanlage Sebastianstraße in Dornbirn, A
Sebastianstrasse Residential Project in Dornbirn, Austria

152 Wohnanlage Achslengut, zweiter Bauabschnitt,
in St. Gallen, CH
Achslengut Residential Project, Second Segment
in St. Gallen, Switzerland

160 Projekt für ein 1.000-Betten-Krankenhaus in Kortrijk, B
1.000-Bed Hospital Projekt in Kortrijk, Belgium

Aktuelle Wettbewerbe / Projekte
Actual Competitions / Projects

166 Move TO, Projekt für die Porta Susa in Turin, I
Move TO, Project for the Porta Susa in Turin, Italy

168 Bürohochhaus Räffel Park in Zürich, CH
Räffel Park High-Rise Office Building in Zurich, Switzerland

170 Städtebauliche Planung für die Docks Prag 8, CZ
Urban Planning Project for the Prag 8 Docks,
Czech Republic

172 Bürohochhaus Hohlstraße in Zürich, CH
Hohlstrasse High-Rise Office Building in Zurich, Switzerland

174 Mega Hall für Peking, China
Mega Hall for Beijing, China

176 Städtebauliches Projekt Oosterdokseiland
in Amsterdam, NL
Oosterdokseiland Urban Development Project in
Amsterdam, The Netherlands

178 Fußball- und Baseballstadion in Sapporo, J
Football and Baseball Stadium in Sapporo, Japan

180 Werkverzeichnis
List of Projects

184 Biographie
Biography

188 Bibliographie
Bibliography

Kenneth Frampton

Die Arbeiten von Carlo Baumschlager und Dietmar Eberle sind, wie Dietmar Steiner in seinem 1996 erschienenen Aufsatz „Architektur vom Nullpunkt" betont, in ihrem Ursprung geprägt von der radikalen Vorarlberger Baukünstler-Bewegung der frühen achtziger Jahre. Zu ihr gehörten eine Reihe junger Architekten aus dieser Region, von denen einige von Roland Rainer beeinflußt waren, obwohl sie nicht alle – wie auch Baumschlager und Eberle – direkt bei ihm studiert hatten. Die beiden ersten gemeinsamen, wichtigen Arbeiten von der Mitte der achtziger Jahre, das *Haus Begle* und die *Wohnanlage Agip* in Lochau, stehen für diese stilistische Herkunft – vor allem die Wohnanlage Agip mit ihren hängenden Gärten und ihrer vom Gemeinschaftsgedanken geprägten Grundhaltung. Dieser mit vielen Grünflächen durchsetzte Gebäudekomplex ist für junge, berufstätige Menschen, wie es die Architekten damals selbst waren, entworfen und steht beispielhaft für ihre Haltung zum Thema Wohnen. Schon hier wird ihre Vorliebe für von oben belichtete Eingangssituationen zu den Wohnungen deutlich – in dieser Wohnanlage durch ein Treppenband, das drei Etagen verbindet und die stufenförmig angeordneten Wohnungen mit ihren großzügigen Terrassen, die einen wunderbaren Blick auf den Bodensee bieten, erschließt. Vorarlberg grenzt an einer Seite an den Bodensee, über etwa 40 Kilometer zwischen Bregenz und Feldkirch erstreckt sich eine lange Grenze zur Schweiz, und das Hinterland bildet primär der Bregenzer Wald. Derzeit leben dort etwa 350.000 Menschen mit einem für Österreich hohen Lebensstandard. Als das Bundesland Österreichs, das am weitesten vom Kernland entfernt und von Deutschland, der Schweiz und Liechtenstein umschlossen ist, mußten die Vorarlberger schon immer über die Grenzen ihrer Region schauen und haben gelernt, mit Hilfe der Tradition ihres Handwerks (das sich heute mit Ausnahme des Bausektors weitestgehend auf High Tech umgestellt hat) und ihren überschaubaren, recht direkten Formen kollektiver Entscheidungsfindung das Beste aus ihrer geographischen Situation zu machen. Regional geprägt, jedoch ohne die engstirnige Selbstgefälligkeit des Provinziellen haben die Architekten dieser Region erkannt, daß hier wie auch anderswo die Bauindustrie tief in der Region, in deren Klima, den zur Verfügung stehenden Materialien, den handwerklichen Fähigkeiten und vor allem in deren Bauvorschriften verwurzelt ist, und alles zusammen bestimmt entscheidend das Wesen dessen, was realisiert wird.
Der große Erfolg von Baumschlager und Eberle basiert eindeutig auf dem sicheren Wissen um diese spezifischen Vorgaben, die in ihren Augen bewußt anzuerkennen sind und in die Arbeit einfließen müssen, wenn der gesamte Berufsstand nicht in eine zunehmende Bedeutungslosigkeit geraten möchte. Zusammenfassen läßt sich dies in den Begriffen Wirtschaftlichkeit, Ökologie und Technologie, die selbst

wiederum mit zwei eng miteinander verbundenen und sehr wesentlichen Faktoren zu koppeln sind, von denen letztlich immer die Realisierung eines Projektes abhängt: die Lösung der politischen und finanziellen Probleme, um das jeweilige Projekt voranzubringen, sowie die schwierige Aufgabe, die gesellschaftliche Akzeptanz der jeweiligen Arbeit zu erreichen, also die Frage, inwieweit sich die Gesellschaft mit dem Ergebnis identifizieren kann.

Bei all dem bevorzugen Baumschlager und Eberle zunächst immer das Gespräch und setzen auf das kreative Potential des Auftraggebers und die Tatsache, daß das Entwerfen von Bauten eine Dienstleistung ist, für deren reibungsloses Funktionieren bestimmte Grundbedingungen erfüllt werden müssen. Beim Entwerfen müssen nicht nur die üblichen Anforderungen an Budget und Zeitrahmen beachtet werden, vielmehr wird der Gesellschaft auch ein gewisses Maß an gesicherter Technik geschuldet. Daher ist es den Architekten auch wichtig, Architektur als kollektive Anstrengung zu sehen, bei der es um eine Neuauslegung der Konventionen geht und nicht so sehr um das bewußte Entwickeln von neuen Formen als Selbstzweck. Mit dieser Absage an den Formalismus sehen sie, in Abwandlung einer Aussage von Adolf Loos, keinen Sinn darin, ein Detail neu zu erfinden, es sei denn, es stellt eine Verbesserung dar. Um im technischen Bereich eine Optimierung zu erreichen, setzen sie während der verschiedenen Herstellungsphasen auf erfahrene Handwerker und Spezialisten wie auch auf ihre eigene Kreativität und Fachkenntnis.

Darüber hinaus ist ihnen sehr wohl bewußt, daß qualitätvolles Entwerfen heute den hochgesteckten Zielen unserer stark von der Mittelklasse geprägten Gesellschaft entgegenkommen muß, wobei dies unterschiedlich stark von örtlichen Gegebenheiten und dem geforderten Maß an Wirtschaftlichkeit abhängig ist. Damit wagen sie den Spagat, einerseits nicht der unrealistischen Hoffnung zu erliegen, in einer solchen Gesellschaft Begeisterung durch die Diskussion weltfremder Architekturtheorie zu wecken, aber andererseits auch ihre Erfahrung einzubringen, daß die Menschen sehr wohl ein gewisses Qualitätsniveau wahrnehmen und sogar einfordern, wie zum Beispiel bei mehrgeschossigen Wohnanlagen einen zumindest kleinen privaten, gut ausgerichteten Außenbereich oder einen qualitätvollen Verarbeitungsstandard für ein individuelles Erscheinungsbild bei gleichzeitig angemessenen Unterhaltskosten. Wie an einigen ihrer Gebäude mit einer Mischnutzung aus den neunziger Jahren deutlich wird, setzen Baumschlager und Eberle bewußt auf den Einsatz von Farbe, Textur und Licht als wichtige Komponenten für ein markantes Erscheinungsbild, auf die handwerklich gute Verarbeitung von Holz, Ziegel und Glas, die je nach Kontext eingesetzt auch zu diesem Bild beitragen, und auf die Verwendung von teuren Materialien wie Kupfer, die aufgrund ihres luxuriösen Aussehens

As Dietmar Steiner points out in his 1996 essay *Architektur vom Nullpunkt*, the practice of Carlo Baumschlager and Dietmar Eberle has its origin in the radical *Vorarlberger Baukunstler* movement of the early '80s, that involved a number of young architects from the region some of whom had been influenced by Roland Rainer, even if, as was the case with Baumschlager and Eberle, they had not studied with him directly. Their first joint works of consequence, their Begle House and Agip Housing, both realized in Lochau in the mid 80s testify to this origin; above all the *Wohnanlage Agip* with its hanging gardens and communal ideals. Designed for young professionals like themselves, this complex interspersed with gardens already typifies these architects' approach to housing, their penchant that is for accessing any apartment building through central top-lit staircases that rise in this case through three floors to serve stepped apartments with generous terraces looking out over Lake Constance.

As the architects remark the Bodensee is not the only prospect that the Vorarlberg looks out on, since running for some 40 kilometers between Bregenz and Feldkirch and backed by the Bregenzerwald, Vorarlberg (encompassing today a population of 350.000 with an exceptionally high standard of living) has always been obliged to look beyond the confines of the region. Isolated from the Austrian heartland and cradled as a narrow strip of land between Germany, Switzerland and Liechtenstein, Vorarlberg has been invariably able to exploit the best aspects of its regional situation through its craft tradition (that today, apart from building, has been largely transposed into high technology) and its intimate, rather direct forms of collective decision making. Provincial without falling into the complacent limitations of provincialism its architects have been brought to acknowledge that, here as elsewhere, the building industry is deeply rooted in the region, that is to say in its climate, its material resources, its craft capacity and above all, in its building regulations that together play a decisive role in determining, in large measure, the generic nature of what is realized.

These architects owe their particular success to their constant recognition of specific constraints which in their view need to be consciously acknowledged and reconciled if the profession is to escape from its currently escalating state of marginalization. One may identify these as economy, ecology and technology, all of which are to be combined with two other closely interrelated and essential factors upon which any realization must ultimately depend, namely negotiating the political and fiscal sanctions to proceed with any given project, together with the delicate issue of assuring the social accessibility of the work in hand, that is the extent to which the society is able to assimilate the result. In all this the key procedure for these architects is dialogical, that is to say they are the first to concede the creative potential of the client and the fact that building design as a service must satisfy certain basic conditions to function effectively. It must not only meet the everyday requirements of budget and schedule but also ensure the society a certain level of technical security. To this end they emphasize the fact that architecture is a collective endeavor and that it turns on the reinterpretation of convention rather than on willful invention of form as an end in itself. Apart from such formalism, as they put it, paraphrasing Adolf Loos, there is no point in inventing a detail unless it is an improvement.

Wohnanlage Mozartstraße
Mozartstrasse Residential Project

Wohnanlage Mitterweg
Mitterweg Residential Project

Thus by way of technological refinement they look as much to skilled craftsmen and to specialists in the various sectors of production as they do to their own creativity and expertise.

Further to this they remain acutely aware that quality design must respond today to the aspirations of our largely middle class society, depending to varying degrees on the locale and the level of the economy. Thus while they are aware that one cannot hope to enlist the enthusiasm of such a society by discussing the somewhat esoteric intangibles of architectural culture, they also know from experience that people do respond and even demand a certain level of quality, such as say some modicum of appropriately oriented, private exterior space in the case of multi-story housing or, say, subject to the same rubric, a quality finish, which while imparting a distinguished image, will also endure over time without incurring high maintenance costs. They are conscious as one may judge from some of their mixed use buildings of the 90s, that color, texture and light play telling roles in the constitution of an arresting image and that precision joinery, brickwork and glazing are all equally reassuring forms of cladding depending on the context and that an expensive material like copper is capable of providing, despite its cost, an arresting and permanent sense of luxury. Sustainability, in every sense of the term, is also a salient factor in their architecture and not least when it comes to the consumption of energy and in this regard, apart from providing adequate insulation, they strive to deploy the latest methods for the re-circulation of heat and for the photovoltaic generation of electricity.

und ihrer Dauerhaftigkeit die hohen Kosten rechtfertigen. Nachhaltigkeit in jeglicher Hinsicht ist ebenfalls ein sehr wichtiges Element ihrer Architektur und dies natürlich insbesondere beim Thema Energieverbrauch. Denn abgesehen von der Verwendung einer geeigneten Wärmedämmung versuchen die Architekten, die aktuellsten Möglichkeiten zur Wärmerückgewinnung und der Stromgewinnung durch Photovoltaik zu realisieren.

Einen großen Teil dieses Wissens haben sich Baumschlager und Eberle über die vergangenen fünfzehn Jahre in ihrer Baupraxis erworben, als sie – wie sie es ironisch nennen – housing-Projekte entwarfen, wobei sie bewußt mit dem englischen Wort spielen, um den vielfältigen negativen Konnotationen, die sich im Lauf der letzten fünfzig Jahre auf diesem Begriff abgeladen haben, eine Absage zu erteilen. Abgesehen von diesen bereits erwähnten bestimmenden Grundsätzen liegt der besondere Beitrag von Baumschlager und Eberle zur Entwicklung des zeitgenössischen Wohnhausbaus in der sehr gefühlvollen Beziehung, die sie zwischen Typenform und Kontext herstellen können und die sich bei ihnen immer in der Auswahl des richtigen Typus für das jeweils spezifische Umfeld ausdrückt, unabhängig von der Frage, ob dies zufällig eine bereits bebaute Umgebung oder eher der Bauplatz auf der grünen Wiese ist.

Es gibt sicherlich kein besseres Beispiel für dieses Prinzip der typologischen Entscheidung in Relation zum topographischen Kontext als die kompakte Form ihres optimierten, mehrgeschossigen Wohnhauses, die sie 1995 bei dem *Projekt am Lindenweg* in Lauterach verwirklichten und die angepaßt an die jeweils anderen Gegebenheiten – einmal kompakter, ein anderes Mal offener – 1997 in der Bebauung einer Baulücke in der *Mozartstraße* in Dornbirn oder in der *Mitterweg-Siedlung* ebenfalls von 1997 sichtbar wird. In beiden Arbeiten zeichnet sich schon das von den Architekten favorisierte Gestaltungselement der Aufteilung der Baumasse auf zwei getrennte Baukörper ab.

Das *Lindenweg-Projekt* war einer der ersten Versuche, nach streng wirtschaftlichen Maßstäben bestmöglich ein mehrgeschossiges Wohnhaus im sozialen Wohnungsbau zu gestalten. Neben dem Erreichen eines möglichst guten Verhältnisses von Bauvolumen und Geschoßfläche – der goldenen Regel für Wirtschaftlichkeit beim Bauen – bestand die Entwurfsstrategie in diesem Fall in der Gestaltung der Außenfassade mit sich wiederholenden Modulen sowie der leichten Drehung der rechteckigen inneren Aufteilung, so daß Küche, Eß- und Wohnzimmer möglichst günstig ausgerichtet werden konnten. Ein umlaufender Balkon von geringer Tiefe garantiert bei den quadratischen Baukörpern einen in gewisser Weise privaten Freiraum für jede Wohnung. Diese recht stereotype Aufteilung wurde aber dann durch ein umlaufendes Band aus schmalen, geschoßhohen, verglasten Öffnungen im Wechsel mit Paneelen gleicher Breite aus senkrecht gestellten Holzelementen und Aluminiumjalousien, die bei Bedarf vor die Glastüren gezogen werden können, in genialer Weise belebt.

Die Planung zeigt bereits deutlich, wie wichtig den Architekten die Gliederung der Außenhaut bei allen Arbeiten ist; für sie bereichert dies die Gestaltung in entscheidender Weise und erhöht die Akzeptanz des Gebäudes in der Öffentlichkeit. Es war sicherlich eine gute Entscheidung, jedes der dreigeschossigen Gebäude am Lindenweg mit einem umlaufenden Dachüberstand mit runden Öffnungen zu versehen, wodurch an der Fassade ein besonders lebhaftes Spiel von Licht und Schatten entsteht. Ein Gespür für einen solch eleganten Touch ist bei jedem weiteren Wohnhausprojekt zu finden. Ebenfalls deutlich wird dies bei der Wohnanlage *Mozartstraße*, hier sind es faltbare, Kupfer verkleidete Fensterläden für die geschoßhohen, schmalen Fensterelemente, die in regelmäßigen Abständen die beiden fünfgeschossigen gemauerten Baukörper gliedern. Die Strategie der Architekten hier wie auch bei anderen Wohnanlagen besteht darin, die Fensteranordnung durch Fensterläden, die die Glasflächen entweder verdecken oder sichtbar lassen, zu beleben, damit sich die Gesamtgestalt des Gebäudes entsprechend den Aktivitäten und Bedürfnissen der Bewohner verändert.

In anderen Fällen, wie etwa bei den senkrecht stehenden

Lagertechnik Wolfurt
Storage Support Wolfurt

Most of this 'know-how' has been acquired through their wide experience over the last decade and a half in the design of what they ironically call house-ing, playing with the English term so as to deny the negative environmental connotations that have accrued to the term over the past half century. Apart from such salient precepts as we have already touched on, the unique nature of their contribution to contemporary residential development turns on the particularly sensitive relationship they have been able to establish between type-form and context, one which they invariably formulate in terms of the aggregation of the type in relation to the character of the immediate environment, irrespective of whether this happens to be built-up fabric or relatively open countryside. There is possibly no better demonstration of this typological principle in relation to the topographic context than the compact form of their optimized, multi-story apartment block as this first appears in their *Lindenweg, Lauterach* development of 1995 and as this type will come to be reworked under different conditions – more cramped in one instance, more open in another – as we may judge say from their *Mozartstrasse* infill blocks, erected in Dornbirn in 1997 or from their *Mitterweg* settlement, Innsbruck of the same year; both works ringing the changes on a twin-block theme which is one of their favorite paradigms.

Lindenweg seems to have been their first attempt to optimize, in strictly economic terms, the provision of multi-story apartments for lower-middle class occupation. In addition to minimizing the amount of exterior wall surface in relation to the floor area – the golden rule for economy in building form – the strategy adopted in this instance also

Wohnanlage Mildenberg
Mildenberg Residential Project

entailed maintaining a regular modular perimeter while skewing the orthogonal geometry of the internal subdivision in such a way as to provide kitchen/dining/living rooms of varying formulation and orientation. A shallow balcony running around all four sides of a square block-plan in this instance afforded some token of quasi-private external space for each unit. This somewhat mechanical provision was thereafter ingeniously animated through the perimeter fenestration, comprising narrow full height, glazed openings, alternating with vertical boarded timber panels of the same width and sliding, aluminum shutters, capable of sliding over the doors at will.

This scheme already demonstrates the importance that these architects have attached to the articulation of the membrane throughout their work, seeing this as a crucial syntactical enrichment, capable of enhancing the reception of a building by the public at large. It is surely a felicitous touch in the case of *Lindenweg* to provide each of the three-story blocks with an oversailing cornice pierced by circular openings, creating a particularly vivacious play of light on the upper face of the structure. A comparable feeling for the decisive elegant move is to be found in one housing project after another. It is only too evident for example in the *Mozartstrasse* development where it assumes the form of full height, folding copper-faced shutters that may be readily drawn over the narrow, floor to ceiling windows that are pierced at regular intervals into the five-story brick prisms from which the scheme is composed. The strategy here as in other residential blocks by these architects is to animate the fenestration by opening and closing shutters so that the overall gestalt will vary according to the movements and desires of the occupants.

In other instances as in the vertically slatted timber brise soleil of the *Mitterweg* blocks, such potential animation will give way to an iterated play of light and shade as the sun moves across the façade. While any change here in the recessed fenestration makes little perceptual difference to the overall image, the overriding, cut-out, slatted screens which constitute the façades permit the subdivision of the exterior periphery into private

Holzlamellen der brise soleil an den Gebäuden am Mitterweg, entsteht durch den sich ändernden Sonnenstand ein beständiges Spiel von Licht und Schatten, das die Fassade belebt. Eine individuelle Gestaltung der zurückgesetzten Fenster durch die Bewohner verändert kaum das Gesamtbild und die prägnanten Fassadenelemente, deren Holzlamellen für die Balkone ausgeschnittenen wurden, schaffen Außenräume mit privatem Charakter und zugleich wird die individuelle Nutzung und Gestaltung solcher Räume optisch abgeschirmt. Diese beiden Grundüberlegungen – Transformation des Fassadenbildes durch Fensterläden versus Verkleidung mit Holzlamellen – werden beim 1998 in Wolfurt errichteten, gemischt genutzten *BTV-Gebäude* kombiniert. Die Fensterläden aus waagrechten Holzlamellen lassen sich hier beliebig über eine in gleicher Weise mit Holzlatten verblendete Außenhaut schieben.

Bei allen diesen Wohngebäuden verändert sich das Leitbild des typischen Grundrisses entsprechend der Frage, ob es sich um ein kompaktes, mehrgeschossiges Wohngebäude handelt oder ob die Wohnungen des Gebäudes stufenförmig und linear angeordnet sind, wie etwa bei der *Agip-Wohnanlage*, was letztlich dann der Fall ist, wenn Baumschlager und Eberle Wohnungen mit einem höheren Standard für einen wohlhabenderen Kundenkreis auf einem freien, hügeligen Bauplatz planen können, wie beispielsweise bei ihrer meisterhaften, mit Schindeln verkleideten *Nüziders-Wohnanlage* von 1996. Gibt es bei der kompakt gestalteten Wohnanlage folgerichtig einen zentralen, großzügig dimensionierten, klar gegliederten und von oben belichteten Treppenaufgang mit Aufzug, um den herum durchgängig die Naßräume wie Bäder und Küchen angeordnet sind, besitzen die aufwendigeren Anlagen komplexere Verbindungs- und Versorgungssysteme, so zum Beispiel die an einer Gebäudeseite angebrachten, asymmetrischen, außen liegenden Zugänge in der *Nüziders-Wohnanlage* oder die mittig eingeschobenen, von oben belichteten Treppenhäuser eines jeden der drei stufenförmig angelegten, fingerartig ausgerichteten Baukörper mit Sichtmauerwerk der *Mildenberg-Wohnanlage* von 1999 in der Nähe der historischen Altstadt von Bregenz.

Die lineare Version mit zentraler Achse wurde auch in dem viergeschossigen Wohnhaus in Bludenz aus dem Jahr 1998 realisiert. Bei diesem Gebäude, das in gewisser Weise zum Prototypen wurde und unter dem etwas kryptischen Arbeitsnamen *V78* lief, wird eine kaskadenartig angelegte Treppenhauszone dreimal wiederholt, um den Zugang zu den 21 Wohnungen zu schaffen. Diese in der Tat recht geniale Möglichkeit, die in ähnlicher Weise auch in der Agip-Wohnanlage umgesetzt wurde, ist sicherlich inspiriert von dem wegweisenden sowjetischen dom kommuna-Bautypus aus den späten zwanziger Jahren. Aber unabhängig davon ist auch hier wieder die Südfassade als veränderbares Relief gestaltet, mit einer Wand aus großen Schiebetüren mit lasierten, naturfarbenen Holzrahmen und breiten, geschoßhohen, aufrollbaren Sonnenschutzmarkisen aus blauem Segeltuch mit Beschlägen aus mattem Aluminium. Dieser Prototyp erinnert daran, daß Baumschlager und Eberle einen Laubengang mit Außenklima als Erschließung in einem mehrgeschossigen Mittelklassewohnhaus aus Überzeugung ablehnen, da dieser weder das gewünschte Maß an Privatheit bietet noch allzu gut bei ungünstiger Witterung nutzbar ist. Darüber hinaus ist diese Erschließungsmöglichkeit eng mit der Vorstellung von Arbeiterwohnhäusern verbunden, die nach heutigen Maßstäben nicht als besonders beliebt gelten.

V78 ist nicht der einzige Prototyp mit experimentellem Charakter, den es im Laufe der unterschiedlichen Bauaufträge für Wohnbauten gab. Ein weiteres Beispiel hierfür sind die viergeschossigen Plattenbauten, die Baumschlager und Eberle für einen *Wettbewerb in Romanshorn* entwarfen, in denen ein zentraler Kern mit von oben belichteten Treppenläufen und Aufzügen paarweise angeordnete, sehr tiefe, durchbindende Wohnungen erschließt, die im Zentrum über Lichthöfe verfügen und damit in praktischer Weise den Wohnbereich vom Schlafbereich trennen.

Natürlich beschäftigen sich Baumschlager und Eberle nicht nur mit großen Wohnanlagen, sondern auch mit freistehenden Einfamilienhäusern, auch wenn ihnen bewußt ist, daß der ursprünglich ländliche Charakter, von dem die Region einmal geprägt war, durch die vielen Einfamilienhäuser grundlegend verändert wird. Sicherlich als Reaktion darauf, versuchen sie häufig, diese Art der Häuser als Metaphern des Landestypischen zu gestalten. So gibt es zum Beispiel einen solchen Bezug bei dem mit Holzlamellen verkleideten *Haus Kern*, das sie 1996 in Lochau bauten, oder bei dem Beton-Megaron in ihrem *Haus Büchel*, das sie 1996 am Fuß eines Alpensteilhangs in Vaduz errichteten. Qualitätvolle Holzverarbeitungstechniken spielen bei beiden Häusern eine wichtige Rolle, wobei es beim Haus Kern die horizontalen Lärchenholzlamellen der Außenhaut sind und beim Haus Büchel eine in Reihen angeordnete Vorhangwand mit Holzrahmen und geschoßhohen Holzläden zum Schieben und Falten ist, durch die die gesamte Südfassade in eine fensterlose Holzscheune verwandelt werden kann. Bei beiden Häusern schaffen streng abstrakte Formen einen leisen Anklang an das verloren gegangene „Ortstypische". Erreicht wird dies durch die Positionierung des Hauses und das Spiel mit Anklängen an ländliche Bauformen, die Baumschlager und Eberle in den jeweiligen Holzverkleidungen und Fensteranordnungen zum Ausdruck bringen. Dieser Kunstgriff ist auch beim *Haus Burger* in Bregenz aus dem Jahr 1994 deutlich sichtbar, bei dem die weitgehend undurchbrochene Nord- und Westfassade mit den traditionellen schmalen Holzschindeln der Region

balconies, while simultaneously screening the random, often cluttered occupation of such spaces. These alternative principles – transforming shutters versus fixed lattice screens – are partially combined in the mixed-use *BTV* block built in Wolfurt in 1998, wherein horizontally slatted shutters, move at random across a similarly louvered timber membrane.

In all this residential work the parti of the typical floor plan will vary according to whether it is a compact multi-story apartment block or whether instead it is arranged as a stepped, linear formation somewhat after the formation of the *Agip* Housing, as is invariably the case when Baumschlager and Eberle are asked to build to a higher standard, for a more prosperous clientele, on open undulating ground, as we find this in their masterly, shingle-clad *Nüziders* housing complex of 1996. Where the former invariably entails a central, generously proportioned and profiled top-lit-stair and elevator, surrounded by a more or less continuous wet-zone of bathrooms and kitchens, the latter is fed by more varied systems of circulation and servicing such as in the one sided, asymmetrical, exterior walkways employed in the *Nüziders* complex or the centralized, top-lit stair cores running down the central spine of each of the three stepped, spread-eagled, apartment blocks in brick that make up their *Mildenberg* housing complex realized close to the historic center of Bregenz in 1999.

The linear version of central axis also obtains in the four-story prototypical apartment block that they built at Bludenz in 1998. In this building, cryptically identified by the rubric *V78*, a single top-lit cascading stair, comes to be repeated, three times successively, in order to access twenty-one apartments. This only too ingenious device, similar to the *Agip* section, may well have been derived from a Soviet dom kommuna prototype of the late 20s. Be this as it may, here again the southern face is rendered as a transformable relief, with large sliding window walls in natural varnished wood and wide, full height roller blinds, with matte aluminum hardware and radiant blue canvas. This prototype reminds one that for Baumschlager and Eberle exterior gallery access in multi-story, middle-class apartment blocks is an anathema, for clearly such a mode, apart from its lack of privacy, is brutally inconvenient in inclement weather. It is moreover commonly associated with working class housing which in today's terms one can hardly consider as popular.

V78 is not the only experimental prototype to surface during the course of their diverse housing forays as we may judge from the four-story, slab blocks developed for their Romanshorn Competition, wherein central cores comprising top-lit access stairs and elevators afford access in pairs to deep apartments with full-height, central atria at the mid-section, conveniently separating the living from the sleeping zones of the apartment. Needless to say for these architects the topic of house-ing also extends to the freestanding house even though they are fully aware that the reiteration of this type is rapidly eroding whatever remains of the original agrarian character that once prevailed in the region. It is surely in response to this that they often attempt to render their one-off houses as vernacular metaphors as we find such a reference in their slatted, timber clad *Kern* House built in Lochau in 1996 or in the concrete megaron of their *Buchel* House

Verwaltungsgebäude Saeco
Saeco Administration Building

completed at the foot of a mountainous escarpment in Vaduz, Liechtenstein in 1996. High quality timber joinery plays a major role in both of these buildings, in the first instance as horizontal louvered larchwood envelope, while in the second it assumes the form of a tiered, wood-framed curtain wall, replete with full height, sliding, folding wooden shutters that are capable of converting its entire southern face into the simulacrum of a windowless timber barn. In both houses rigorously abstract forms make a subtle reference to the 'lost' vernacular by virtue of their siting and the agrarian allusions that are implicit in their respective forms of timber revetment and fenestration. This ploy is also evident in the *Burger* House, Bregenz (1994) where the cladding of the largely blank, northern and western façades, in the traditional narrow wooden shingles of the region, makes a reference which is even more direct, particularly since local farmers are still engaged in making these shingles during the winter months.

Apart from their continual permutation of a whole range of relatively economic residential forms from which the depth of their expertise so evidently stems, Baumschlager and Eberle have also played a major role as public architects, designing within the megalopolitan Vorarlberg region, one carefully appointed signature building after another, irrespective of whether it is a parish hall or a mixed use commercial structure, having an ingeniously contrived civic presence. This last surely accounts for the compelling character of the *Saeco* office building erected in Lustenau in 1998. Here we encounter a translucent variation on the theme of the layered, transformable skin, for in this instance a glistening, flush, steel-framed plate glass membrane is open to a potential play with full height, off-white curtains that are set some 90 cm behind the glass, running along the line of the free-standing structure. The result is an exceptionally graceful relief of uncertain depth, luminous and reflective by day and back-lit at night; an advertisement in itself for the elegant coffee machines marketed by the company and more than a match for the pink stucco lustro wall, enriched with a sheet of jade, that alerts the visitor to the welcoming presence of a cafeteria adjacent to the entry.

verkleidet sind. Diese Verbindung zum Ortstypischen ist besonders gelungen, da die örtlichen Bauern diese Schindeln in den Wintermonaten immer noch selbst herstellen.
Neben ihrem beständigen Bemühen, eine breite Palette von Wohnhaustypen, die sich wirtschaftlich realisieren lassen und die sie zu absoluten Experten auf diesem Gebiet haben werden lassen, kreativ umzusetzen, spielen Baumschlager und Eberle jedoch auch eine bedeutende Rolle als Architekten öffentlicher Bauten, und sie entwerfen für die durchaus großstädtisch geprägte Region Vorarlberg ein markantes Gebäude nach dem anderen, wobei die Nutzungen vom Gemeindesaal bis zum Gewerbebetrieb reichen und sie immer in genialer Weise Gebäude mit einer urbanen Präsenz schaffen. Ganz besonders trifft dies auf das bestechende Bürogebäude der *Firma Saeco* in Lustenau aus dem Jahr 1998 zu. Es ist die transluzente Variante des Themas einer wandelbaren, mehrschichtigen Gebäudehaut. Denn in diesem Fall läßt sich die glänzende, umlaufende, in einen Stahlrahmen gefaßte Glasmembran durch geschoßhohe, gebrochen weiße Vorhänge, die sich etwa 90 cm hinter der Glasfassade befinden und die Skelettkonstruktion nachbilden, verändern. Das Ergebnis ist ein außergewöhnlich eleganter Baukörper mit ungewisser Tiefe, glänzend und reflektierend bei Tag und von innen heraus leuchtend in der Nacht. Damit wird das Gebäude selbst schon Werbung für die eleganten Kaffeemaschinen dieser Firma, die ihre Besucher gleich in Eingangsnähe in eine Cafeteria mit einer lachsfarbenen Wand in Stuccolustro-Technik in Verbindung mit Jade-Elementen einlädt.
Eine ähnlich glänzende Eleganz besitzt das *Pfarrheim in Satteins*, hier befindet sich im oberen Teil eines langen Glaskubus ein Mehrzwecksaal und im Erdgeschoß ein Kindergarten. In beiden Geschossen gibt es entlang der Fenster rote Samtvorhänge, die als vertikales Element in einem gewissen Abstand von der horizontal angeordneten Glasaußenhaut aufgehängt sind und zusammen mit den regelmäßig angeordneten Deckenelementen mit integrierter Beleuchtung und Lüftung diesen von einer breiten Öffentlichkeit genutzten Räumen Würde und Ansehen verleihen. Wie auch beim *Saeco-Gebäude* besteht hier die Möglichkeit, die Gesamtgestalt des Gebäudes durch Zuziehen einzelner oder aller Vorhänge zu verwandeln. Schräg versetzt zu diesem kristallinen Baukörper steht ein viergeschossiges Bibliotheksgebäude als weißer, weitgehend opaker Kubus. Verbunden werden diese beiden Gebäude durch einen eleganten Vorplatz, überdeckt vom auskragenden Dach des Pfarrsaales.
Ein weiteres Aushängeschild des Büros von Baumschlager und Eberle neben dem *Saeco-Gebäude* und dem *Pfarrheim Satteins* ist der *Gemeindesaal Mäder*, der sowohl aufgrund seiner äußeren Gestalt als auch durch seine Außenhaut urbane Präsenz vermittelt. Die orange-rote Verkleidung der geschwungenen Form dieser Halle setzt durchaus ein beein-

druckendes Zeichen, dem die monumentale, atemberaubende Schlichtheit des weißen, kubusförmigen Eingangsgebäudes entgegensteht, das selbst wiederum durch seine klare Sprache an den strengen nordischen Stil in seinen besten Zeiten erinnert. Hier wie auch bei ihren anderen Planungen für öffentliche Bauten dient alles dem Anliegen, stützenfreie, flexible Innenräume zu schaffen, die unterschiedlichen Nutzungen angepaßt werden können und nicht nur einseitig als Konzerthalle verwendbar sind – auch wenn das fast schwebende, geneigte Dach und die schräg gestellten Wände besonders für diese Nutzung entworfen wurden.

Wie in *Mäder* bestimmt die Farbe Orangerot, eine absolute Signalfarbe, die Fassade einer über zwei Gebäude gelegten Brücke aus Verwaltungsbüros, die ein verbindendes Element in einem heterogenen Anbau ist, den die Architekten für die Dornbirner *Elektronikfirma Graf* 1995 planten.

Noch atemberaubender als gut gestaltetes, markantes Gebäude ist der Kupfer verkleidete *Gewerbepark Achpark* in Lauterach aus dem Jahr 1998. Vereinigendes Element dieses relativ großen Baus mit seiner sehr lebendigen Form voller Bezüge sind die horizontalen Stehsäume der Kupferverkleidung. Im Bauprogramm waren unter anderem ein Einkaufszentrum, eine Bank und zwei Ausstellungsräume für einen Autohändler entlang der Straße gefordert. Alle diese Elemente wurden geschickt in ein Atriumgebäude integriert, dessen oberen Abschluß Büroräume und sogar Penthousewohnungen bilden. Auf diese Weise wird aus der banalen, weltweit gleichen Gestaltung der Einkaufszentren auf der grünen Wiese fast so etwas wie eine Stadt im Miniformat.

Die Palette der Arbeiten aus dem Büro Baumschlager und Eberle wird sich sowohl in programmatischer Hinsicht als auch hinsichtlich der städtebaulichen Bedeutung der Aufträge erweitern, da die Aufträge von institutioneller Seite zunehmen, beispielhaft dafür stehen der *Gewerbebau* in Wolfurt von 1995 und das *Öko-Schule-Projekt* für die Innenstadt von Mäder von 1998. Beiden Arbeiten liegen quadratische, bezugsreiche Ausgangsformen zugrunde, innerhalb derer die unterschiedlich gestalteten Fassaden dem Betrachter immer neue Ansichten eröffnen. Beim *Gewerbebau* in Wolfurt ist diese variantenreiche Gestaltung weitgehend eine Reaktion auf das sehr heterogene Umfeld um den Gebäudekomplex. Die auf eine Autobahn ausgerichtete Nordfassade zum Parkhausanbau ist vollständig mit Gußglas verkleidet, während die Südfassade des Anlagenkerns einem Wohnhauskomplex gegenüber steht und ihr auf ganzer Höhe großformatige, verstellbare Aluminiumlamellen vorgelagert sind. Die Ostfassade wiederum schaut auf eine Autobahnüberführung und ist als massive Betonwand mit Fensterschlitzen ausgestattet, während dagegen die Westfassade auf freies Feld blickt und durch geschoßhohe Fenster und verschiebbare Fensterläden aus horizontal gelegten Holzelementen den Anschein von Tiefe

Gewerbepark Achpark
Achpark Shopping Center

A similar luminous elegance can be found in the *Satteins Parish Center* where a multi-purpose parish hall in a long glazed prism is combined with a nursery school on the ground floor. Both the hall and the nursery school are equipped with vertical banks of red velvet curtains which, suspended some distance behind the horizontal plate glass skin, impart to these public volumes a richly honorific status, mediated at intervals by the play of square, top-hung ventilating lights. Once again as in the Saeco building there is a potential for transforming the overall gestalt of the structure by drawing either some or all of its curtains. This crystalline envelope of the library is set at an angle to a four story library block that, assuming the form of white prism that is largely opaque towards the main approach, a form which counterbalanced by an honorific 'cornice' suspended above the leading edge of the parish hall.

As much a billboard building as *Saeco* or *Satteins*, the community center at *Mader* asserts its civic presence as much through its gestalt as through its skin, even though the orange red revetment of the sweeping form of the hall establishes a compelling icon that is countered by the monumental, arresting blankness of a white entry cube that with its raised metal lettering recalls the laconic style of Nordic Doricism at its best. Everything here as in their other public works stems from providing a column-free, flexible interior, one that may be adapted for purposes other than optimally serving as a concert hall for which its oversailing, inclined roof and canted walls have been so expressly designed.

As in *Mader*, the signal color of orange-sienna red is applied to the face of an oversailing 'bridge' of administrative offices which also serves as a unifying trope in a rather heterogeneous addition designed by the architects to an electronics factory, trading in Dornbirn under the name of *Graf* (1995).

Even more arresting as a well-dressed, billboard building is the copper clad *Achpark Shopping Center* in Lauterach of 1998. This relatively large structure is unified as a dynamic pin-wheeling form by the horizontal standing seams of its copper revetment.

Öko-Schule Mäder
Ecological School in Mäder

Umspannwerk Hörbranz
Hörbranz Transformer Plant

Programmatically it consists of a shopping center, a bank and two automobile showrooms facing the street, all these elements being deftly integrated into an atrium plan formation that at its highest point is capped by offices combined with penthouse apartments. In this way a banal feature of the universal motopian strip comes to be transformed into something approximating to a city-in-miniature.

The scope of the Baumschlager and Eberle practice will be amplified at both a programmatic and a civic level by commissions of a more institutional nature such as the flatted-factory complex completed at *Wolfurt* in 1995 or their *Öko School* projected for the center of Mader in 1998. Both of these works take off from square pin-wheeling formats, wherein their correspondingly rotating façades generate different aspects as one turns around the building. In the case of the *Wolfurt* complex this differentiation is largely a response to the different contextual conditions obtaining on the four faces of the building. Thus the north elevation to the parking annex, facing onto a federal autoroute, is clad throughout in cast glass while the southern face of the basic half cube, fronting on to a nearby housing complex, is screened throughout its height by adjustable, large scale aluminum louvers. Similarly the east face confronting a motorway overpass is rendered as a thick concrete wall with slatted windows, while conversely, the west face, set before open fields, is given a partly illusory depth by floor to ceiling windows and sliding, horizontally boarded timber shutters. While each elevation suggests a different inner content, varying from stacked parking to warehousing, laboratories and offices, there is no consistent correspondence between the differentiated articulation of the skin and the functional character of the space within. The sole exception to this is the parking annex which, accommodating the principal means of vertical access, is exclusively a mechanical agent, and here is appropriately clad in obscured glass throughout.

Given that the façades of the *Öko School* are essentially the same on all four sides of a square plan, the only visible rotary inflection is a recessed wood-paneled wall, at each of the four corners. The didactic intention lying behind this arrangement is succinctly expressed by the office description wherein we read: Both the volume of the four-

erweckt. Jede Ansicht vermittelt zwar den Eindruck, daß sich dahinter immer andere Inhalte – vom mehrgeschossigen Parkhaus bis zu Lagern, Labors und Büros – verbergen, jedoch gibt es keine logische Übereinstimmung zwischen den unterschiedlichen Gestaltungsformen der Außenhaut und den Nutzungen im Innenraum. Die einzige Ausnahme bildet der Parkhausanbau mit seinen vertikal ausgerichteten Zufahrten, er ist ein Bau mit einer klar ausgerichteten Funktion und ist entsprechend durchgängig mit verdunkeltem Glas verkleidet.

Bei der *Öko-Schule* dagegen, mit ihren im wesentlichen gleichen Fassaden an allen vier Seiten des quadratischen Grundrisses, ist das einzig wahrnehmbare, immer wiederkehrende Element eine abgesetzte, Holz verschalte Wand an jeder der vier Gebäudeecken. Die Botschaft hinter dieser Gestaltung wird sehr treffend in einer Beschreibungs des Projekts wie folgt dargelegt: Sowohl das viergeschossige Schulhaus als auch die flache, mit einem Drittel ins Erdreich abgesenkte Sporthalle sind kompakte Baukörper mit einer möglichst geringen Außenfläche und damit geringem Energieverlust. Der Entwurf orientiert sich an den engen Zusammenhängen zwischen Form, Funktion, Ökonomie und Ökologie. Die gesamte Fassade der Schule besitzt einen zweischichtigen Aufbau: eine Innenhaut aus Holz und Glas, außen ein hinterlüfteter Mantel aus geschuppten Glaslamellen. Das transparente Erscheinungsbild des Gebäudes verändert sich mit dem Stand der Sonne: „Erscheint es vage und unscharf bei niederem Sonnenstand, kehrt sich dieser Eindruck ins Gegenteil, wenn sich zu einer anderen Tageszeit die gesamte Umgebung darin spiegelt ..." (nach Wolfgang Jean Stock).

Nicht unerwähnt bleiben sollte aber auch, daß Sonnenblenden zwischen der Außen- und Innenhaut der doppelt verglasten Süd- und Westfassade angebracht sind, um eine zu starke Erwärmung der Innenräume durch Sonneneinstrahlung zu verhindern.

Wie bereits herausgearbeitet wurde, gestalten Baumschlager und Eberle großartige Industriebauten unabhängig von deren Nutzung, so ist es einmal ein Holz verarbeitender Betrieb und ein anderes Mal ein Versorgungsunternehmen, wie beispielsweise das *Kraftwerk von Alberschwende* von 1993, bei dem die zwei Flügelseiten als Bruchsteinwände ausgebildet sind und die Frontseite eine geschwungene Glasfassade mit vorgelagerten Aluminiumlamellen ist – eine Gestaltung, die an das fast fensterlose, vollständig mit Kupfer verkleidete *Umspannwerk in Hörbranz* von 1998 erinnert.

Absoluter regionaler Höhepunkt der Vorliebe von Baumschlager und Eberle für eine Außenhaut mit Latten und Lamellen ist der Bau für einen Holz verarbeitenden Betrieb. Dieses Thema erlaubte es ihnen, ein rechteckiges Gebäude zu entwerfen, das über seine gesamte Länge wie in eine Röhre aus Lärchenholzlamellen geschoben ist. Mit Ausnahme des Daches ist der als Konsequenz dieser Idee entwickelte, etwas bunkerähnliche, zweigeschossige Glasbau im gesamten Obergeschoß mit dünnen, eng übereinander liegenden Holzlatten verkleidet. Dieser Kubus mit seinen Holzlatten liegt auf einer Betonwand auf, die im Boden verankert ist und eine transparente, lamellenfreie Membran mit vollverglasten Schiebetüren als Zufahrtstore für die Laster zu den Holzlagern im Erdgeschoß darstellt.

1999 wurde Dietmar Eberle als ordentlicher Professor an die ETH in Zürich berufen. Dieser Berufung ging eine Entwicklung voraus, die das Unternehmen von einem regionalen, ausschließlich in Vorarlberg tätigen Büro zu überregionalen Aufträgen führte, was sowohl für die Größe der Bauten wie auch für die Bedeutung der Bauaufgaben gilt. Eine Reihe von Aufträgen und Projekten waren die Folge, deren Umfang und Bedeutung wesentlich größer ist und bei denen sowohl die Beachtung auf internationaler Ebene als auch die städtebauliche Bedeutung – sofern eine solche Dichotomie hier überhaupt möglich ist – größer geworden ist. Unmittelbar sichtbar wird dies an einem Projekt zur Erweiterung der *ETH Forschungsgebäude* auf dem Hönggerberg. Hier wurde ein sechsgeschossiger, freistehender Gebäudeblock um ein langgestrecktes, rechteckiges, von oben belichtetes Atrium mit zwei ebenerdigen Hörsälen für je 100 Personen geplant. Über diesen Rücken an Rücken gelegenen Sälen befindet sich die Cafeteria, und in den weiteren drei Geschossen darüber befinden sich Seminarräume, die in gewisser Weise „im Atriumraum hängen". Licht fällt kaskadenartig durch Lichtkästen im Dach in den verbliebenen Raum des Atriums. Die auf jedem Geschoß um das Atrium verlaufenden Galerien sind von den unterteilbaren Bürobereichen durch einen Versorgungsbereich mit Toiletten, Fluchttreppenhäusern, Aufzügen und Lagerräumen abgetrennt – eine räumliche Anlage, die bis zu einem gewissen Grad von den kompakten Wohnungsgrundrissen des Büros abgeleitet ist. Die Wände des Versorgungsbereichs haben zum Teil tragende Funktion und sind daher mit dem freistehenden Tragskelett, an dem die *façade libre* des Gebäudes befestigt ist, verbunden. Die vorspringende Außenhaut besteht aus einer Doppelverglasung und besitzt geneigte, geschoßhohe Sonnenblenden aus Gußglas. Das zusammen mit dem deutschen Architekten Hans Ullrich Grassmann, der seit 2000 Partner im Büro ist, entworfene Gebäude ist eines der drei in jüngster Zeit in der Schweiz geplanten Bürogebäude, bei denen ein zentrales Atrium ein wichtiges Element der Planungsidee ist. Sehr deutlich wird dies an der Machbarkeitsstudie, die das Team für die Rentenanstalt Swiss Life in Binz durchführte. Geprüft wurde die Möglichkeit von drei untereinander verbundenen, teilweise

storey school and that of the gymnasium, low in height and with a third of its mass below ground, are compact, with a minimum of exposed surface and thus less energy wastage. The design is conceived by taking the strict relationship of form, function, economy and ecology into account. The entire perimeter of the school façade is double-layered: the interior layer is of wood and glass, while the outer sheath-like layer is porous and constructed of vertical glass louvres. The transparent look of the building changes in relation to the position of the sun: "a diffuse aspect in low light gives way to its opposite, when the entire surroundings are reflected in it ..." (Wolfgang Jean Stock). Although the architects do not remark on it, it is perhaps important to note that sun blinds are installed within the double-skin of the southern and western faces in order to mitigate the greenhouse effect that may be induced by the impact of direct sunlight.

As I have already suggested these architects are naturally adept at handling industrial structures irrespective of whether this happens to be a wood workshop or let us say the occasional power facility that they have been asked to design, such as the *Alberschwende power plant* (1993), faced in rubble stonework and glazed on one curved side with aluminum louvers that follow the same profile or in the virtually windowless *Hörbranz Energy Conversion Plant* faced entirely in copper in 1998.

Baumschlager and Eberle's penchant for louvered membranes reaches a kind of local apotheosis in a timber workshop; a subject that would permit them to indulge in the idea of a rectangular building ostensibly covered throughout its length in a 'tube' of larchwood louvers. While the roof is presumably free of this conceit the resultant glazed, but somewhat bunker-like, two-story structure is louvered throughout its upper story with thin timber louvers set at close intervals. This slatted prism is poised on top of a concrete retaining wall which, set into the ground, provides for a transparent, louver-free membrane with fully-glazed sliding doors to facilitate truck access to the timber storage accommodated at the lower level.

Prior to Dietmar Eberle's appointment in 1999 to a full professorship at the ETH in Zurich the firm had evolved from being a regional, exclusively Vorarlberg practice in both scope and scale to one whose new commissions increasingly emanated from elsewhere, too. A series of commissions and projects followed which were not only larger in physical size and scope but also pitched at a broader international and civic level if such a dichotomous opposition may be momentarily entertained. This is immediately visible in a project to enlarge an *ETH* research facility on the *Hönggerberg campus*, that amounting to a six-story, free-standing block, is planned around an elongated rectangular, top-lit atrium which accommodates two, 100-seat lecture halls at the grade. The top surface of these back-to-back halls serves at a cafeteria on the second floor, while as the third, fourth and fifth levels there are seminar rooms which are similarly suspended within the atrium space. Light cascades down from rooftop monitors through the remaining interstitial space of the atrium. Derived in some measure from the firm's compact apartment plans, the galleries encircling the atrium on every floor are separated from the subdividable perimeter office space by a service zone, containing lavatories, escape stairs, elevators and storage. The walls of this zone are partially structural and as such are linked to the free-standing columnar system from which the façade libre of building is projected. This cantilevered membrane is double-glazed throughout and shielded by angled, floor height brise soleil in cast glass.

This building, designed in collaboration with the German architect Hans-Ullrich Grassmann, partner since 2000, is but one of three office structures recently projected for Switzerland which are based on planning strategies derived from a similar atrium parti pris. This is only too evident with the feasibility study evolved by the same team for the Swiss Life insurance company at Binz wherein three interconnected rectangular redent blocks are disposed in a continuous undulating formation in plan about equally rectangular atria, within which, as in the ETH project, certain seminar spaces and recess rooms come to be suspended. The exterior syntax in this instance is a total departure from their former practice in that the perimeter comprises structural mullions in reinforced concrete, set at close centers. Any thought of brise soleil has evidently been dispensed with and its function replaced by triple-layered, anti-solar glass.

The competition entry for the *WHO/UNAIDS* offices on the outskirts of Geneva is ultimately the most picturesque of the three propositions in that it responds to the mature bourgeois parkscape in which it is situated with linear landscaped atria that insinuate themselves ingeniously into the body of the office structure, raised five floors above the surrounding land with the grade level varying somewhat from one end of the block to the other. The paved foyer that penetrates as a promenade of semi-public space beneath the elevated office accommodation is flanked by the gardens of the linear atria, while beyond this top-lit green space lie additional bands of offices that faced in plate glass afford panoramic views over the surrounding landscape. The upper floors that crown the complex are conceived as being faced of serigraphic glass that while screening the sun and cutting down on reflection also imparts a deceptive, somewhat uncanny minimalist gestalt to the overall mass of building.

Baumschlager and Eberle's recent winning competition for a large addition to the existing airport of Vienna, designed in association with Bernese firm of Itten + Brechbühl, more than crowns, one might say, their career to date, since this commission will clearly be with them for a long time to come. There is something vaguely neo-constructivist about this project, which is also perhaps distantly inspired by the pre-war Tyrolean master architect Lois Welzenbacher, for the plastic energy of this scheme, partly derived from the dynamism of the autoroute and the rotary forms of the existing terminal, somehow also recalls the kind of landscape configurations engendered by Welzenbacher's architecture. The sweep of this project, conceived so as to encompass the potentially circular form of a pre-existing office park also gives rise to a large glazed structure housing all the multiple, multi-level facilities required by an international airport, while running out to feed two standard finger buildings, capable of handling some thirty aircraft.

It is hard to sum up the trajectory of this remarkable partnership for while they have long since secured their reputation as regional realists, they have also assumed from time to time, against their preferred image, positions which one could only describe as theoretical if not, at times bordering on the critical. In my view, they are to be as much valued

vorstehenden rechteckigen Gebäudeblöcken, die einen wellenförmigen Grundriss und rechteckige Atrien umschließen, in die wie beim Projekt für die ETH, einzelne Seminarräume und Aufenthaltsräume gehängt werden. In der Außengestaltung weichen Baumschlager und Eberle hier vollkommen von ihrer bisherigen Praxis ab und planen umlaufend tragende, regelmäßig angeordnete Stahlbetonpfosten. Sonnenblenden standen hier offenbar nicht zur Debatte, und ihre Funktion übernimmt eine Dreifachver-glasung aus Sonnenschutzglas. Der Wettbewerbsbeitrag für das *WHO/UNAIDS-Bürogebäude* im Großraum Genf wirkt im Vergleich zu den anderen beiden Entwürfen geradezu pittoresk, weil das Gebäude auf die gediegene, stilvolle Parklandschaft, in der es steht, reagiert. Dies geschieht durch linear geformte, schön angelegte Atrien, die sich großartig in den Baukörper des Bürogebäudes einfügen. Das Gebäude selbst erhebt sich mit fünf Geschossen über bewegtem Gelände mit unterschiedlichen Höhen. Neben dem gepflasterten Foyer, das wie eine Promenade als halböffentlicher Raum unter den erhöhten Büroräumen verläuft, befinden sich die Gärten der linear aufgereihten Atrien, während sich jenseits dieses von oben belichteten grünen Raumes zusätzliche Büroreihen befinden, die verglast sind und einen wunderbaren Blick auf die umliegende Landschaft ermöglichen. Die oberen Geschosse des Komplexes werden mit siebbedruckten Glasplatten verkleidet, wodurch zum einen die Blendwirkung der Sonne und die Wärmeeinstrahlung reduziert werden soll, und zum anderen dem gesamten Gebäudekörper eine trügerische, in gewisser Weise unheimliche, minimalistische Gestalt gegeben wird.

Der siegreiche Entwurf von Baumschlager und Eberle in dem erst kürzlich durchgeführten Wettbewerb für eine große *Erweiterung des Wiener Flughafens*, der in Zusammenarbeit mit dem Berner Büro Itten + Brechbühl entstand, stellt gewissermaßen die Krönung des bisherigen Werkes dar, und sicherlich ist dieser Auftrag eine langfristige Aufgabe. Der Entwurf wirkt neokonstruktivistisch und ist aufgrund der spannungsvollen plastischen Gestaltung möglicherweise auch inspiriert von dem Tiroler Meisterarchitekten der Vorkriegszeit Lois Welzenbacher. Die plastische Energie leitet sich zum Teil aus der Dynamik der Autobahn und den radialen, gerundeten Formen des bestehenden Flughafenterminals ab, was in gewisser Weise an die Verbindung von Architektur und Landschaft in den Arbeiten Welzenbachers erinnert. Die schwungvolle Gesamtanlage dieses Projekts, das auch den runden, schon bestehenden Büropark einbinden soll, ließ ein großes verglastes Gebäude entstehen, in dem die vielfältigen Angebote eines internationalen Flughafens untergebracht sein werden und das sich zugleich auch mit zwei fingerartigen Gebäudeteilen auf das Rollfeld als Andienungsgebäude für etwa dreißig Flugzeuge ausdehnen soll.

Es ist schwer, die Linie dieser bemerkenswerten Partnerschaft in wenigen Worten zusammenzufassen, denn während sie schon lange den Ruf als die Realisten der Region haben, vertreten sie auch manchmal, entgegen ihrem bevorzugten Image, Positionen, die sich nur als theoretisch, wenn nicht gar als kritisch beschreiben lassen. Meiner Ansicht nach, sollte man sie sowohl wegen dieser überraschenden Haltung als auch wegen der hervorragenden Eleganz und des Verantwortungsbewußtseins ihrer besten realisierten Werke schätzen. Die Tatsache ist offensichtlich, daß sie bei jedem Projekt das Potential der umliegenden Landschaft einbeziehen, und begleitet wurde diese Haltung bis jetzt auf jeden Fall von einem kompromißlosen Engagement für Nachhaltigkeit am Bau, nach modernsten und wirtschaftlichen Gesichtspunkten. Darüber hinaus sind sie bereit, die von unserer spätkapitalistischen Gesellschaft auferlegten Bedingungen, wie sie gegenwärtig in der sogenannten entwickelten Welt vorherrschen, offenzulegen, und deshalb mahnen sie uns zur Vorsicht gegenüber übertrieben romantischen Versuchen, die Lebensverhältnisse der Stadt des 19. Jahrhunderts zurückzuholen, die in vielfacher, nicht nur in formaler Hinsicht, sondern auch im Lebensvollzug verloren gegangen sind. Wie ein spätmoderner Architekt auf realistische Weise danach streben sollte, diesen kulturellen Verlust auszugleichen, ist noch lange nicht geklärt, insbesondere angesichts der allmächtigen, entpolitisierenden Macht der Medien. In einer sehr nüchternen Betrachtung haben Baumschlager und Eberle auf das sozio-kulturelle Elend eines nimmer müden Schaffens hingewiesen, das dazu dient, bestimmte Aspekte unseres ungleich verteilten Reichtums zu stützen. Aber – und das ist kein Zufall – alle diese Überlegungen finden ihren Ausdruck in der bis heute nicht zu leugnenden Lebenskraft und Redlichkeit ihrer Leistungen, da sie sich in neue Gefilde mit größeren Möglichkeiten und Herausforderungen aufmachen. Festzuhalten sind von ihrer Zeit in Vorarlberg, die sicherlich noch nicht beendet ist, ihre außerordentlich lebendigen baulichen Leistungen, die weltweit die vollste Anerkennung verdienen.

Bürogebäude Flughafen Wien-Schwechat
Office Building Vienna-Schwechat Airport

for this inadvertent stance as they are for the exceptional elegance and responsible character of their finest realized works. That they have always conceived of every project in terms of its landscape potential is surely self-evident and along with this has gone, most certainly until now, their unequivocal commitment to the realization of a sustainable environment with the latest and most economical means available. Moreover they have been prompt to expose the conditions imposed by our late capitalist, consumerist economy, as it currently prevails in the so-called developed world and to this end they have cautioned us against unduly romantic attempts to evoke the mores of a nineteenth century urbanity that in many respects is already lost, not only as a form but also as a way of life. How a late modern architect should realistically endeavor to compensate for this cultural loss is far from clear, particularly given the omnipotent, depoliticizing power of media. In their more somber moments Baumschlager and Eberle have even conceded the socio-cultural plight of the amphibian labor that serves to support certain aspects of our unevenly distributed prosperity. But all of this is but coincidental to the undeniable vivacity and probity of their achievement to date, as they now turn to tack into a different wind, upon the surface of a wider and more challenging sea. We can only say of their Vorarlberg career which may, as yet, be far from over, that it has been an exemplary vital, tectonic achievement that deserves to receive the fullest recognition at a world-wide scale.

VIE Skylink in Wien-Schwechat, A
VIE Skylink of Vienna-Schwechat, Austria

Erweiterung des Vienna International Airport und der Flughafenstadt Ziel des Realisierungswettbewerbes: die langfristige (bis zum Jahr 2015), zukunftsorientierte Neugestaltung und Erweiterung des gesamten Flughafenareals (einschließlich Flughafenstadt) und die Verbesserung der Verkehrsanbindung (S-Bahn).

Erster entscheidender Teilaspekt des Gesamtvorhabens: Der Flughafen Wien ist ein wichtiger Verkehrsknotenpunkt zwischen Ost und West. Die prognostizierte Entwicklung in den nächsten zehn Jahren soll eine Verdoppelung des Passagieraufkommens auf 20 Millionen pro Jahr erreichen. Trotzdem hält der Flughafenbetreiber an der in Europa einzigartigen „Minimum Connecting Time" von 25 Minuten fest. Das war eine wichtige Voraussetzung für die geplante Terminalerweiterung und den Pier Süd, der in einem ersten Bauabschnitt verwirklicht werden wird. Der Pier Nord, integriert in ein umfassendes, sehr langfristiges Gesamtkonzept, ist als Entwicklungsmöglichkeit von vornherein mitgedacht.

Zweiter entscheidender Teilaspekt: Die Flughafenstadt wird immer mehr zum wichtigen Wirtschaftsstandort, wo sich aber seit Jahren auch Hotels etc. ansiedeln.
Maßnahme in letzter Minute: ein städtebauliches Gesamtkonzept, das dieser bisher ziemlich beiläufigen Entwicklung einen definierten, urbanen Rahmen vorgibt. Das Projekt sieht eine ringförmige Umfahrung der Flughafenstadt vor und eine Durchwegung, die das Areal – trotz seiner ubanen Dichte – erschließt und überschaubar gliedert.

Schließlich als dritter Teilaspekt – die verkehrstechnische Lösung: Hauptzubringer von der Innenstadt ist heute ein kurztaktiger Busverkehr, dessen Zuverlässigkeit naturgemäß von der Verkehrssituation im städtischen Bereich abhängt. Die auch heute schon vorhandene Alternative einer S-Bahn-Verbindung wird dennoch wenig genützt, weil der heutige Flughafen-Bahnhof relativ unattraktiv und eher versteckt ist. Für die Zukunft wird es daher wichtig sein, diese Verbindung zu entwickeln, auszubauen und vor allem aufzuwerten. Der Flughafen Wien-Schwechat könnte vom Bahnhof Wien-Mitte aus in 25 Minuten zu erreichen sein.

Expansion of the Vienna International Airport and the Airport Town The project realisation objective: the long-term, future-oriented (by 2015) re-design and expansion of the entire airport area (including the airport town) and improving City Rail (S-Bahn) access.

The first decisive aspect of the overall project: The Vienna Airport is an important traffic hub between East and West. The projected development over the next ten years foresees a doubling of passenger volume to 20 million per year. However, the airport operator still maintains a 'Minimum Connecting Time' of 25 minutes, which is unique in Europe. That was one important requirement for the planned Pier Süd (South Pier) expansion. The Pier Nord (North Pier) is already integrated as a development possibility in a comprehensive, very long-term overall concept.

The second decisive aspect: The airport town is becoming an increasingly important economic hub that has also led to an increase in the number of hotels etc., built in the area. The last minute measure: an overall urban development concept that gives the rather coincidental development to date a defined urban framework. The project includes a traffic bypass ring around the airport town and pathways that structure and offer clear access to the area, despite the high urban density.

Finally, the third aspect – the traffic solutions: a short-interval bus service supplies the main transportation service into town. Naturally, its reliability is dependent on the urban traffic situation. An S-Bahn City Rail option exists, but it is rarely used since the airport station currently in use is unappealing and rather hard to find. It will therefore be important for the future to develop this connection and most of all, upgrade it. It would be possible to reach Vienna Airport from the Wien-Mitte S-Bahn station in 25 minutes.

Bauherr | client **Flughafen Wien AG** Planung | planning **ARGE Itten+Brechbühl AG./B&E Baumschlager-Eberle GmbH c/o P.ARC Baumschlager Eberle Gartenmann Raab GmbH** Projektsteuerung | construction manager **Drees & Sommer und FCP Fritsch, Chiari & Partner ZT GmbH** Projektleitung | project architect **Jost Kutter** Mitarbeiter | assistance **alle Wiener Mitarbeiter | the viennese office** Landschaftsarchitekt | landscape architect **Vogt Landschaftsarchitekten** Statik | structural engineer **Pauser-Thumberger ZT GmbH** Grundstücksfläche | site area **656.000 m²** Bebaute Fläche | built up area **44.000 m²** Nutzfläche | floor area **161.000 m²** Umbauter Raum | building volume **1,010.000 m³** Planungsbeginn | commencement of planning **2000** Baubeginn | commencement of work **2005** Fertigstellung | completion **2007**

Der Flughafen Wien-Schwechat wurde seit seiner Eröffnung im Jahr 1960 mehrfach umgebaut – und damit den jeweils neuen technischen Standards im Luftverkehr angepaßt – er wurde aber auch deutlich erweitert. Dieser – architektonisch teilweise höchst problematische – Bestand ist mit dem aktuellen Erweiterungsprojekt durch ein sogenanntes „One Roof Konzept" verbunden, so daß sowohl optisch als auch funktional eine Gesamtanlage entsteht. Die neuen Bauteile liegen östlich des heutigen Terminals 2 und bestehen aus einem neuen Terminal, einem Verbindungsbauwerk und den beiden Piers Süd und Nord. Die sichelförmige Gestalt des neuen „Skylink" setzt dabei auch städtebaulich einen äußerst signifikanten Akzent und wird durch seine direkte Verbindung mit dem erweiterten Bahnhof, zu den Parkhäusern und zur wachsenden Flughafenstadt das attraktive Herzstück, die dynamische Drehscheibe des gesamten Flughafengeländes.

Aus der Nutzerperspektive läßt sich die Problematik einer Flughafenneuplanung knapp zusammenfassen: Der Passagier möchte möglichst kurze, auf jeden Fall effiziente Verbindungen vom jeweiligen Transportmittel (Bus, Bahn, PKW) zum Flughafen bzw. umgekehrt, er möchte sie aber vor allem im Flughafen selbst; und er möchte sich orientieren können, obwohl die naturgemäß horizontale Organisation eines Flughafens und die additive Aneinanderreihung gleicher Funktionen (mit allerdings wechselnden Destinationen) diese Anforderung schwierig erscheinen läßt; und dann möchte er natürlich die anfallenden Wartezeiten komfortabel überbrücken.

Aus der Betreiberperspektive kommt zu diesem Anforderungsprofil noch einiges, vor allem in technischen, auch in funktionellen Belangen hinzu. Es geht um Fragen der Fassadentechnologie, der Haustechnik, der Klimatechnik; es geht um Sicherheitsfragen, um Schengen und Nicht-Schengen; um Transfer; und vor allem auch darum, welcher Flugzeugtyp (welche Flugzeuggröße) wo andocken kann. Aber das ist in Wirklichkeit nur ein ganz kleiner, lapidarer Ausschnitt aus dem Fragenkatalog, den es bei einer Flughafenplanung zu beantworten gilt.

Vienna Airport has been refurbished a number of times since it opened in 1960 – and thus been adapted to meet the newest technical standards of the respective time. However it has also been expanded continuously as well. This in part extremely problematic state of the structure is linked to the current expansion project via a 'One Roof Concept', to insure that one overall facility is created visually and functionally. The new construction segments lie to the east of the current terminal and the north and south piers. They consist of a new second terminal and a connecting structure. The sickle-shaped form of the new 'Skylink' emphatically underlines the project's urban planning aspects and will feature a direct connection to the larger City Rail station, the parking lots and the growing airport town. Hence it will be the appealing centrepiece, the dynamic hub of the entire airport area.

The problems surrounding airport planning **from a user perspective** can be summarised quickly: The passenger wants connections that are as short as possible and efficient inter-connections between the respective transport modes (bus, rail, cars) on the way to the airport and back, but most of all, in the airport itself. Passengers also want orientation to be easy, although the horizontal organisation of an airport and the additive alignment of identical functions (with changing destinations) make this a difficult requirement to meet. And of course he wants to spend any waiting time that may arise comfortably.

A number of additional requirements emerge **from the operational and functional point of view**, especially with respect to technical matters. These issues include the façade technology, the building's technical equipment and the air conditioning. Other aspects include whether the Schengen Agreement is in effect, transfers and most of all: where which type of aircraft (aircraft size) can dock on to the pier. But this is only a very small excerpt from the list of issues that have to be dealt with when planning an airport.

Städtebau

Das Bebauungskonzept gliedert den Bestand größtenteils ein, es schreibt ihn fort. Wichtigste Maßnahme: die ringförmige Umfahrung der Flughafenstadt, die eine klare geometrische Grenze, auch eine Stadtkante formuliert. Sie ist als Einbahn vorgesehen, die rasterförmige Erschließung innerhalb des Office Parks wird hauptsächlich gegenläufig befahrbar sein. Das Gestaltungskonzept sieht hochwertige, dauerhafte, pflegeleichte Materialien für die Gebäudefassaden vor, die durch ihre gläserne Transparenz – und eine sorgfältig ausgebildete Erdgeschoßzone – großstädtische Eleganz vermitteln. Ein umfassendes Grünkonzept – mit kleinen „Pocketparks" innerhalb des Business Parks – bindet das Flughafenareal in die natürliche Landschaft der Umgebung ein.

Urban Construction

The construction concept integrates most of the existing structures and continues them. The most important measure: the traffic bypass ring surrounding the airport town creates a clearly formulated edge of town. It is conceived as a one-way road while the grid-like access routes within the office park will be set in alternating directions. The design concept includes the use of high quality; long lasting easily cared for materials on the building façades. The glass transparency of these elements – and the carefully structured ground level area – convey a metropolitan sense of elegance. A comprehensive green areas concept with small 'pocket parks' located within the business park, links the airport site to the natural scenery of the landscape.

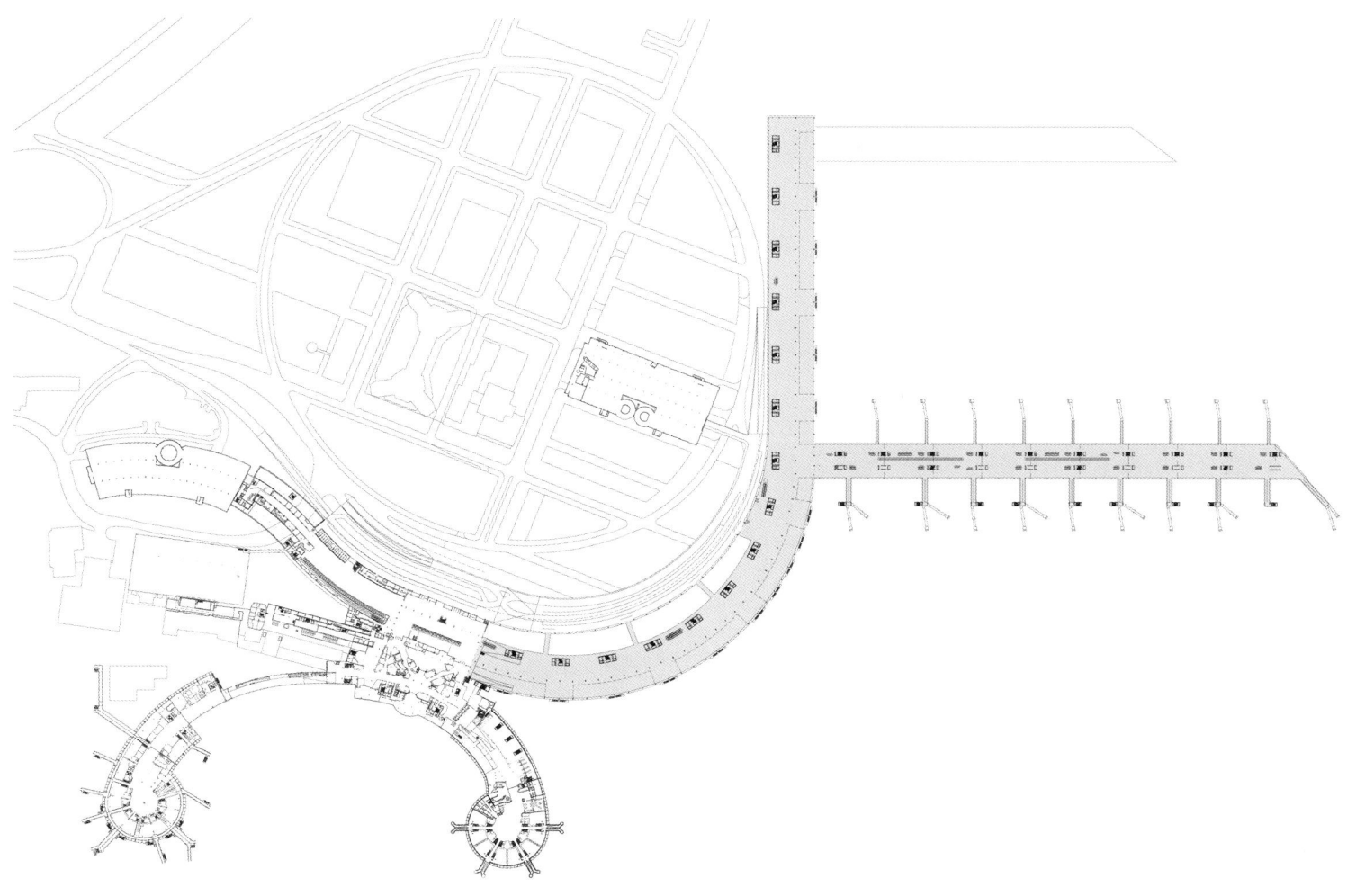

Lassen wir die organisatorischen, funktionellen Fragen im Detail beiseite. Architektonisch bemerkenswert ist am neuen **Gesamtkonzept**, daß die schwungvolle Figur des Terminalgebäudes sowohl landseitig als auch luftseitig aus einem Kontinuum ineinandergreifender Räume besteht, die natürlich belichtet sind und nicht nur den Außenbezug sondern auch innen drinnen vielfältige Durchblicke ermöglichen. Der Weg durch diesen Flughafen wird auf jeden Fall auch zum Raumerlebnis, und zwar zu einem differenzierten Raumerlebnis. Denn die einzelnen Abschnitte im Gebäude selbst werden trotz großer Einheitlichkeit der eingesetzen materiellen Mittel sehr unterschiedliche atmosphärische Raumqualitäten beinhalten. Das ist zur Identifikation und auch als Erinnerungsposition im Gedächtnis des Passagiers auf seinem Weg durch einen ihm fremden Flughafen enorm wichtig. Dazu gibt es auch jetzt schon, im Vorentwurfsstadium, sehr detaillierte Vorstellungen und Vorschläge.

Klar, daß eine solche Anlage auf der Basis einer modularen Bauweise errichtet werden muß. Das hat nicht nur ökonomische Gründe, es hat auch mit der erforderlichen Flexibilität einer solchen Gebäudestruktur zu tun. Und Flexibilität ist im Flughafenbau oberstes Gebot: Selbst die genauesten Prognosen bieten keine letzte Gewissheit.

Es geht also um Nutzungsneutralität und darum, die Gebäude „in übersichtliche Einzelteile" zu zerlegen. Der hohe Wiederholungsgrad steigert sozusagen die Betriebsfähigkeit, und die Vereinheitlichung von Materialien und Details steigert die Wiedererkennbarkeit des Einzelnen im Ganzen und wie nebenbei auch die Ökonomie.

Die Haut der Terminalerweiterung wird zweischalig sein, wobei die großformatigen, liegenden Gläser einen uneingeschränkten Ausblick bilden. Diese Haut ist eine äußerst filigrane Konstruktion, wobei die horizontalen, geschlossenen Tragelemente der Gläser die Fassade beschatten. Das Dach wird als fünfte Fassade aufgefaßt. Das Luftbild des künftigen Flughafens ist eine vereinheitlichende Haut, die den Hauptbau überzieht. An dieses Hauptvolumen stoßen die Piers an, ihre Eigenständigkeit wird dadurch ablesbar.

Let us put the detailed organisational and functional matters aside. What is remarkable architecturally about the new **overall concept** is that the forceful figure of the terminal building consists of a series of inter-locking spaces when looked at from the landside and from the airside. The spaces are naturally lit and allow for a number of different views and perspectives both inside and outside due to the building's relation to the exterior. Walking through this airport will definitely be a spatial experience. It will be a differentiated spatial experience since the individual segment designs are characterised by greatly differing atmospheric room qualities despite the great uniformity of the materials used. This is intended to serve for identification and location recognition, which are very important in helping a passenger find his way in an unfamiliar airport. Very detailed proposals and suggestions were made as early as the preliminary draft phase to augment this aspect.

Clearly, a facility such as this has to be built on the basis of a modular construction method. There are economical reasons for this, but it also has to do with the flexibility such a structure requires. And flexibility is key in airport construction: not even the most accurate forecasts offer absolute certainty.

The concern is a neutrality of use and being able to take the buildings apart in clearly understandable individual parts. The high degree of repetition helps economise and increases operational ease. The uniformity of materials and details increases the ease of recognition of individual parts within the whole as well.

The skin of the terminal extension will consist of two shells with the large-format horizontal glass panels offering an unimpaired view. This is an extremely delicate construction in which the horizontal, closed glass support elements provide shadow for the façade. The roof can be perceived as the structure's fifth façade. From the air, the future airport will feature a unifying skin that covers the main building. The piers meet with this main volume, which in turn helps delineate their independence.

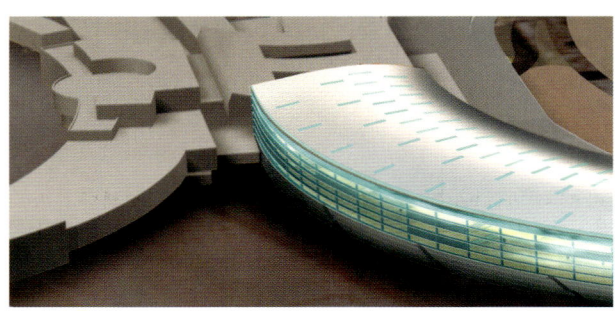
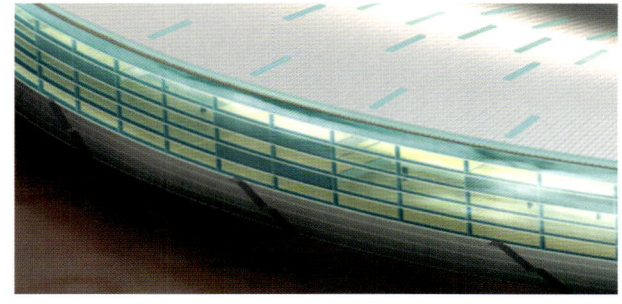

Zum Thema Gebäudehülle:
Transparent – transluzent – leuchtend. Zu allen Tageszeiten und aus jeder Perspektive wird der neue Skylink ein Erlebnis. Vom Vordach kommend, tritt man durch eine zum Windfang aufgeweitete Zone der Fassade in das Terminalgebäude ein. Nach dieser relativ niedrigen Schleuse ist man in einer hohen – landseitigen – Halle. Richtung Airside inszenieren die Hallen entlang der transparenten Fassade die Zusammenhänge zwischen dem Geschehen auf dem Flugfeld und dem im Gebäude eindrucksvoll, aber auch selbstverständlich und informativ. Was auf einem Flughafen wirklich geschieht, erlebt man hier. Dach und Fassade bilden dabei eine homogene Fläche.

On the subject of the building shell:
Transparent – translucent – illuminated. The new Skylink will be an experience at any time of day and from any perspective. Coming from the canopy, one enters the terminal via a zone of the expanded façade that acts as a porch. After entering this relatively low gate area one arrives in a large hall facing the land. The halls facing the departure side along the transparent façade offer impressive vistas of the happenings on the tarmac and in the building while remaining matter-of-fact and providing information. One experiences what happens in an airport here. The roof and façade create a homogeneous surface to do this on.

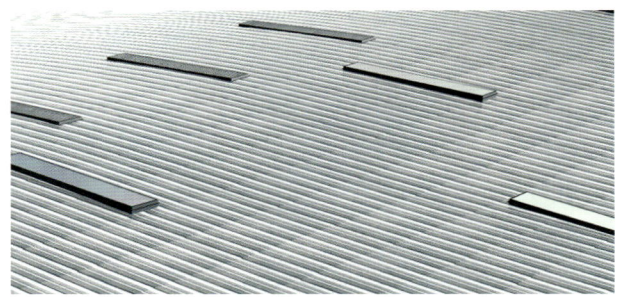

Zum Thema Primärstruktur:
Grundstrategie: eine modulare Systematik, die dem hohen Wiederholungsgrad und der (wirtschaftlichen) Notwendigkeit der Vereinheitlichung von Materialien, Details und Funktionseinheiten entspricht. Es gibt vier Ebenen über Niveau und in Teilbereichen (durch die nur in einfacher Tieflage geführte Bahn) eine unter Niveau. Die Hauptkonstruktion ist ein Stahlbetonskelettbau, die Decken sind (bis auf die Kernbereiche) als Fertigteildecken projektiert – eine, auch bei großen Spannweiten, sehr wirtschaftliche Lösung. Oberer Gebäudeabschluß: eine Kaltdachkonstruktion mit Blechdeckung. Gebäudehöhe an den Fassaden: 21 Meter. Am First: 24 Meter. Wichtig: Die Obergeschosse im Terminal sind durch vertikale Lufträume von der Fassade abgesetzt.

On the subject of the primary structure:
Basic strategy: a modular system that is suited to the degree of repetition and addresses the (economic) need for uniform materials, details and function. Four levels are above ground and there is one under the ground in certain segments (where the train runs on one subterranean level). The main construction is a ferroconcrete skeleton structure and the roof is to be built with prefabricated units (except for the core areas). This is an extremely economical solution – even in the case of large spans. The upper building closure: a cold forge construction with a plate roof. Building height along the façades: 21 metres. At the ridge: 24 metres. Important, the upper levels in the terminal were separated from the façade on the inside with vertical air spaces.

Das eigentliche **Terminal-Gebäude** besteht aus konzentrischen Schichten. Zwei außenliegende Hallen umfassen die innere, dichtere Struktur. Verbindungsglied zwischen den zwei Hallen: die offene Abflugsebene. Landseitig ist das Schwergewicht auf die Orientierung Richtung Verteilerebene gelegt. Wichtig: die Doppelhautfassade und die eingespannte, mehrschichtige, lichtdurchlässige Decke. Luftseitig öffnet sich die Halle zum Flugfeld, eingehängte Volumen strukturieren sie. Die Piers sind ganz einfach organisiert: Die Erschließung liegt in der Mitte, links und rechts davon, zwischen zwei statischen Scheiben sind die Aufgänge, Nebenräume, Fluchtwege und die Haustechnik gefaßt, die Warteräume liegen außen. Die Primärstruktur ist also äußerst signifikant. Durch die hohe Transparenz der Fassade wird diese Charakteristik der Räume noch weiter gesteigert.

Landseitig wird die Anbindung durch ein Verkehrsbauwerk und die Verteilerebene bewerkstelligt. Rund zehn Meter unter Terrain: der erweiterte Bahnhof und der neue Airportexpress, die das Terminalgebäude in einer eigenen Geometrie unterqueren. Die Ankunftshalle kippt an beiden Seiten zur Verteilerebene ab, dadurch ist die Sichtbarkeit der neuen Anbindung an die Bahn gesichert. Der Passagier wird ganz selbstverständlich und unmittelbar geleitet: zur Bahn, hinüber zu den Parkhäusern, auch zur Flughafenstadt.

Sicher ist: Allein schon das Vordach Richtung Vorfahrt, das in voller Länge die Sichelform des Terminalgebäudes aufnimmt, wird zum Spezifikum des neuen Flughafens werden. Die besondere Fassaden- und Dachlandschaft kommt noch dazu. Bei solchen Bauwerken geht es doch immer um die Signifikanz: Stadträumlich prägt die neue Figur das Areal, und ihre Form spiegelt die Dynamik des heutigen Verkehrs wieder. Zu Lande und zur Luft.

The actual **terminal building** consists of concentric layers. Two halls on the outer periphery surround the dense inner structure. The connecting link between the two halls: the open departures area. On the landside, the main focus was on offering orientation on the way to the distribution level. Important: the double glazed façade and the trussed, multi-layer, transparent roof. On the departure side, the hall opens to the tarmac and the suspended volumes define its structure. The piers are organised in a very simple manner: the access is located in the middle. The stairways lie to the right and left of two static glass panels as well as the ancillary and technical equipment rooms, the waiting rooms are located on the outside. Hence the primary structure is especially significant. The façade's high degree of transparency helps underline the characteristics of these rooms.

A transportation building and the distribution level provide access **on the landside**. Around ten meters under the ground lies the expanded train station and the new Airport Express, which traverse the underground section of the building geometrically. The arrivals hall slopes down from the distribution level on both sides, making it possible to see the new train connection. The passenger is guided in an immediate, yet matter-of-fact way to the train, over to the parking houses and to the airport town.

A certainty: The full-length of the sickle-shaped canopy facing the driveway of the terminal building will become the specific feature of the new airport. The special façade and roofing effect adds to this. Buildings such as this are always about significance: In terms of urban space, the new figure dominates the area and the shape reflects the dynamics of today's transportation, on land and in the air.

Erster eigener realisierter Beitrag im neuen Bebauungskonzept der Flughafenstadt:
ein Bürohaus, in dem auf der vierten Etage auch das Planungsbüro P.ARC Baumschlager Eberle Gartenmann Raab GmbH seinen Sitz hat. Die Fassade ist zweischalig, die Büros und Besprechungsräume „wickeln" sich um den Kern des Gebäudes als offenes Raumkontinuum, das nur durch Glaswände gegliedert wird.
Seit Vorliegen des Bebauungskonzeptes für die Flughafenstadt wurden übrigens zahlreiche Verfahren mit unterschiedlichen Inhalten durchgeführt – alle aber mit einem Ziel: Man wollte architektonische Lösungsvorschläge für Einzelmaßnahmen erlangen, die qualitativ dem Bedeutungsstatus des Areals rund um den Vienna International Airport adäquat sind.

B&E's first realised contribution to the new airport town construction concept:
The first contribution to the new airport town construction concept: an office building in which the P.ARC Baumschlager Eberle Gartenmann Raab GmbH planning office is located on the fourth floor. The façade consists of two shells; the offices and meeting rooms are wrapped around the core of the building, functioning as an open continuum of space that is only structured by glass panels.
A number of processes with varying contents have been implemented since the airport town construction concept was introduced, all with one goal: the goal was to achieve architectural solutions that are in keeping with the significance of the site surrounding Vienna International Airport and adequate in terms of quality.

Verwaltungsgebäude Saeco in Lustenau, A
Saeco Administration Building in Lustenau, Austria

Die Österreich-Niederlassung eines erfolgreichen italienischen Unternehmens (z.B. Kaffeemaschinen). Errichtet auf der grünen Wiese, aber unweit des Betriebsgebäudes der Firma Alcatel (ebenfalls B&E, 1992). Thema: eine maximal offene Struktur, die in der Zukunft alles zulässt.
Die Primärkonstruktion – extrem minimiert. Ein ökonomisch sinnvoller Stützenraster hinter der Fassade, pro Geschoß jeweils eine durchgehende Decke gespannt, zwei Erschließungskerne: einer als eigener (schwarzer) Baukörper aus dem Gebäude herausgeschoben, einer (mit Lastenaufzug) zur Aussteifung in das Gebäude eingeschoben. Das Haus hat eine Glasfassade. Mit sehr hochwertigen Gläsern, die wenig Wärmeeinstrahlung zulassen. Zusätzlich – psychologisch, nicht klimatisch bedingt – gibt es öffenbare, dunkel gefärbte Fassadenelemente, die eine eigene Geometrie formulieren. Sie hat mit dem Szenario einer möglichen anderen Nutzung des Hauses zu tun. Man könnte auch Einzelbüros realisieren, dann hätte jedes ein solches Fensterelement.

The Austrian branch headquarters of the Italian company (that produces coffee machines, for example) was built on a green meadow not far from the Alcatel building (also by B&E, 1992). The theme: a structure that is as flexible as possible to allow for anything and everything in the future.
The primary structure is extremely minimised. An economically sound grid of supports lies behind the façade. A single, continuous ceiling covers each level. There are two core access areas: one is a separate (black) structure that protrudes slightly, the other (including the service elevator shaft) is set in the building in order to stiffen it. The building has a glass façade, made of high-quality glass paneling that minimises thermal radiation. There are additional operable, tinted façade elements – for psychological reasons, not climactic ones – that create their own geometry. This has to do with other possible uses for the building. It would also be possible to create individual offices, then each office would have one of the window elements.

Bauherr | client **Saeco Handels Ges.m.b.H**   Projektleitung | project architect **Elmar Hasler**   Landschaftsarchitekt | landscape architect **Vogt Landschaftsarchitekten**   Haustechnik Konzept | mechanical engineer **GMI Gasser & Messner Ingenieure**   Elektro Planung | electrical engineer **HECHT Elektroplanung**   Statik | structural engineer **D.I. Ernst Mader**   Grundstücksfläche | site area **6.191 m²**   Bebaute Fläche | built up area **910 m²**   Nutzfläche | floor area **2.397 m²**   Umbauter Raum | building volume **11.087 m³**   Planungsbeginn | commencement of planning   Juli | July **1995**   Baubeginn | commencement of work   Juli | July **1997**   Fertigstellung | completion   Oktober | October **1998**

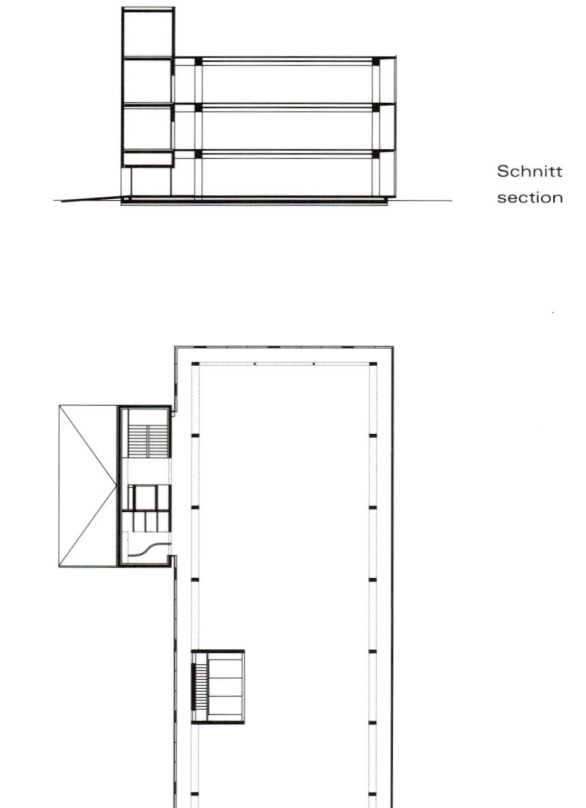

Schnitt
section

Regelgeschoß
standard floor

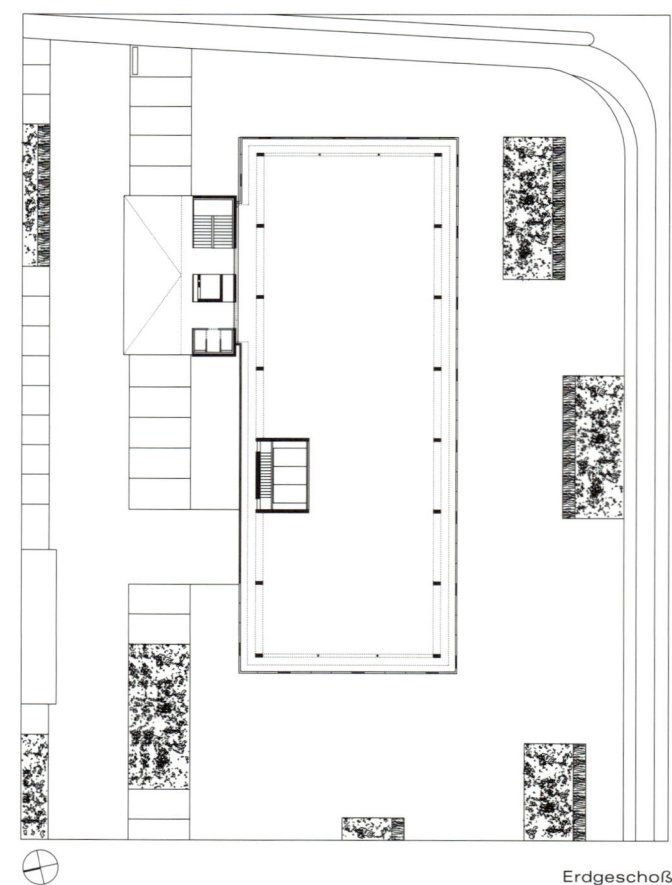

Erdgeschoß
ground floor

Derzeit wird das Haus so genutzt: Es gibt den großzügigen Kundenempfang mit Stucco-Lustro-Theke, es gibt Bürozonen und den Werkstättenbereich, die durch Glaswände strukturiert sind. Interessant ist, daß die Arbeitsplätze selbst von der Fassade abgerückt wurden. Zwischen Glashaut und Stützen verläuft ein interner Kommunikationsweg, der durch ganz simple Vorhänge, je nach der Bedürfnislage der einzelnen Mitarbeiter, modifiziert werden kann. Wesentlich dabei: Auch bei geschlossenen Vorhängen und trotz großer Trakttiefen ist die natürliche Belichtung garantiert.

Zusatz: **Die Freiflächengestaltung** rund um das Gebäude. Es steht in einer reizvollen Riedlandschaft. Günter Vogt aus Zürich hat das natürliche Erscheinungsbild dieses Landschaftstyps aufgenommen und formalisiert: Das Haus ist in eine Feuchtwiesenlandschaft mit „Paketen" von Baumpflanzungen und Wasserbecken eingebettet. Rundherum gibt es das in Form von Kanälen, von natürlich gewachsenen Baumgruppen. Vogts Entwurf ist fast besser.

Currently, the building is used as follows: there is a large customer reception area including a stucco-lustro counter, this is followed by the office area and the workshop area, which are structured with glass walls. It is interesting that the work places themselves are set at a slight distance to the façade. An internal communication path lies between the glass skin and supports that can be modified with simple curtains according to the need of the individual employees. An important feature is the guaranteed natural lighting despite the great wing depth, even when the curtains are closed.

An additional feature: **the landscaping** around the building. It stands in an appealingly marshy landscape. Günter Vogt from Zurich created a formal theme with these surroundings: the house is imbedded in a moist meadowy landscape along with 'thickets' of forestation and water pools. This theme is followed up with the channels of tree clusters that have grown naturally. Vogt's design is almost better.

Bürohaus und Lkw-Werkstätte Ospelt
in Vaduz, FL
Ospelt Office Building and Auto Repair Shop
in Vaduz, Duchy of Liechtenstein

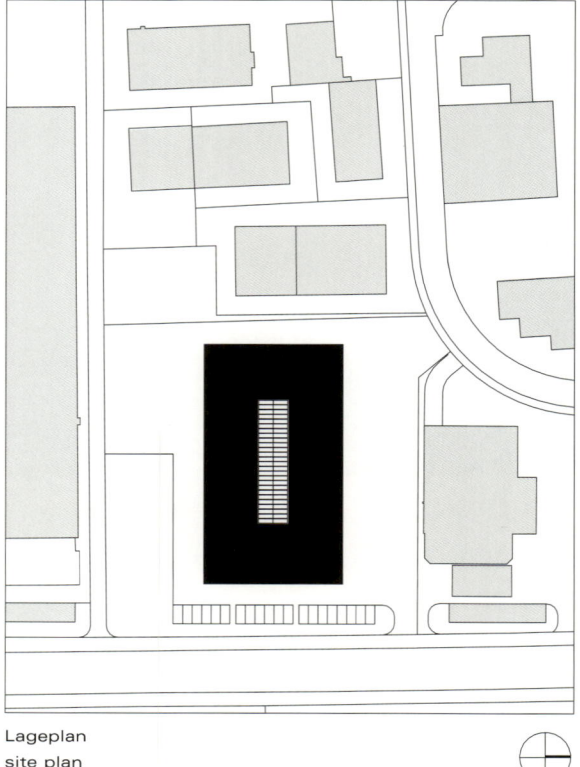

Lageplan
site plan

Die Vorgeschichte: Ursprünglich stand auf dem Areal eine große Werkstättenhalle und vorne, an der Straße, ein schmaler Bürotrakt, in dem u.a. das Büro von B&E untergebracht war. Das Bürohaus fiel einem Brand zum Opfer, B&E erhielten den Auftrag einen Neubau zu errichten.
Vorgabe war: eine bessere Ausnutzung des Grundstücks. Daher wurde die Lkw-Werkstätte überbaut. Folge: sehr große Trakttiefen bei den Büros. Trotzdem sind sie natürlich belichtet. Über eine große verglaste Erschließungshalle und Oberlichtverglasungen in den Wänden zur Halle fällt selbst in die innenliegenden Räume Tageslicht. Wie ein solcher Bürotyp optimal genutzt werden kann, führen B&E übrigens in ihrem eigenen Büro – mit Trennwänden aus Glas – beispielhaft vor.

Prologue: originally, a large workshop stood on the site with a small office wing facing the street up front that also contained the B&E offices. The building burned down and B&E were contracted to build the new facility.
The objective: to use the site more efficiently. Office levels were built over the auto repair shop. The effect: a very deep office wing. However, they are nonetheless naturally lit. Daylight reaches even the rooms farthest to the back via the large access hall and transom lighting along the walls leading to the hall. By the way, B&E show how such an office type can be used in their own office in an exemplary fashion – by installing glass separating walls.

Bauherr | client **Bruno Ospelt**   Planung | planning **Baumschlager Eberle Anstalt**   Projektleitung | project architect **Elmar Hasler**   Mitarbeiter | assistance **Christoph Ruegg**   Haustechnik Konzept | mechanical engineer **Ospelt Haustechnik**   Statik | structural engineer **Frick & Gattinger AG**   Grundstücksfläche | site area **5.887 m²**   Bebaute Fläche | built up area **1.853 m²**   Nutzfläche | floor area **6.221 m²**   Umbauter Raum | building volume **41.888 m³**   Planungsbeginn | commencement of planning **Jänner | January 1999**   Baubeginn | commencement of work **Juni | June 1999**   Fertigstellung | completion **März | March 2001**

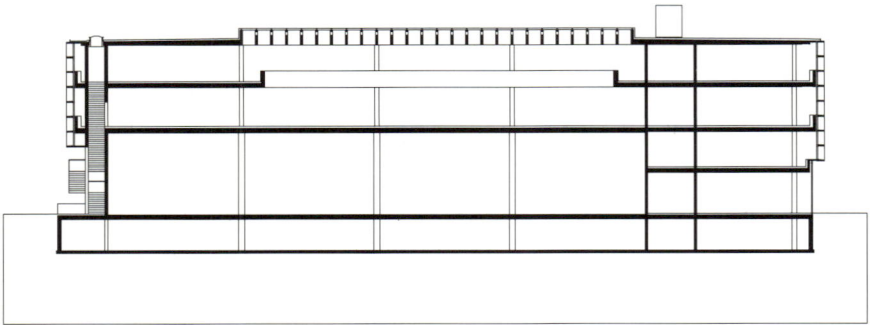

Schnitt
section

Es gibt **drei Themen** bei diesem Gebäude: die Neutralität der Struktur, organisiert um einen Lichtraum, dabei aber offen für jede erdenkliche Nutzung; die Nutzung innerhalb dieser Struktur – mit einem Innenausbau, der durch den Tageslichteinfall diktiert wird; schließlich die Fassade.
Es ist eine Glasfassade, der ein fixer Beschattungsraster (Kupfer) vorgeschaltet ist. Die Tiefe dieses Rasters ist das Ergebnis mehrfacher Simulationen. Sie läßt nur einen geringen Wärmeeintrag zu. Der starre Sonnenschutz ist die Corporate Identity des Gebäudes.

This building is characterised by **three themes**: the structure's neutrality, organised around a lit space but open for any conceivable purpose within this structure, as well as the interior design that is dictated by the amount of daylight that streams in and finally, the façade.
It is a glass façade with a fixed shadow-providing grid (copper) in front of it. The depth of this grid is the result of a number of simulations. It only allows for very little thermal heat build up. The immovable sun protection is the building's corporate identity.

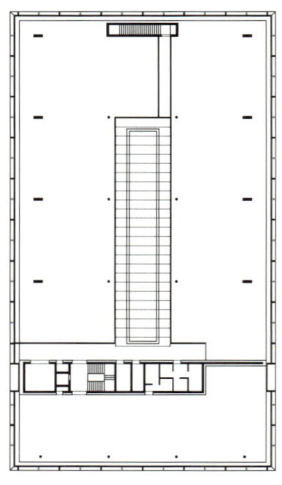

Regelgeschoß
standard floor

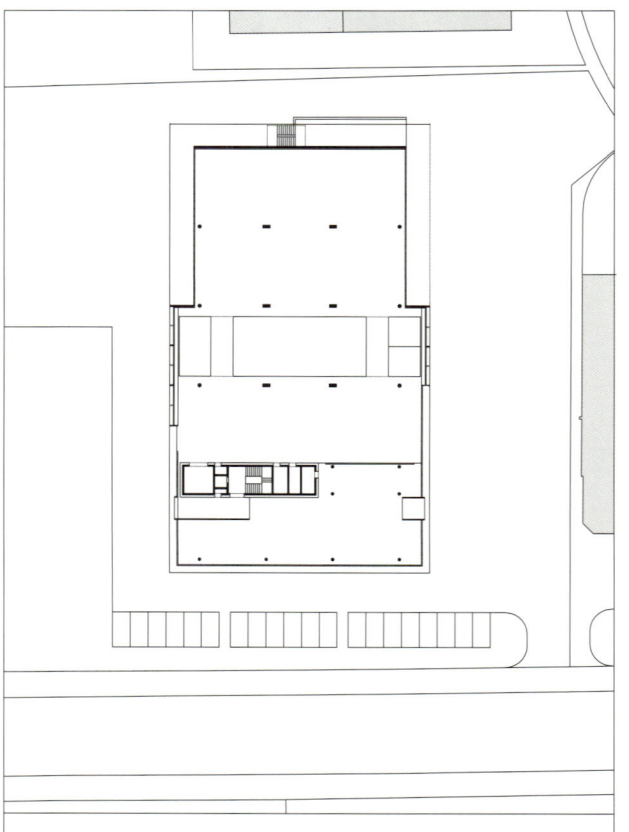

Erdgeschoß
ground floor

B & E > Bürohaus und LKW-Werkstätte Ospelt_FL

Bürogebäude IT Data Center Zumtobel AG
in Dornbirn, A
Office Building IT Data Centre Zumtobel AG
in Dornbirn, Austria

Der Neubau ist Teil eines größeren Werksgeländes von Zumtobel, das seit den sechziger Jahren gewachsen ist. Eines der beiden älteren Gebäude wurde von B&E schon vor Jahren umgebaut, ebenso ein Geschoß im zweiten. Mit dem Rechenzentrum nimmt nun **eine städtebauliche Lösung** Gestalt an, die zwar Entwicklungspotentiale für die Zukunft offen hält (im Anschluß an das Rechenzentrum), aber auch dem spezifischen Ort und seiner Geschichte Rechnung trägt. Kuriosum: Mithilfe der Wasserkraft des kleinen Baches, der am Gelände vorbei fließt, wurde früher Strom erzeugt. Das technische Relikt dieser Historie haben die Architekten zwar ein wenig verschoben, aber entsprechend wirkungsvoll inszeniert.

The new building is part of a larger Zumtobel industrial complex that has grown since the sixties. B&E was responsible for the refurbishment of one of the two older buildings a few years back and also did such work on the second floor of the other building. With the computer centre, **an urban construction solution** took shape that allows for potential future developments (in connection to the computer centre). However, it also pays tribute to the specific place and its history. A curious feature: electricity used to be generated with energy from the creek that flows past the site. The architects shifted this historical relict a bit, but it still has effect from its new location.

Bauherr | client **Zumtobel AG** Generalunternehmer | general contractor **IBM Österreich** Planung | planning **B & E Baumschlager-Eberle GmbH** Projektleitung | project architect **Oliver Baldauf** Mitarbeiter | assistance **Christine Mayr** Landschaftsarchitekt | landscape architect **Vogt Landschaftsarchitekten** Haustechnik Konzept | mechanical engineer **IBM Österreich** Statik | structural engineer **Moosbrugger Ingenieure** Grundstücksfläche | site area **11.592 m²** Bebaute Fläche | built up area **856 m²** Nutzfläche | floor area **2.735 m²** Umbauter Raum | building volume **13.161 m³** Planungsbeginn | commencement of planning **Jänner | January 2001** Baubeginn | commencement of work **April | April 2001** Fertigstellung | completion **März | March 2002**

Das eigentliche Rechenzentrum spielt sich **unterirdisch** ab, auf insgesamt zwei Geschossen. Darüber wurde ein Bürohaus errichtet. Entscheidend ist die städtebauliche Konfiguration, die durch den Neubau definiert wird: im Zentrum ein halb/öffentliches Areal, das eine Art Mitte, das Herzstück zwischen Alt und Neu darstellt. Hier gibt es auch einen Parkplatz, von dem eine sehr flache (behindertengerechte), einmal geknickte Rampe hinauf zum Haupteingang führt.

Daß der Haupteingang über dem 00-Niveau liegt, hat mit dem unterirdischen Rechnungszentrum, vor allem auch mit Sicherheitsvorschriften zu tun. Man tritt ein wenig über Bodenniveau ins Gebäude ein, kommt in die Eingangshalle und von dort über den Erschließungskern in die Büros. Dieser Kern, ebenso wie jener mit dem Lastenaufzug an der straßenabgewandten Seite, erfüllt statische Fuktionen. Außerdem gibt es Stützen, die hinter der Fassade liegen. Der eigentliche Büroraum ist aber völlig offen, also beliebig ausbau- und interpretierbar.

Die Fassade ist zweischalig. In der thermischen Haut – raumhoch verglast – sitzen auch öffenbare Fenster, davor gibt es eine Schicht aus grün eingefärbten, sehr hochwertigen Sonnenschutzgläsern. Im Zusammenwirken mit all den anderen (architektonischen, haustechnischen) Maßnahmen der aktiven Bauteilkühlung und der kontrollierten Gebäudelüftung wurde so eine klimatisch angenehme Arbeitssituation geschaffen, die zusätzlich nur noch einen innenliegenden Blendschutz braucht.

Die äußere Fassadenschicht der grün eingefärbten Gläser wirkt ausgesprochen spektakulär. Im Vorbeifahren verändert sie sich von geschlossen zu transparent, aber sie schillert auch farblich in vielen Nuancen. Das wurde einerseits durch das Format der Scheiben, andererseits durch den Grad der Schrägstellung erreicht.

The actual Computer Centre is located **underground**, on a total of two levels. An office building was erected above it. The decisive aspect here is the configuration in terms of urban planning that defines the new building. At the centre lies a semi-public open space, a heart resting between old and new. The parking lot is also located here, with a very flat ramp (adequate for the disabled) that leads to the main entrance.

The fact that the main entrance lies over the 00 level has to do with the underground Computer Centre and safety regulations. Thus the visitor enters the building a bit above ground level, reaches the entrance hall and continues to the offices via the distribution hub at the core of the building. This core and the service elevator shaft facing away from the street address structural requirements. There are also supports located behind the façade. The actual office space is completely open and it can therefore be freely expanded or re-interpreted.

The façade consists of two layers. Operable windows were also placed in the thermal skin, which features ceiling-to-floor glass paneling. In front of this layer are green-colored, very high-quality sunshade glass panels. Hence a climatically pleasant work environment that only needs supplemental shades was created in conjunction with all the other (architectural, building-technical) measures.

The green-coloured glass outer façade layer achieves a spectacular effect. They change from closed to open as one drives past, but also shimmer with many colorful nuances. This was achieved with the format of the windows and the angle at which they were set.

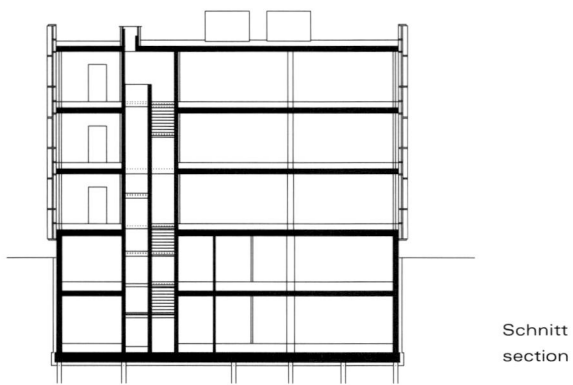
Schnitt
section

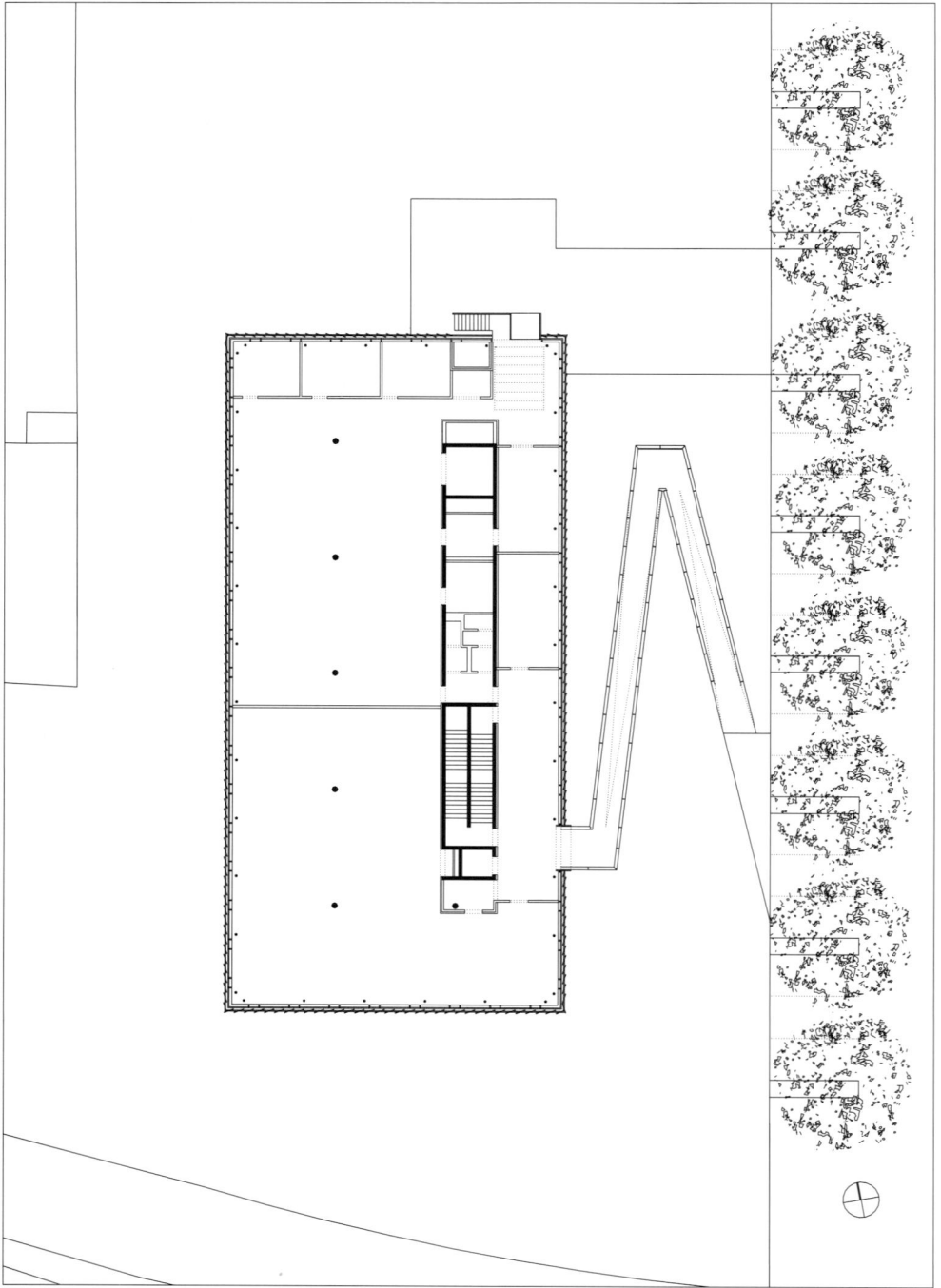

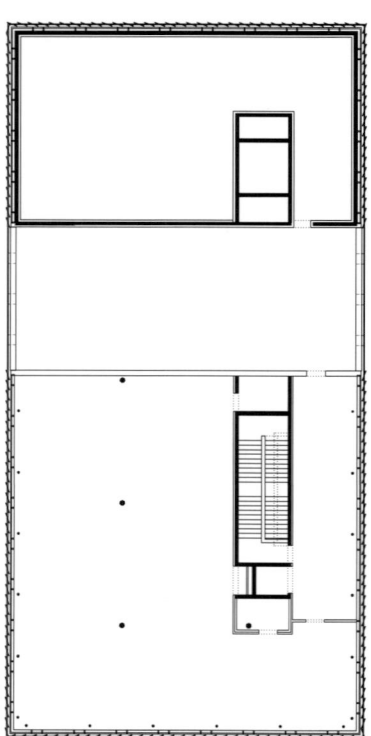

1. Obergeschoß
1st floor

Erdgeschoß
ground floor

B & E > IT Data Center Zumtobel AG_A

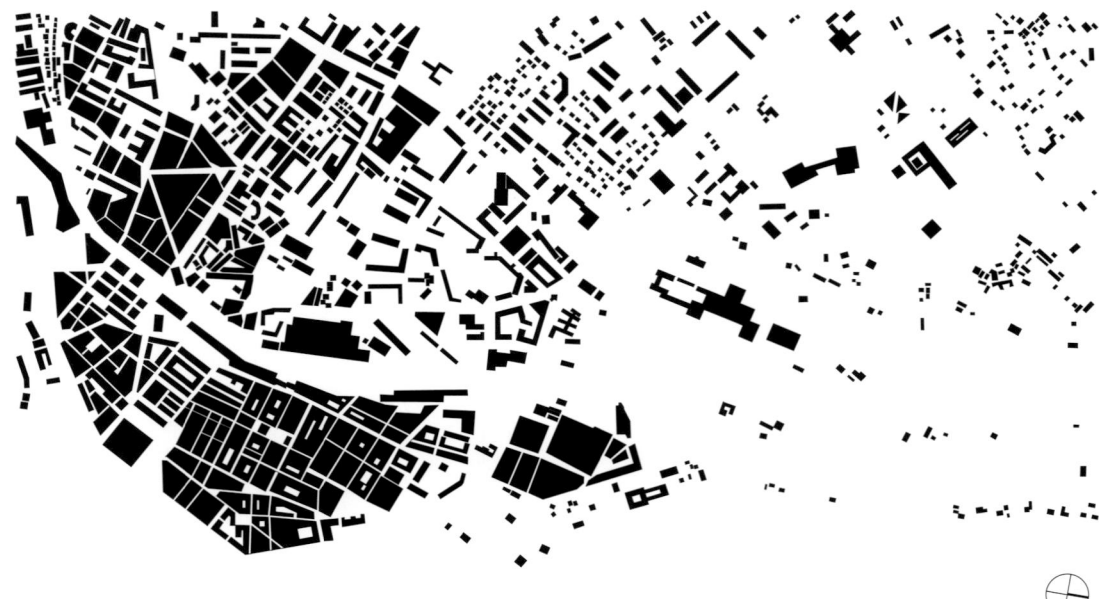

Verwaltungsgebäude für WHO und UNAIDS in Genf, CH
WHO and UNAIDS Administration Building in Geneva, Switzerland

Ein prominenter Standort: mitten in der Parklandschaft der internationalen Organisationen, auf einem Hügel über Genf, Blick auf die Altstadt und den See. Hier liegt das WHO-Gelände, ein überzeugendes Beispiel für „Neues Bauen".

Themen des aktuellen Entwurfs: die Auseinandersetzung mit diesem gebauten Bestand und mit dem parkartigen Naturraum des Geländes; natürlich auch die Maximierung von Büroflächen mit Außenbezug, trotz aller städtebaulichen Vorgaben. Architektonisch nimmt B&E's Antwort auf die hochhausartige Scheibe des WHO-Bestandes Parameter dieses Hauses auf: Es ist eine Art „liegende", horizontale Version davon, artikuliert mit heutigen Mitteln. Beim Altbau geht das Gelände unter dem aufgeständerten Haus durch, beim Neubau setzt sich der Naturraum durch Einschnitte und Höfe im Gebäude fort. Wichtig dabei: Die beiden Hauptbürogeschosse sind nur an drei Stellen durch kompakte Bauvolumen im Terrain verankert. Im übrigen ist die große, erdgeschossige Halle höhenmäßig (6 bis 10 Meter) entsprechend dem Geländeverlauf gestaffelt. Sie dient mit Restaurant, Konferenzräumen, Ausstellungsbereich als fließendes Raumkontinuum beiden Institutionen, die ansonsten – bis hin zu den Eingängen – völlig getrennt organisiert sind.

A prominent location: right within the setting of international organisations on a hill overlooking Geneva with a view of the historical centre of the city and the lake. This is the site of a convincing example of 'Neues Bauen' (new building).

The themes of the current project: an appreciative study of the existing substance and the park-like natural area the terrain offers. Of course another theme is the maximisation of offices with outside views, despite all the urban planning requirements. Architecturally, B&E's answer to the high rise-like slab of the existing building dissolves the parameters of its counterpart: it is a 'lying', horizontal version of it articulated in modern terms. The terrain continues under the raised ground floor of the old building and incisions and courtyards in the new structure expand the green area. Important, the three main office storeys are only anchored in the grounds at three spots as a result of the compact building volume. The height of the large, ground level hall is staggered according to the lie of the terrain (6 to 10 metres). This hall is a flowing continuum of space comprising a restaurant, conference rooms, and exhibition space integrating both organisations – which are otherwise separately organised entities – right up to the doors.

Bauherr | client **WHO-UNAIDS** Planung | planning **B & E Baumschlager-Eberle GmbH** Projektleitung | project architect **Hans Ullrich Grassmann, Oliver Kaps** Mitarbeiter | assistance **Kai-Uwe Bergmann, Alexia Monauni, Julja Nägele-Küng** Landschaftsarchitekt | landscape architect **Vogt Landschaftsarchitekten** Haustechnik Konzept | mechanical engineer **HL Technik AG** Statik | structural engineer **D.I. Ernst Mader, D.I. Bruno Rissi** Grundstücksfläche | site area **14.065 m²** Bebaute Fläche | built up area **3.956 m²** Nutzfläche | floor area **14.479 m²** Umbauter Raum | building volume **105.990 m³** Planungsbeginn | commencement of planning **Februar | February 2002** Baubeginn | commencement of work **Februar | February 2003** Fertigstellung | completion **Oktober | October 2005**

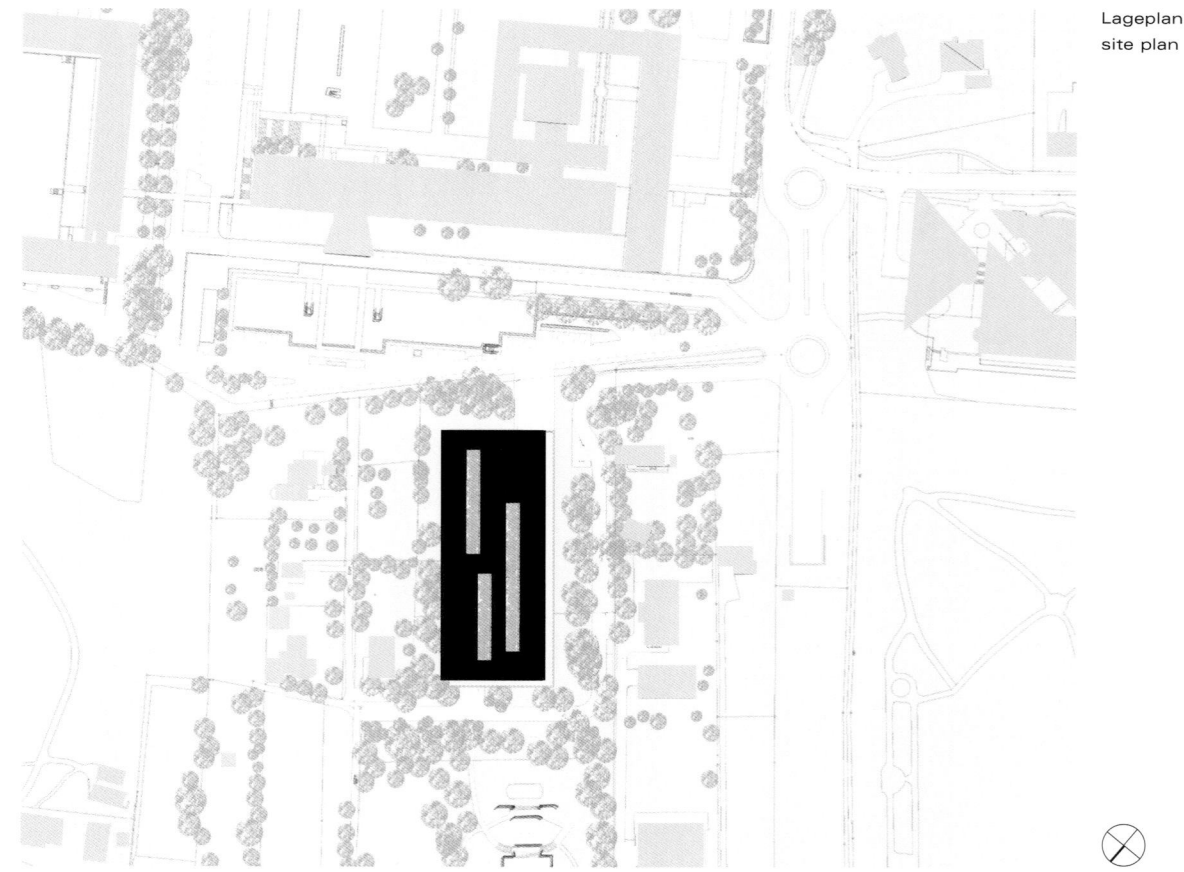

Lageplan
site plan

Ein integrativer Entwurf: Mit seiner differenzierten Glasfassade verhält er sich kontrapunktisch zum WHO-Bestand; andererseits wird mit der Durchgängigkeit des Naturraums durch beide Gebäude auch eine Art Dialog eröffnet. Mit respektvollem Abstand: Zwei Solitäre schauen sich an.

An integrating design: with its differing façade elements it acts as a counterpoint to the existing WHO building; on the other hand, the easily traversed natural space creates a form of dialogue between the two buildings: two solitary structures eyeing each other at a respectful distance.

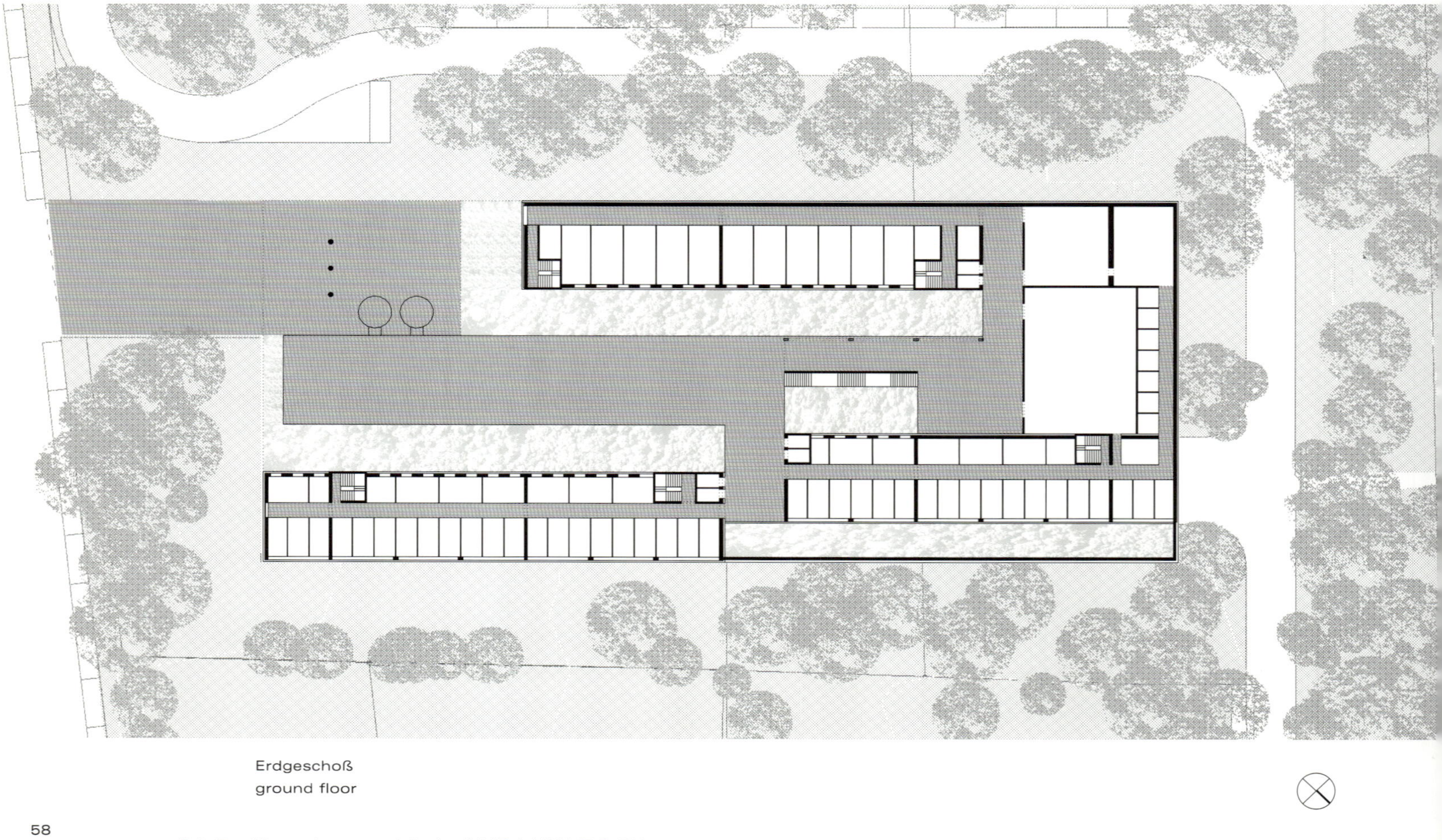

Erdgeschoß
ground floor

B & E > Verwaltungsgebäude WHO | UNAIDS_CH

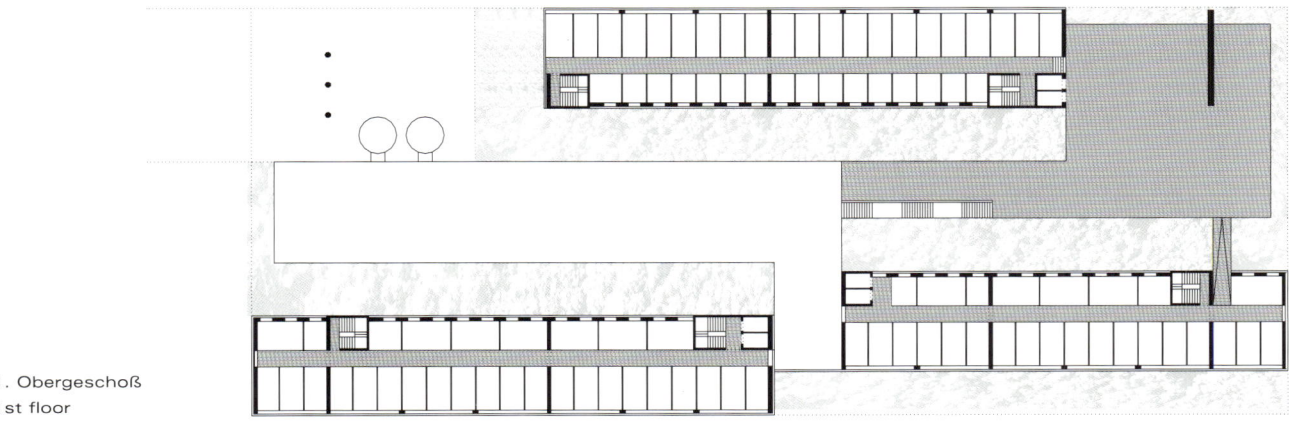

1. Obergeschoß
1st floor

Regelgeschoß
standard floor

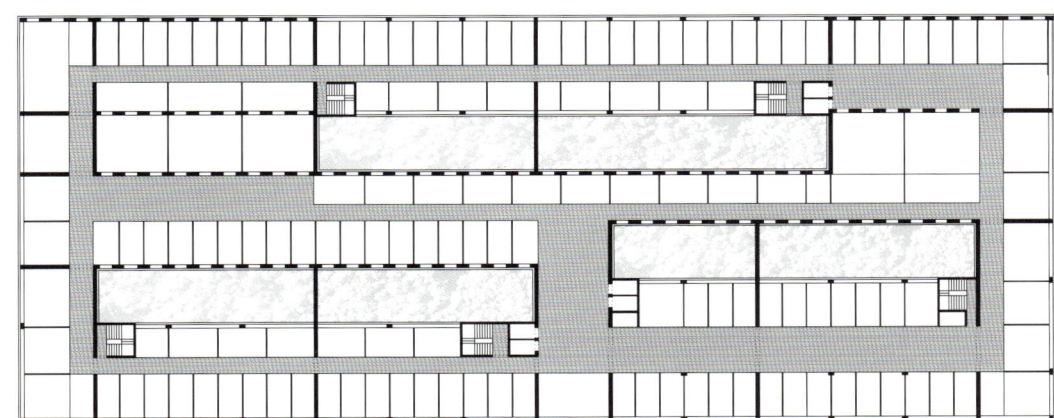

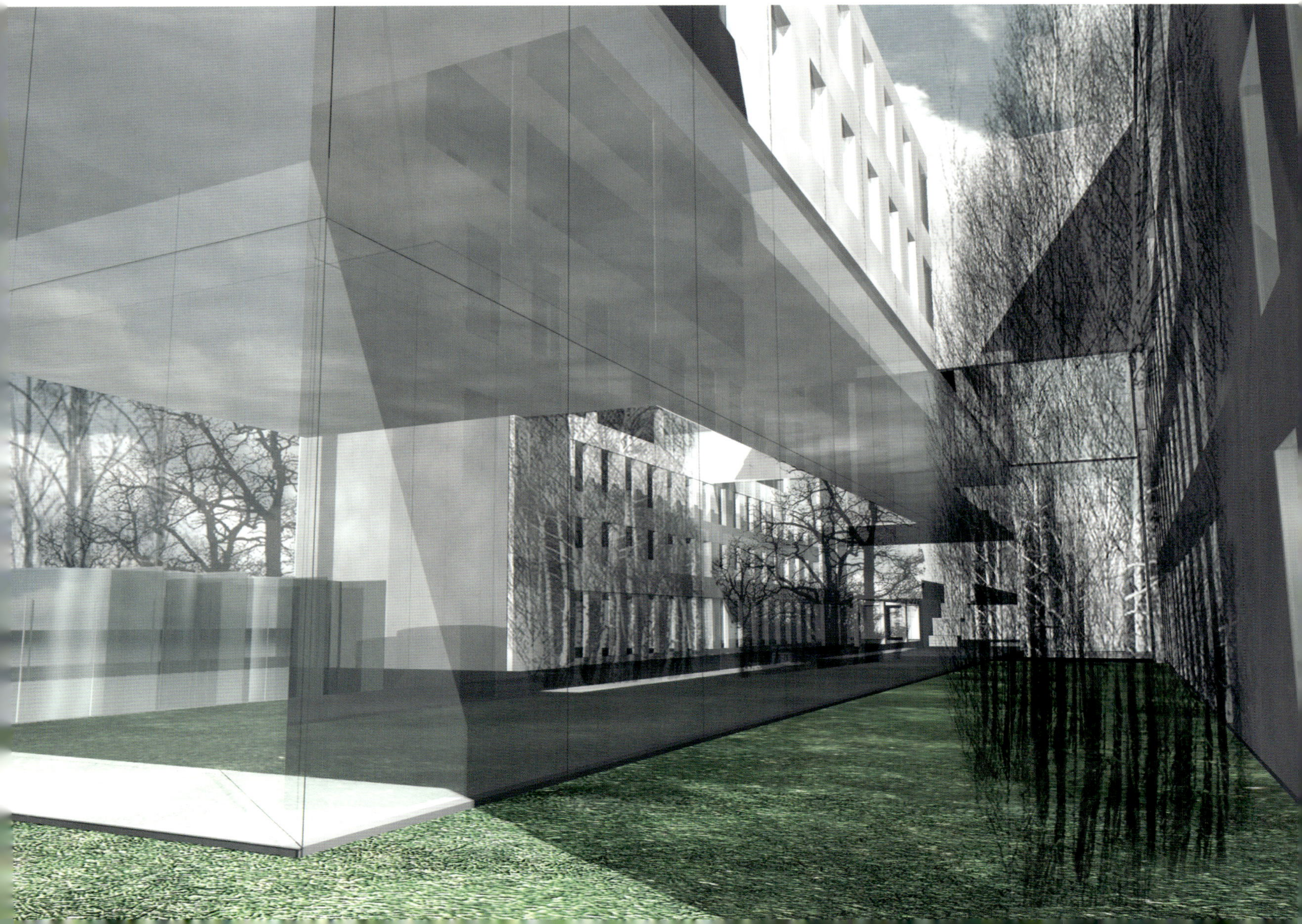

Bürogebäude Münchener Rückversicherung, D
Münchener Rück Office Building, Germany

Um- und Neubau, Stadtreparatur, ökologisches Vorzeigeprojekt, Aufwertung überkommener Bürowelten, imageprägendes Demonstrationsobjekt. Viel Inhalt für ein einziges Vorhaben, das noch dazu innerhalb der Primärkonstruktion eines Bestandes vom Ende der sechziger Jahre (1968 bis 1973) realisiert werden mußte. Gegenüber: Das alte Stammhaus der Münchener Rück, ein Hôtel de Ville mit Ehrenhof und schöner Gartenanlage. Und: ein Standort mitten in Schwabing, zwischen Leopoldstraße und Englischem Garten. Staffelbauweise charakterisiert dieses Viertel, also Einzelbauten, große Bürgerhäuser, mit begrünten Höfen und Hofeinfahrten, die den Eindruck von Durchlässigkeit vermitteln.
Der Bestand: ein maroder Stahlskelettbau mit Waschbetonfassade, dreiachsig, mit dunkler Innenzone und umlaufenden Büros. Die Idee: Anbau einer vierten Gebäudeachse und dadurch die Möglichkeit – trotz Büroflächengewinns – das Gebäude aufzuschneiden. Eingeschnitten wurden der Haupteingang und der gartenhofseitige Nebeneingang – so wird die Gliederung des Viertels aufgenommen und das Gebäude mutiert vom 80 Meter langen Betonkoffer zur S-förmigen Konfiguration –, eingeschnitten wurde aber auch die große, zweigeschossige Eingangs-, Verteiler-, Aufenthalts- und Veranstaltungshalle.

Refurbushment and new building, an exemplary ecological project, an enhancement of overrun office environments and an image-defining, demonstrative object. This is a lot of content for a single undertaking, especially for one that had to be realised within the primary structure of an existing building from the sixties (1968 to 1973). Across the way: the old *Münchener Rück* building, a *Hôtel de Ville* with a ceremonial court and a beautiful garden, and: a location set in the middle of Schwabing, between Leopoldstrasse and the English Gardens.
Staggered construction characterises this area, individual large houses with landscaped courtyards and driveways that convey a sense of permeability abound.
The existing building: a decrepit steel skeleton structure with a washed cement façade set on three bays with a dark interior zone surrounded by offices. The idea: to build a fourth bay and thus open the building while still gaining office space. The main entrance and garden-side entrance were created as incisions in the structure. This reflects the organisation of the neighbourhood, and allowed the building to mutate from a 80-meter cement suitcase to a structure featuring a S-shaped configuration. The large, two-storey entrance, distribution, living and event space was also cut into the building.

Bauherr | client **Münchener Rückversicherungsgesellschaft** Planung | planning **Baumschlager Eberle Anstalt** Projektleitung | project architect **Eckehart Loidolt, Christian Tabernigg** Mitarbeiter | assistance **Bernhard Demmel, Marc Fisler, Elmar Hasler, Alexia Monauni, Marlies Sofia, Daniela Weber** Bauleitung | construction supervision **BIP - Beratende Ingenieure für das Bauwesen VBI GmbH München** Sanitärplanung | sanitary engineering **CAE - Ingenieurbüro für Haustechnik** Bauphysik | physics relating to construction **ZP - Zumbach & Partners SA** Medienplanung | media planning **P.I.- Projekt Innovations, Müller BBM GmbH** Landschaftsarchitekt | landscape architect **Vogt Landschaftsarchitekten** Elektroplanung | electrical engineer **OvM-Oskar von Miller/Beratende Ingenieure** Haustechnik Konzept | mechanical engineer **GMI Gasser & Messner Ingeniure** Statik | structural engineer **FSIT-Friedrich Straß Ing. Büro Tragwerksplanung** Grundstücksfläche | site area **4.331 m²** Bebaute Fläche | built up area **2.718 m²** Hauptnutzfläche | net floor area **6.758 m²** Umbauter Raum oberirdisch | building volume overground **47.873 m³** Umbauter Raum unterirdisch | building volume underground **27.300 m³** Planungsbeginn | commencement of planning Oktober | October **1998** Baubeginn | commencement of work Oktober | October **1999** Fertigstellung | completion Dezember | December **2001**

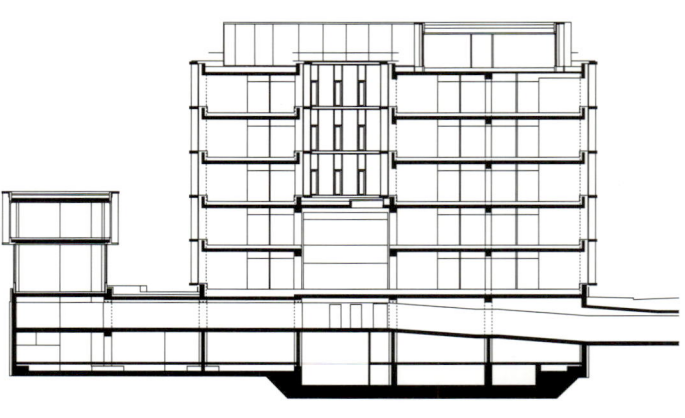
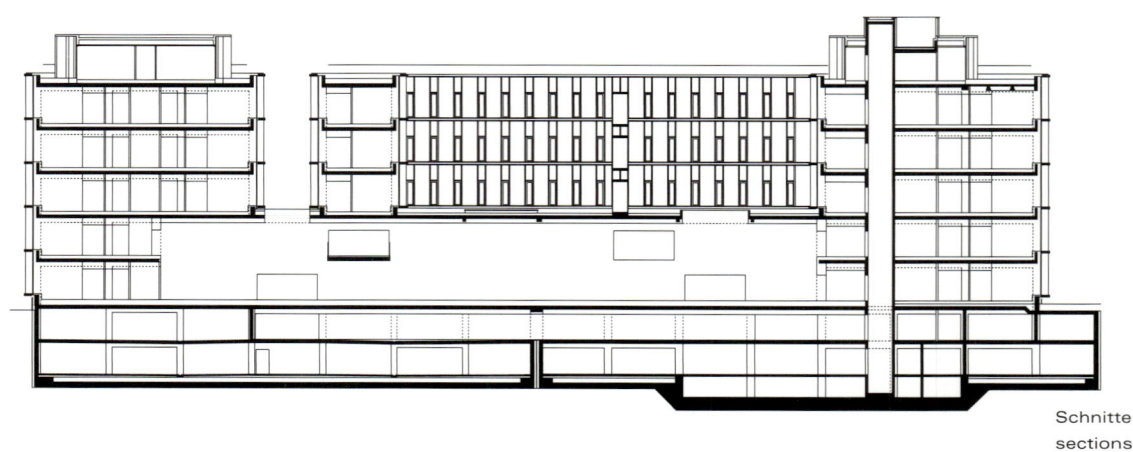

Schnitte
sections

B & E > Bürogebäude Münchener Rückversicherung_D

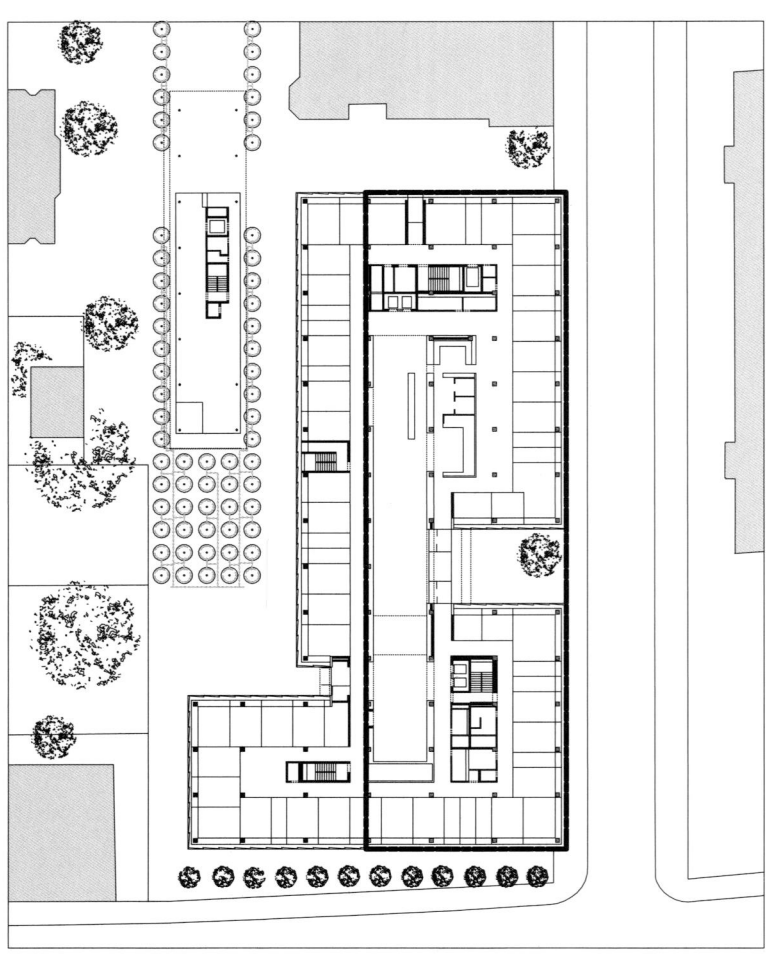

Erdgeschoß
ground level

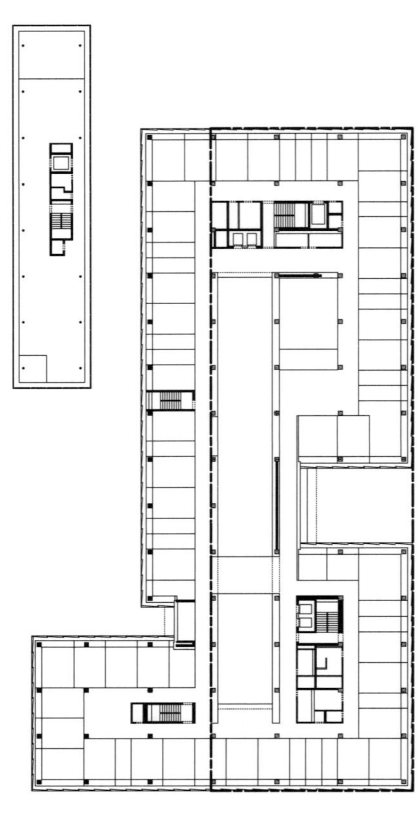

1. Obergeschoß
1st level

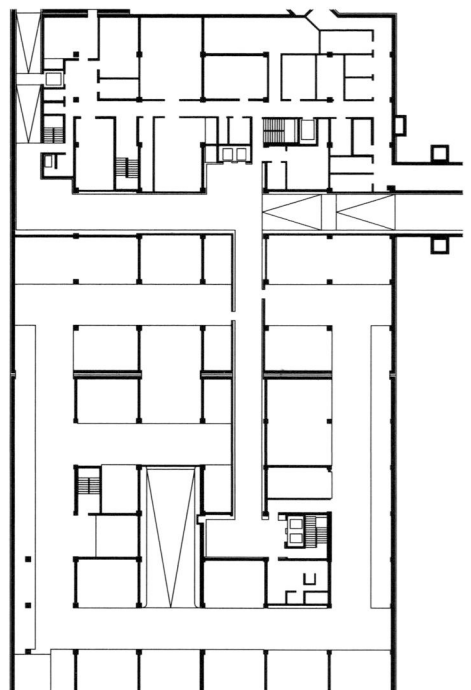

1. Untergeschoß
1st lower level

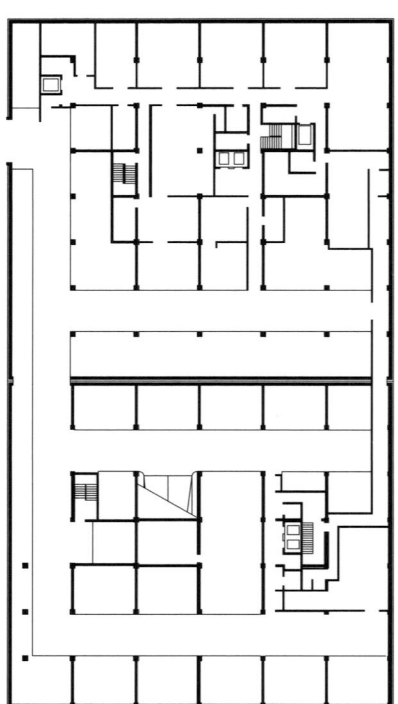

2. Untergeschoß
2nd lower level

B & E > Bürogebäude Münchener Rückversicherung_D

Die Halle ist ein **Highlight des Gebäudes**. 55 Meter lang, sieben Meter breit und sechs Meter hoch, rundum verkleidet mit kanadischem Ahorn im Stäbchenformat und durch drei Oberlichten natürlich belichtet. Die Mitarbeiter kommen durch einen gläsernen Windfang hinein, und von dort verteilen sie sich. Links oder rechts. Die Kerne mit den Liften wurden so verschoben, daß man von jedem Liftlanding einen Blick nach draußen hat: entweder in den Innenhof über der Halle oder nach draußen, in den Garten. Eine Orientierungsmöglichkeit also, auch atmosphärischer Gewinn.

This hall is **one of the building's highlights**. 55 metres long, seven metres wide and six metres high, it is fully clad with strips of Canadian maple and naturally lit by light from the ceiling skylight. Employees enter the building via a glass porch and continue from there, to the left or right. The elevator shafts were shifted to allow a view of the outside from every landing: either of the interior courtyard above, of the hall beyond, or of the garden outside. Thus it is an orientation aid and it enhances the building's atmosphere.

Die neue Büroatmosphäre: hell, freundlich, angenehm, zeitgemäß. Die Erschließungskorridore durch den Innenhof natürlich belichtet, Wand- und Türelemente der Büros aus transluzentem Glas, der Boden massives Ahornparkett. Herausforderung für die Architekten: die Interpretation der Zellenbüros.

Der Bestand, die Primärkonstruktion basiert auf einer besonders engen Rasterstruktur, einem Rastermaß von 62,5 Zentimetern. Eine einachsige Bürozelle ist also nur 1,875 Meter breit (eine Gebäudeachse besteht aus drei solchen Büroachsen) – das ist sehr schmal und führt zu extrem kleinen – etwas über zehn Quadratmeter – Bürozellen. Wobei es natürlich auch zweiachsige und in manchen Fällen sogar größere Büros gibt. Versucht wurde jedenfalls eine „Zonierung" dieses Miniraumes zwischen schalltechnisch optimierten, in der Materialstärke minimierten Trennwänden: Eingangsbereich mit Garderobe und Schrank, dabei niedrigere Raumhöhe durch einen ahornverkleideten „Deckenkoffer", der die Technik aufnimmt; höherer Arbeitsbereich mit Schreibtisch, Computer und Flachbildschirm; Brüstungsbereich an der Fassade mit öffenbarem Fenster und natursteinverkleidetem – Anröchter Dolomit – Hochzug der Primärkonstruktion des Bestandes.

The new office atmosphere: light, friendly, pleasant, contemporary. The access corridors are naturally lit by the courtyard. The office's wall and floor elements are made of translucent glass, the floors are of solid maple parquet. The next challenge for the architects: the interpretation of the cell-like office spaces.
The existing building's primary structure is based on a particularly tight grid structure with a grid space size of 62.5 centimetres. Hence a one bay office cell is only 1.875 metres wide (a building bay consists of three of these office bays) this is very narrow and leads to extremely small, slightly over ten square metre-sized offices. However, naturally there are also two bay and even larger offices in some cases. The attempt was made to 'zone' the miniaturised space by dividing it into an acoustically dampened area using slender, minimised separating panels: the entrance area features a wardrobe and closet and lower ceilings, above which lies technical equipment, in a maple-paneled roof 'cradle'. Then follows the elevated work space with a desk, computer and flat monitor, the balustrade section of the façade with an opening window and the vertical rise of the existing building's primary structure, which is clad in natural 'Anröchter' Dolomite stone.

Die Fassade: Sie ist zweischalig und die optische Visitenkarte dieses Hauses. Grün-gläsern schimmernd wertet sie das gesamte Umfeld auf. Es gibt die thermische Haut des Gebäudes – mit den öffenbaren Fenstern und den natursteinverkleideten Brüstungshochzügen des Bestandes –, und es gibt die zweite Haut. Geschoßhohe Gläser, die leicht schräg und im Abstand von etwa 60 Zentimetern (Putzbalkongröße) in einer Kragplatte, ebenfalls aus Anröchter Dolomit, sitzen. Auch diese zweite Fassadenhaut bringt thermischen Gewinn: Sie hält Wind und Wetter ab. Im übrigen wird im gesamten Haus mit Quelllüftung, Wärmerückgewinnung und Fußbodenkühlung der Energieaufwand minimiert.

Besonderheit auf dem Dach: die beiden – fast organisch geformten, gekurvten, irgendwie amöbenartigen – Aufbauten mit Besprechungsräumen und Vorstandsbüros. Sie ersetzen die Technikaufbauten des Bestandes und sind eingebettet in eine minimalistische Dachterrassenbepflanzung des Züricher Landschaftsplaners **Günter Vogt**.

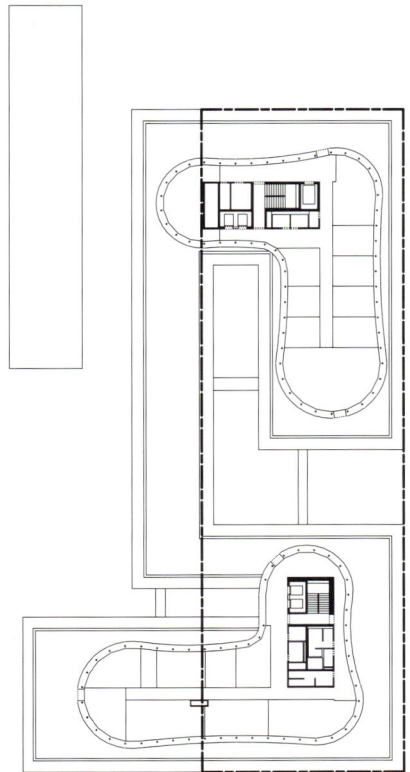

Attikageschoß
attic level

The façade: it is made of two layers and is the building's visual calling card. Its shimmering green glass upgrades the entire surrounding area. There is the thermal skin of the building with the opening windows and the natural stone-clad vertical balustrade lengths and the second skin layer. Ceiling-to-floor glass panels that are spaced around 60 centimetres apart (service balcony size) in a supporting collar also made of Anröchter Dolomite stone. This second façade layer also has thermal advantages: it offers protection from wind and weather. The entire building is ventilated with *Quelllüftung*. Energy consumption was minimised by using heat recovery and floor cooling systems.

Special features on the roof: The two almost organically shaped, curved, amoeba-like structures contain meeting rooms and the boards' offices. They replace the structures of the old building that housed the technical equipment and are imbedded in minimalist roof terrace greenery designed by the Zurich-based landscaping specialist **Günter Vogt**.

Vogt hat überhaupt einen wichtigen Beitrag geleistet. Von ihm stammen die künstlich bemoosten Tuffsteine auf dem Hallendach – darauf bezieht sich der Künstler **Olafur Eliasson** mit seinen ebenfalls bemoosten Tuffsteinwänden über den Eingängen –, von ihm stammen auch die urban-formalisierte, aber nicht aufdringliche Bepflanzung mit nordamerikanischem Ahorn und die schmalen, strengen Wasserbecken der Freiraumgestaltung.

Eingebettet in diesen Freiraum – nachdem zwei kleinere Objekte auf dem Areal gefallen sind – ist ein niedriges, nur zweigeschossiges Dienstleistungszentrum für die Münchener Rück. Das Musterhaus, das in der Realisierungsphase als Baubüro diente, hatte von vornherein nur begrenzte Lebenszeit. B&E konnten hier jedenfalls 1:1 überprüfen, was die zweischalige Fassade, was die Bürolösung wirklich leistet.

Das Gebäude ist natürlich ein Sicherheitstrakt. Als Besucher kommt man nicht direkt hinein. Man wird am Haupteingang des Stammhauses in Empfang genommen und über das unterirdische Passagensystem, das alle Objekte der Münchener Rück in diesem Quartier verbindet, hinüber geleitet. Kein Schaden. So sieht man wenigstens die neue Passage mit der wunderbaren Lichtarbeit von **Keith Sonnier**.

Vogt made an important contribution overall. He created the artificially mossy tuff stones on the roof of the hall which the artist **Olafur Eliasson** cites with his own artificially mossy tuff stone surfaces above the entrances. Eliasson was also responsible for the urbanely formed, but unobtrusive landscaping with North American maple and the slender, stringently shaped water pools that characterise the open space's design. Imbedded in this open space after two smaller objects landed on the lot is a low, only two-storey high service centre for the *Munich Rück*. The sample house, which acted as the building office during construction, had a limited life cycle from the beginning. B&E were able to examine what would really happen with the double façade and how the office solution would work on a 1:1 scale in this way.

Naturally, the building is a secure wing. Visitors do not have direct access. One is received at the main entrance of the main building and guided across via a system of underground passages that connects all the *Munich Rück* buildings with this structure. No harm done, at least one can admire the new segment with **Keith Sonnier**'s wonderful light work.

Aribert von Ostrowski

Keith Sonnier

Felice Varini

Peter Kogler

B & E > Bürogebäude Münchener Rückversicherung_D

Werbeagentur Baschnegger,
Sanierung und Zubau in Dornbirn, A
Baschnegger Advertising Agency,
Refurbishment and Expansion in Dornbirn,
Austria

Ursprünglich eine Barackensituation, in der früher eine Schneiderei war. In einem ersten Bauabschnitt wurde diese Substanz saniert und innen entsprechend der neuen Nutzung umgebaut. **Im zweiten Bauabschnitt** wurde das Gebäude erweitert.
Es gibt jetzt ein zusätzliches Geschoß, das um die Erschließung der neuen Bürozone im Obergeschoß verbreitert wurde. Diese Maßnahme zeichnet sich in der Faltung der Fassade ab und liegt außerhalb des konstruktiven Systems im Bestand. Die neue Fassadenschicht – aus vorpatiniertem Kupfer – lenkt außerdem auf die geänderte Eingangssituation hin: Sie wurde von der Schmalseite des Gebäudes an die Längsseite verlegt, davor wurden Parkplätze geschaffen.

Originally this was a barracks building that had been a tailoring factory. In the first construction phase, this existing structure was refurbished and adapted on the inside in accordance with its new purpose.
The annex was built during **the second construction phase**.
Now the building has an additional level that was widened to include access to the new office area. This measure is indicated by the wrinkle in the façade and lies outside the structural system of the existing building. The new façade layer – made of weathered copper – attracts attention to the new entrance: it was moved from the narrow side of the building to a location along the length of the building and parking spaces were placed in front of it.

Bauherr | client **Hansjörg Baschnegger** Planung | planning **Architekturbüro B & E Ziviltechniker GmbH** Projektleitung | project architect **Paul Martin** Mitarbeiter | assistance **Marika Marte, Tobias Reichart** Statik | structural engineer **D.I. Ernst Mader** Grundstücksfläche | site area **834 m²** Bebaute Fläche | built up area **466 m²** Nutzfläche | floor area **601 m²** Umbauter Raum | building volume **2.853 m³** Planungsbeginn | commencement of planning Juni | June **1997** Baubeginn | commencement of work Juli | July **1998** Fertigstellung | completion September | September **1998**

Man kommt jetzt durch den neuen Eingang in ein Foyer und von dort über eine Stiege ins Obergeschoß. Im Bestand wurde die Tragkonstruktion belassen, Zwischenwände wurden entfernt und die Decken teilweise aufgeschnitten. Dadurch entstand einerseits ein zweigeschossiger Besprechungsraum, andererseits ein großer, ebenfalls zweigeschossiger Arbeitsraum, dem außerdem die Kellerräume zugeschlagen wurden. Über großflächige Verglasungen, die zur Gartenseite orientiert sind, wird dieser Raum natürlich belichtet. Hierher, Richtung Garten, ist auch die neue Bürozone im Obergeschoß orientiert. Den Chefbüros vergeschoben: eine Terrasse.

Der Umbau ist ganz auf das Anforderungsprofil des Unternehmens zugeschnitten: Erreicht wurde ein weitgehend offenes, fließendes Raumkontinuum, das die innere Organisationsform dieser Agentur architektonisch, vor allem aber atmosphärisch entsprechend zum Ausdruck bringt.

Now visitors enter the building and find themselves in a foyer that leads them to a staircase and the upper level. The supporting structure of the existing building remained in place. Separating walls were removed and the ceilings were cut open in part. Thus a two-level meeting room and a large two-level working area that also includes the basement area were created. This space is naturally lit via large, glass-paneled surfaces facing the garden. The new office area is also aligned facing the garden and the management office features a terrace.

The refurbishment was undertaken in complete accordance with the company's requirements. What was achieved is a largely open, flowing space continuum that adequately expresses the organisational form of this advertising agency in terms of architecture. Most of all, it also does justice to the atmosphere of the company.

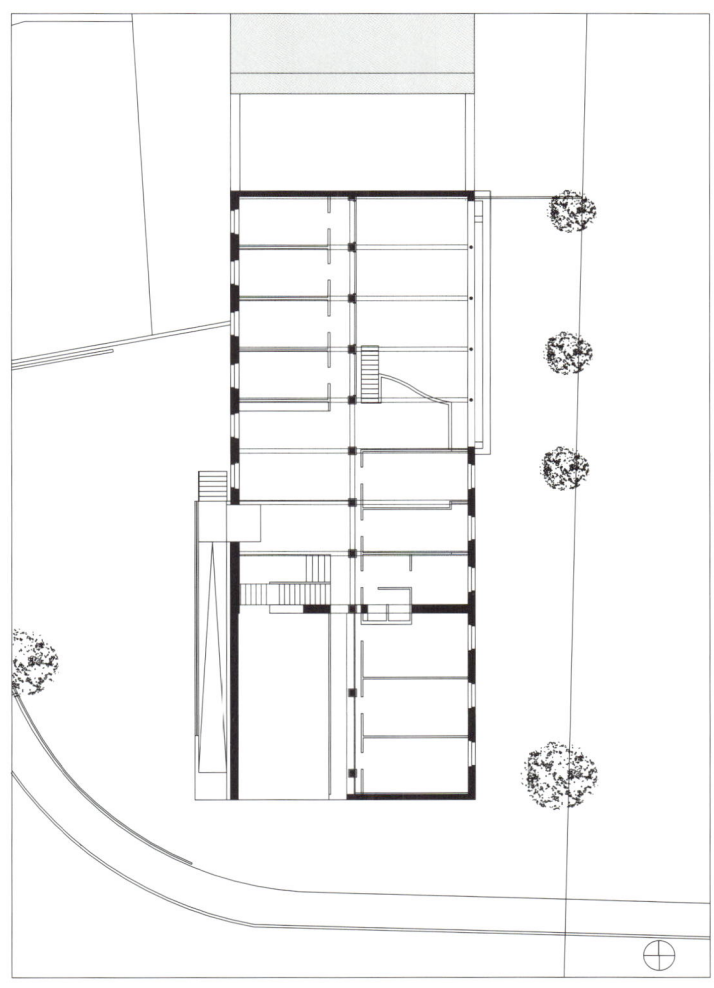

Erdgeschoß
ground floor

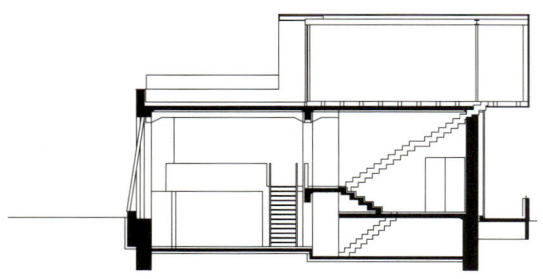

Schnitt
section

B & E > Werbeagentur Baschnegger_A

Hafengebäude Rohner in Fussach, A
Rohner Port Building in Fussach, Austria

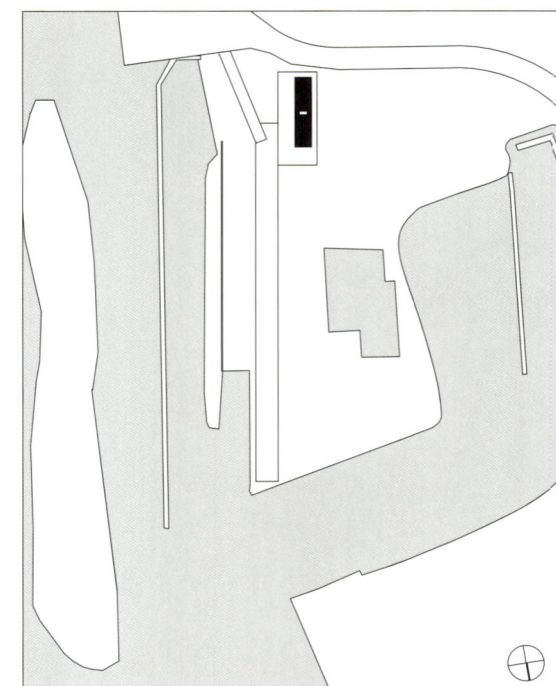

Lageplan
site plan

Ein Hauch von Sichtbeton. Licht, Luft, Wasser, Wind, Wetter. Und das Ufer des Bodensees: der Rand eines geschützten Naturraumes. Ehemaliges Werftgelände, heute vor allem als Privathafen genutzt, für mietbare Liegeplätze von Booten.
Der Bedarf: eine sinnvolle Gestaltung des Geländes – samt Zufahrt und Parkplätzen für die Bootseigentümer –, ein Minimum an Serviceeinrichtungen – hauptsächlich eine ebenerdige Entsorgungsanlage für die Toiletten der Boote und zusätzliche Toiletten für die Mieter –, schließlich ein Raum für die Verwaltung.
Hintergrundbilder für den Entwurf: die Impression eines Vogels, der auf dünnem Bein im Wasser steht und Beute sucht, bestrebt, nicht naß zu werden. Und: Segelboote auf dem See, von denen man aus der Distanz den Bootskörper kaum wahrnimmt, nur das Segel. Dieses Haus steht auch auf dünnem Bein. Und es steht auf einem Gelände, das bei Hochwasser überflutet sein kann. Aber naß werden will es nicht. Daher spielt sich (fast) alles oben ab, im auskragenden (acht Meter!) Obergeschoß. In einer Betonröhre. Sie ist nach hinten (da ist ein Wartebereich für Kunden vorgeschoben) und nach vorne zum See verglast. Und sie spottet – wie das Segel im Wind – der Schwerkraft.
Es ist ein „Ding" in Stahlbeton. Rohbauqualität gewissermaßen. Insofern sehr kostengünstig. Aber wie ein Lebewesen hat es seinen inneren Organismus: eine eingeschobene Holzkiste, die atmet und beinahe Wohnkomfort bietet.
Die Bauherrin überblickt jedenfalls ihr Terrain: Durch schmale, liegende Sichtschlitze an den Seiten sieht sie, wer kommt, durch die Verglasung Richtung See, was sich dort tut.

A touch of unfinished cement. Light, air, water, wind and weather. And the shore of Lake Constance: this is the edge of a protected area of nature, here lies a former shipyard, which is mostly used as a private port now, with berths for rent.
The requirements: the need for a useful design of the surrounding land, including the driveway and parking spaces for boat owners, as well as a miminum of service facilities. These include a boat waste disposal system and additional toilets for the respective owners, and finally, space for the administration. A bird standing on thin legs while it searches for prey and avoids getting wet. This impression constituted **the design's background**. And: the sails of the sail boats on the lake, the hulls of which can barely be seen. The building also stands on a slender leg. It stands on terrain that could be flooded in the case of high water, but it doesn't want to get wet. Therefore, (almost) everything takes place upstairs, on the upper level that projects forward (eight metres!), a cement shaft. It is clad with glass in the back (where there is a customer waiting area) and in the front, facing the lake. And it scorns gravity, like a sail in the wind. It is a ferroconcrete 'thing', with an unfinished quality of sorts, which therefore makes it cost-efficient. But it has an inner organism akin to that of a living creature: an ensconsed wooden box that breathes and offers almost residential living comfort.
In any case, the client can survey her terrain: she can see who is coming via the small, horizontal view slits and she can see the goings on on the lake via the glass panels set in that direction.

Bauherr | client **Maria Rohner** Planung | planning **Architekturbüro B & E Ziviltechniker GmbH** Projektleitung | project architect **Rainer Huchler** Mitarbeiter | assistance **Marika Marte** Statik | structural engineer **D.I. Ernst Mader** Bebaute Fläche | built up area **87 m²** Nutzfläche | floor area **51 m²** Umbauter Raum | building volume **352 m³** Planungsbeginn | commencement of planning Juli | July **1999** Baubeginn | commencement of work März | March **2000** Fertigstellung | completion Juli | July **2000**

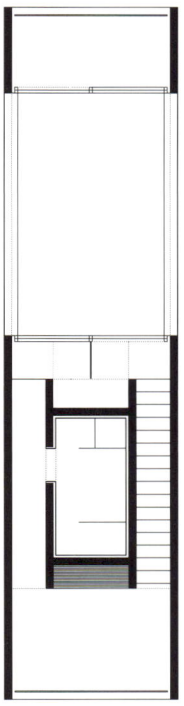

Obergeschoß
upper floor

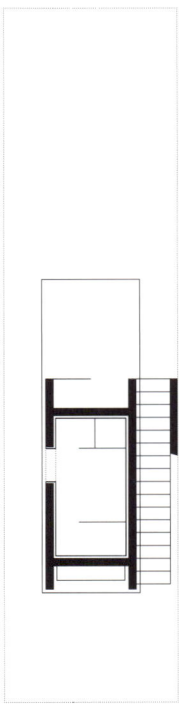

Erdgeschoß
ground floor

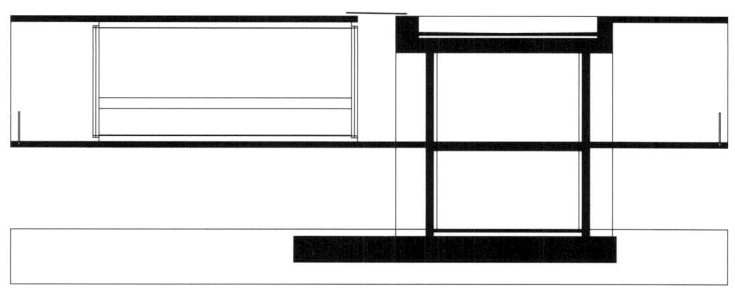

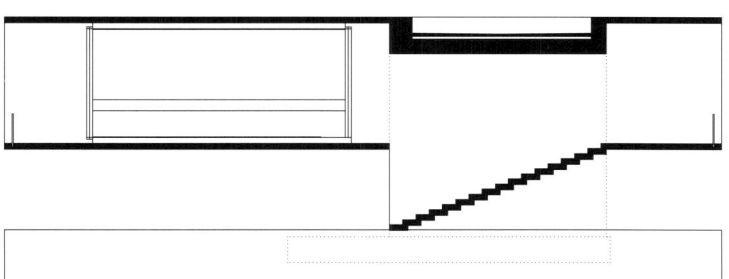

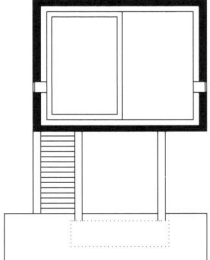 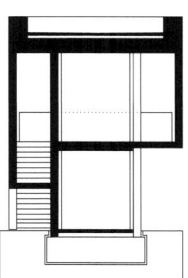

Schnitte
sections

Betriebsgebäude Sirch in Böhen, D
Sirch Industrial Building in Böhen, Germany

Das Haus steht im Allgäu, in einer dünn besiedelten Voralpenregion. Hier werden teils Industriepaletten, zum überwiegenden Teil aber Rodeln erzeugt. Der Neubau ist Teil einer kleinen Gebäudeagglomeration mit einem Wohnhaus, Lagergebäuden, Werkhallen und Anlieferungshöfen. **Übergeordnetes Thema:** architektonische Intervention in einer weitgehend intakten Landschaft.

Das Gebäude ist in bzw. auf einem ansteigenden Gelände situiert. In den Hang eingeschnitten: ein Anlieferungs- und Lagerbereich auf dem Niveau des Umfelds. Wo er ins Gelände eingeschnitten ist, wird er – dreiseitig – von Betonwänden geschützt. Auf der Anlieferungsseite (großes Schiebetor) und darüber: eine Fassade aus Doppelstegplatten, die den aufgesetzten, als Röhre formulierten und vorspringenden Hauptbaukörper schwebend erscheinen läßt. Oben: der Werkstättenbereich und die Abholung.

The house is in the *Allgäu* area of Germany, which is a sparsely populated region at the foot of the Alps. Industrial pallets are made here, but the larger part of production is dedicated to trolleys. The new building is part of an assembly of uses consisting of a residential building, storage facilities, workshops and delivery courtyards.
The guiding theme: architectural intervention in a largely pristine landscape.
The building is located on a rising incline. The delivery and storage area was cut into the slope at the level of its surroundings. The site of the incision is protected by cement walls on three sides. The delivery side is defined by a large sliding gate with a façade made of double-ridge panels that make the projecting, tubular main building appear to be hovering. On top lies the workshop and outbound delivery area.

Bauherr | client **Wolfgang Sirch** Planung | planning **Architekturbüro B & E Ziviltechniker GmbH** Projektleitung | project architect **Rainer Huchler** Statik | structural engineer **D.I. Ernst Mader, Merz und Kaufmann** Bebaute Fläche | built up area **583 m²** Nutzfläche | floor area **1.171 m²** Umbauter Raum | building volume **8.059 m³** Planungsbeginn | commencement of planning Oktober | October **1997** Fertigstellung | completion Oktober | October **1998**

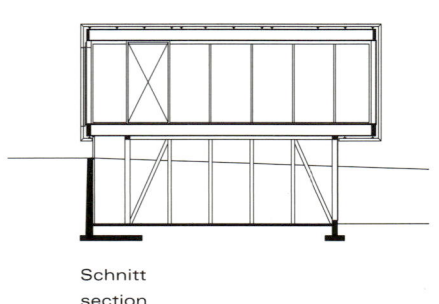

Schnitt
section

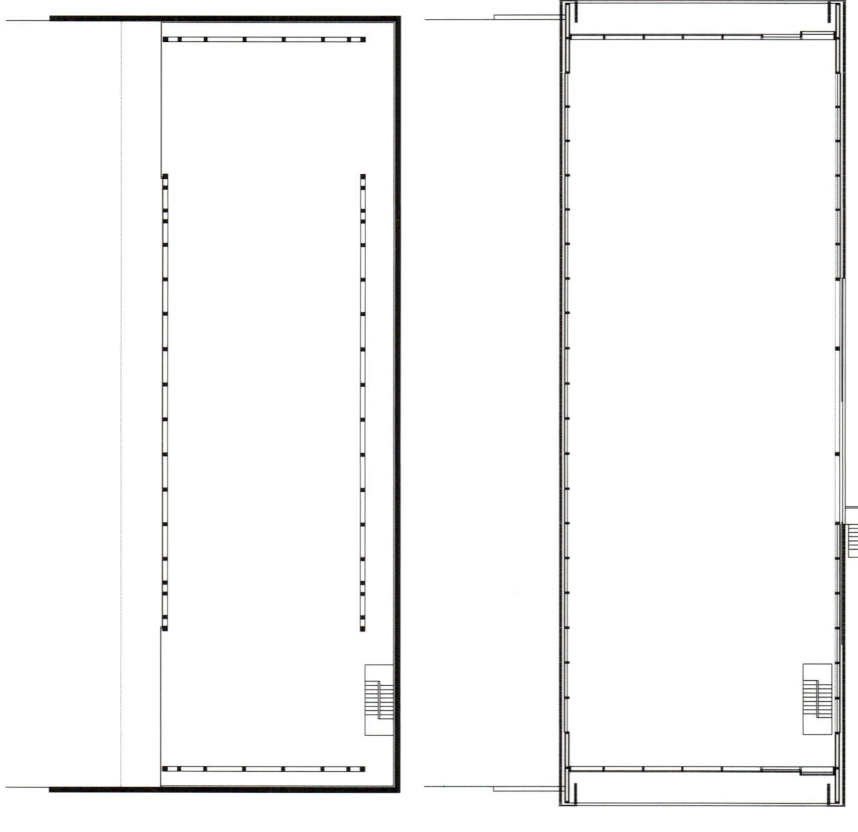

Erdgeschoß
ground floor

Obergeschoß
upper floor

B & E > Betriebsgebäude Sirch_D

Die „Röhre" ist an beiden Stirnseiten wie ein Schaufenster verglast, den gläsernen Längsfassaden wurde eine Lamellenhaut aus Lärchenholzbrettern (Eigenbau des Unternehmens) vorgeschaltet. Eine doppeldeutige Maßnahme übrigens: Auch bei den hier produzierten Rodeln spielen diese gewissen Lattenroste eine wichtige Rolle.
Spannend ist jedenfalls, wie sich mithilfe einer sehr einfachen Konstruktion – zwei Fachwerkträgern, auf denen die „Röhre" scheinbar schwebend aufsitzt – ein sehr nachdrücklicher Effekt erzielen läßt. Man sieht überhaupt nur von Osten wie das Gebäude wirklich funktioniert. Aus allen anderen Richtungen hat man den Eindruck: Etwas schwebt über dem Gelände.

The 'tube' features glass paneling akin to that of showcase on the gable ends. The glass façade along the length of the structure is protected by larch timber boarding (produced by the company). This was a double-edged measure, by the way: these lathes also play an important role in the production of the company's trolleys.
What is exciting in any case is how, with the help of a very simple construction – two open-web girders, it was possible to make the 'tube' seem to hover, which creates a lasting effect. It is only possible to see how the building really works from the east. Something seems to be hovering over the site from any other perspective.

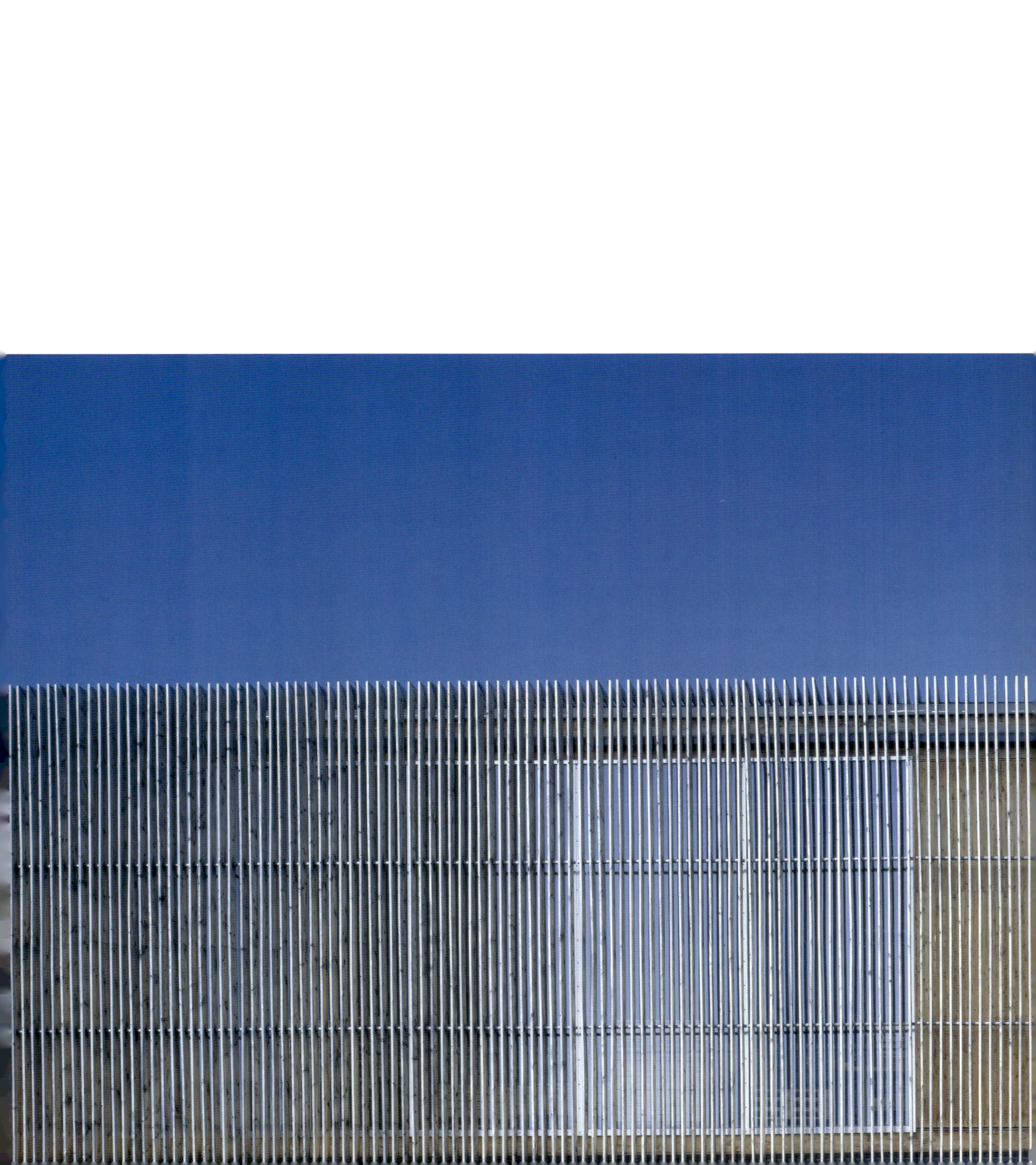

Einfamilienhaus Flatz in Schaan, FL
Flatz One-Family House in Schaan,
Duchy of Liechtenstein

Ein skulpturales Haus aus maisgelbem Sichtbeton. **Die Umgebung:** ein zersiedeltes Einfamilienhausgebiet. Trotzdem hat der Ort eine entscheidende Qualität: seine Fernbezüge. Man sieht ein spektakuläres Gebirgspanorama. Daher sind zwei Themen miteinander verschnitten. Erstens, die Abschottung nach außen; zweitens, die inszenierte Komposition der Öffnungen Richtung Bergwelt.
Schon der Sichtbeton ist eine lesbare Geste nach außen: Vom Umfeld setzt sich das Haus dadurch unmissverständlich ab. Und die komplexe Verschachtelung der verschiedenen Volumina bzw. die teilweise Einfriedung mit einer (durchbrochenen) Mauer schafft Räume – außen und innen –, die sehr subtil differenzieren. **Außen:** ein ganz intimer, tiefliegender grüner Hof, zu dem Gäste- und Arbeitszimmer orientiert sind; etwas höher gelegen eine dem Wohnbereich zugeordnete Terrasse, ein Swimmingpool, eine Grünfläche, in die nur jene Einblick nehmen können, die als Besucher hinauf zum Eingang gehen; eine überdachte Terrasse im Obergeschoß. **Innen:** ebenerdig Wohnraum und Eßzimmer ein Kontinuum, verbunden mit der Küche; darüber die verschiedenen Schlafräume und Badezimmer; aber jede Öffnung (Fenster, Fixverglasung zum Pool) im Haus so präzis gesetzt, daß sie den Rahmen für ein ganz bestimmtes Blickfeld bietet.
Sicher keine offene, beliebig nutzbare Struktur, sondern maßgefertigte Haute Couture. Hier läßt sich die Belegung der Räume nicht einfach verändern. Dafür ist die Banalität des Umfelds bestenfalls als Randposition präsent. Der Fernblick dominiert.

A maize-yellow sculpted house made of unfinished cement. **The surroundings:** a sprawling, overdeveloped single-family house area. But the location nonetheless has a decisive quality: its far-reaching views. One sees a spectacular mountain panorama, therefore, two themes are intertwined here. First, closing off the outside and second, the composition of the openings facing the mountains.
The unfinished cement is in itself a readable gesture to the environment outside. The house stands out unmistakably among its surroundings. The complex arrangement of the varying structure volumes and the partial enclosure with a (broken through) wall creates spaces – on the inside and outside – that are characterised by subtle differentiations. **Outside:** a very intimate, low-slung green courtyard with the guest and work rooms facing it. Somewhat higher lies a terrace belonging to the living space, a swimming pool and a green area that can only be seen by those visitors who walk up the entrance. A roofed terrace is located on the uppermost level.
Inside: the ground level living spaces and the dining room create a continuous structure connected to the kitchen. Above it are the various bedrooms and bathrooms. But every opening (the windows and fixed glass paneling facing the pool) is set so precisely that it frames a specific, individual view.
This certainly isn't an open structure that can be used for any purpose. Instead, it is a custom-made, *Haute Couture* project. The rooms' purposes cannot be changed at will, and the banality of the surroundings is only perceptible on the periphery.
The far-reaching views are the dominant feature.

Bauherr | client **Dr. Dietmar Flatz** Planung | planning **Architekturbüro B & E Ziviltechniker GmbH** Projektleitung | project architect **Marlies Sofia, Paul Martin** Mitarbeiter | assistance **Eckehart Loidolt, Christian Tabernigg** Landschaftsarchitekt | landscape architect **Vogt Landschaftsarchitekten** Haustechnik Konzept | mechanical engineer **GMI Gasser & Messner Ingenieure** Statik | structural engineer **Ferdy Kaiser** Grundstücksfläche | site area **698 m²** Bebaute Fläche | built up area **277 m²** Nutzfläche | floor area **244 m²** Umbauter Raum | building volume **1.665 m³** Planungsbeginn | commencement of planning August | August **1998** Baubeginn | commencement of work September | September **1999** Fertigstellung | completion Juli | July **2000**

98
99 >   B & E > Einfamilienhaus Flatz_FL

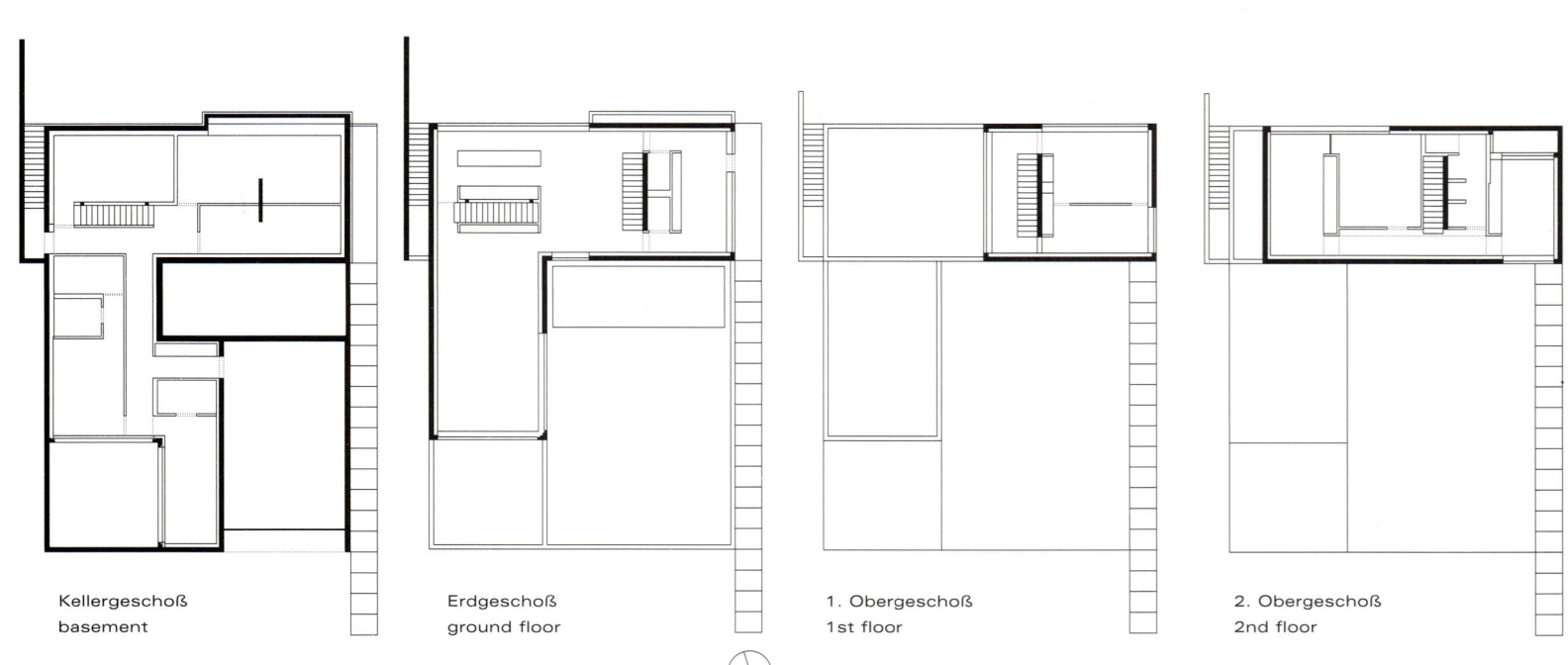

Kellergeschoß
basement

Erdgeschoß
ground floor

1. Obergeschoß
1st floor

2. Obergeschoß
2nd floor

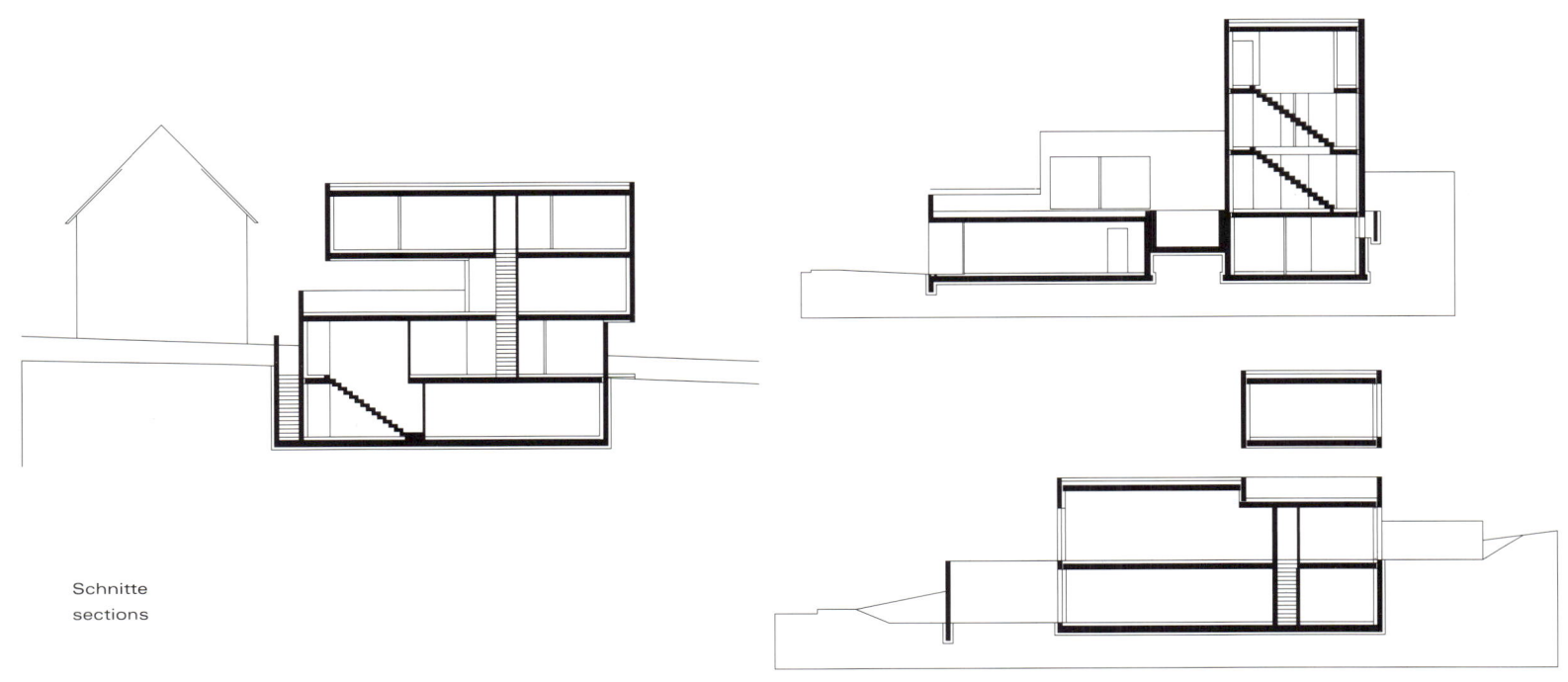

Schnitte
sections

Einfamilienhaus in H, D
One-Family House in H, Germany

Die zeitgenössische Interpretation des **klassischen Villentyps**. Ein Haus auf einem Hügel, von dem man bis hinunter zum Bodensee sieht. Die Anfahrt ist nicht zu knapp und führt zuletzt an ein paar Bauernhäusern vorbei. Eine Referenz an den ländlichen Charakter des Umfelds – die Schindeln an der Fassade. Es ist ein kubisches Haus auf einem großen Grundstück. Und es umfaßt alle Elemente einer Villa – von den parkartigen Außenanlagen (Vogt, Zürich) über die Zugangssituation bis zur repräsentativen Halle, in und um die dann die verschiedensten Funktionen wie Wohnen, Essen – einschließlich Bibliothek und Kaminzimmer – gelagert sind.
Die individuellen Bereiche im oberen Geschoß sind wie kleine Häuser organisiert. Theoretisch könnten sie auch ganz autark funktionieren. Beim Bereich des Kindermädchens ist es schon fast so: Sie hat sogar eine eigene Stiege. Wichtig ist die skulpturale Überformung des Obergeschosses durch Einschnitte, kleine Balkone, die jeder Einheit zugeordnet sind, und durch die Träger darüber. Damit wird hier jene Bereicherung, die beim traditionellen Villentyp der Dekor leistet, durch die Lichtführung erreicht.
Draußen gibt es einen großen Pool und eine kleine Box, das ist die Grillstelle. Und es gibt einen gestalteten Park. Der Eingang ist mit grünem Stein formuliert, drinnen ist dann alles sehr weiß und voller edlem Nußholz (auf dem Boden, beim eingebauten Mobiliar). Die Wand, der Hintergrund des Wohnens in diesem Haus, hat also wirklich noch den Architekten gehört.

A contemporary interpretation of a **classical villa**. A house on a hill from which one has a view that reaches all the way down to Lake Constance. The access route isn't short and visitors drive past a few farms towards the end of the road. The shingles on the façade are a reference to the rural character of the surroundings. It is a cubic house on a large plot of land and it comprises all the villa elements – from the park-like facilities outside (Vogt, Zurich) to the representative entrance access, around which a large variety of functions such as living, dining and even the library and chimney room are aligned.
The individual areas on the upper level are organised as little houses. Theoretically, they could function in complete autonomy. This is almost the case with the nanny's quarters: she even has her own staircase. An important feature is the sculpted shape of the upper level that includes incisions and the small balconies allotted to each unit, as well as the stays above. Hence the building is enhanced by the organisation of light within as opposed to the decorations in a traditional villa.
A large pool and a small box, the barbecue area, are located outside, as well as a landscaped park. The entrance was made with green stone, while everthing inside is very white and full of refined walnut wood (used on the floor and on the built-in furniture). The wall, the residential backdrop in this house, really did belong to the architects after all.

Planung I planning **Architekturbüro B & E Ziviltechniker GmbH** Projektleitung I project architect **Rainer Huchler** Mitarbeiter I assistance **Marika Marte** Landschaftsarchitekt I landscape architect **Vogt Landschaftsarchitekten** Haustechnik Konzept I mechanical engineer **GMI Gasser & Messner Ingenieure** Statik I structural engineer **D.I. Ernst Mader, D.I. Bruno Rissi** Grundstücksfläche I site area **4.260 m²** Bebaute Fläche I built up area **396 m²** Nutzfläche I floor area **542 m²** Umbauter Raum I building volume **3.965 m³** Planungsbeginn I commencement of planning August I August **1997** Baubeginn I commencement of work Oktober I October **1998** Fertigstellung I completion April I April **2000**

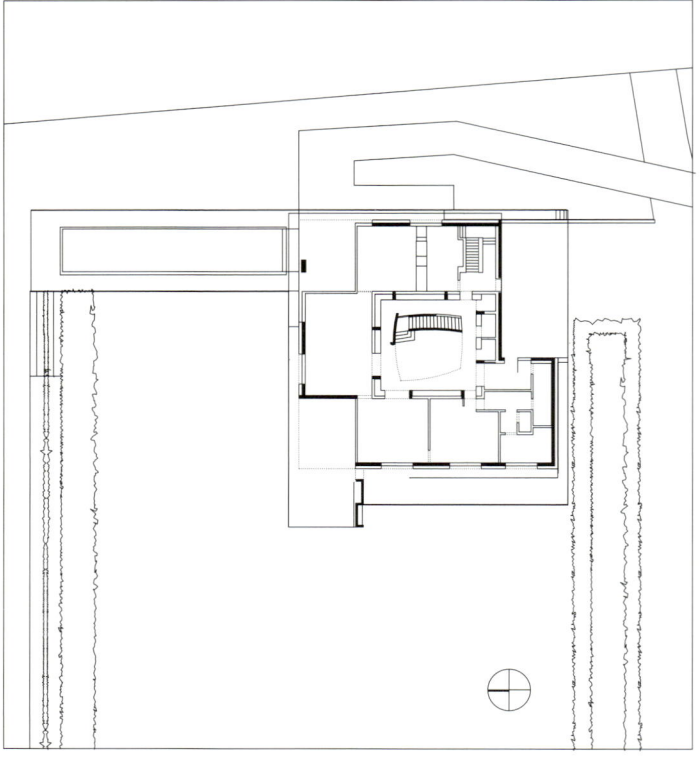

Erdgeschoß
ground floor

1. Obergeschoß
1st floor

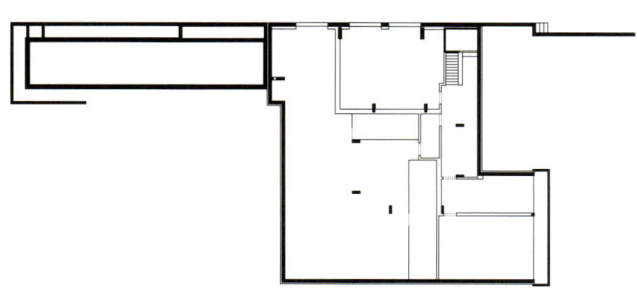

Kellergeschoß
basement

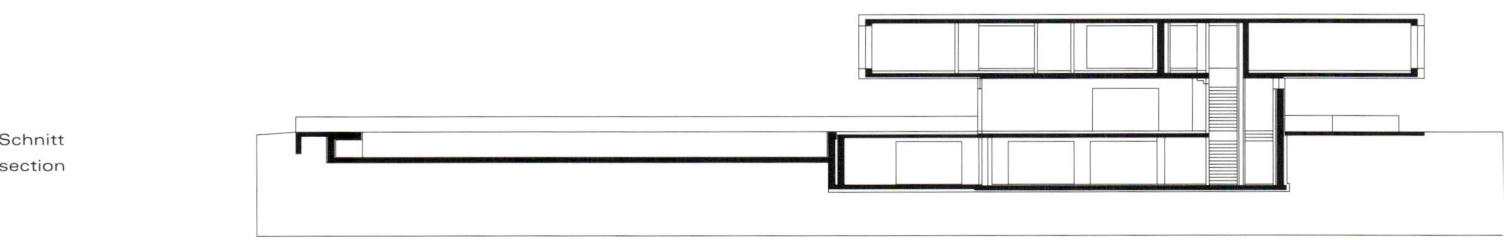

Schnitt
section

Öko-Hauptschule in Mäder, A
Ecological School in Mäder, Austria

Ein städtebaulicher Wettbewerb. Aufgabe: die Neuordnung des Zentrums von Mäder. Es ging um den Neubau eines Gemeindezentrums mit größerem Veranstaltungssaal und den Neubau einer Hauptschule; ein bestehendes Schulhaus und ein Kindergarten waren in die Planung einzubinden; ein kleines Schulgebäude vom Ende der fünfziger Jahre war eventuell zu erhalten und neu zu nutzen. Wichtiger zusätzlicher Aspekt: Das vorhandene, dichte Fahrrad-, Fußwege- und Grünraumsystem sollte sinnvoll in die Planung einbezogen werden.

In der ersten Bauetappe wurde **das Gemeindezentrum mit dem großen Vorplatz** errichtet, auf den das bestehende Wegesystem orientiert ist. Die alte Schule wurde saniert und für Vereinszwecke genutzt. In der zweiten Bauetappe wurde die Hauptschule realisiert.

Es ist eine sehr große **Schule in Verbindung mit einem Doppelturnsaal**. Das Thema „Öko" kam erst nachträglich hinzu, nachdem sich die Gemeinde um spezielle Förderungen beworben und den Zuschlag erhalten hatte. Die Folge war eine vollständige Neuplanung des Wettbewerbsprojekts. Ziel war ein Gebäude, das als Energieverbraucher auch selbst ökologischen Ansprüchen genügt.

An urban construction competition. The task: the reorganisation of the centre of *Mäder*. This meant the construction of a new community centre with a larger event facility and building a new school. An existing school house and a kindergarten were to be integrated in planning. A small school building stemming from the end of the fifties was to be preserved and used for new purposes. An important additional task was to include the existing, dense cycling, pedestrian and green belt system usefully in the new plans.

The community centre and a large forecourt were built during the first construction phase. The existing network of paths is directed towards this square. The old school was refurbished and used for association meetings. The new school was built during the second construction phase.

It is a very large **school with a double gymnasium**. The "ecological" theme was only added later, after the community had applied and received special subsidies. The consequence was the complete redrafting of the competition project. The objective was to create a building that meets ecological requirements in terms of energy consumption.

Bauherr | client **Gemeinde Mäder** Planung | planning **Architekturbüro B & E Ziviltechniker GmbH** Projektleitung | project architect **Rainer Huchler** Landschaftsarchitekt | landscape architect **Vogt Landschaftsarchitekten** Haustechnik Konzept | mechanical engineer **GMI Gasser & Messner Ingenieure** Statik | structural engineer **Rüsch, Diem + Partner** Grundstücksfläche | site area **5.860 m²** Bebaute Fläche | built up area **2.010 m²** Nutzfläche | floor area **3.728 m²** Umbauter Raum | building volume **23.171 m³** Planungsbeginn | commencement of planning Mai | May **1994** Baubeginn | commencement of work November | November **1996** Fertigstellung | completion August | August **1998**

B & E > Öko-Hauptschule_A

Die Schule ist ein kompakter Würfel, der innen wie ein Windrad – geschlossener Teil, Klassentrakt, geschlossener Teil, Klassentrakt usw. – organisiert ist. Der Zugang zu den einzelnen Klassen ist als Nischeneinzug in Nußholz – Eingang plus Garderobe – formuliert. Durch die Mittelzone ist ein Lichthof durchgesteckt, der von oben das Tageslicht bis hinunter transportiert. Sie wird als Pausenfläche genutzt. Angelagert: der Lift. Das Stiegenhaus – von oben belichtet, die Podeste gehen nicht bis an die Wand – liegt in einer der vier Ecken.

The school is a compact cube whose organisation within is akin to that of a wind mill – enclosed façade, open classroom, enclosed façade, open classroom, etc. The individual classroom access niches were finished in walnut wood – entrance and wardrobes. An atrium that transports light from the top down was set in the middle zone. This space is used as a recess area. Stored away: the elevator. The stairway is lit from the top, the steps do not reach the walls and it lies in one of the four corners.

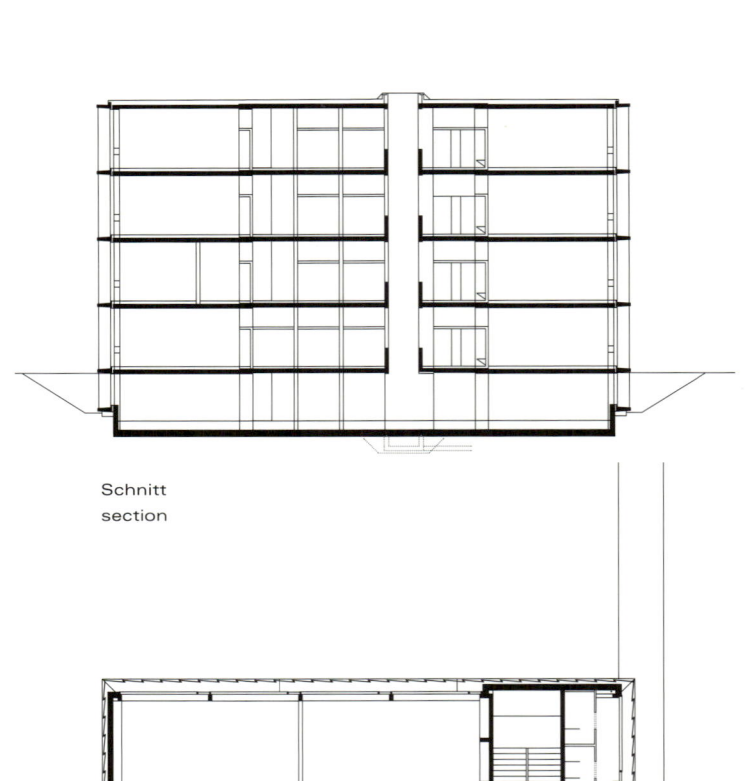

Schnitt
section

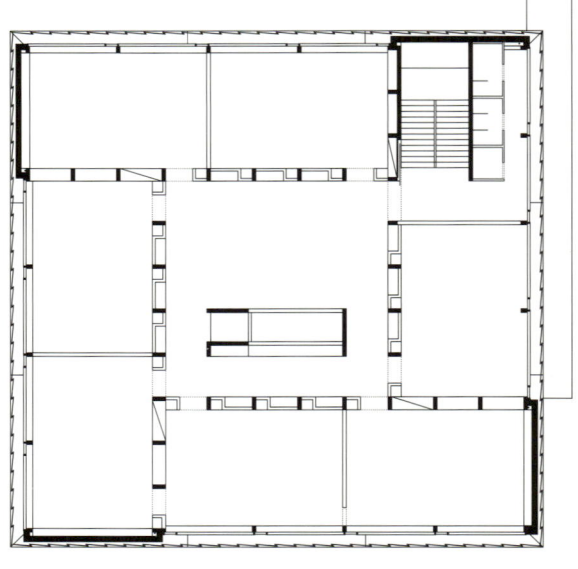

Regelgeschoß
standard floor

Erdgeschoß
ground floor

Die Doppelturnhalle ist teilweise in die Erde eingegraben. Von außen sieht man also nur das umlaufende Band der gläsernen Fassade. Dadurch ist das große Gebäudevolumen, das die Dimensionierung in der Umgebung sprengen würde, weitgehend relativiert. Man sieht durch das Gebäude durch, das Dach hat fast den Charakter eines Flugdaches. Von außen ist die Turnhalle über einen asphaltierten Platz – bei außerschulischen Veranstaltungen Parkplatz – zugänglich. Es gibt ein kleines Foyer, eine eigene kleine Küche, Zuschauertribünen. Mit der Schule ist die Turnhalle über einen Tunnel im Untergeschoß verbunden, hier liegen auch die Umkleidekabinen.

Trotz rigoroser Kostenbeschränkung – das Gebäude durfte nicht mehr als eine herkömmliche Schule dieser Größenordnung kosten – wurde das ökologische Ziel einer Minimierung des Energieverbrauches beispielhaft umgesetzt. Schulhaus und Doppelturnhalle verbrauchen nicht mehr Energie als ein Einfamilienhaus. Erreicht wurde das hauptsächlich durch die architektonische Form und durch einfache technische Mittel – geringe Abstrahlflächen, Ausnutzung der Wärme, die im Gebäude (durch die Schüler) erzeugt wird, Ausnutzung von Erdwärme und Erdkühle (durch ein Luftsystem unter dem Vorplatz) –, also ohne den Einsatz von High Tech. Für die Schüler funktioniert das Haus außerdem als „gebautes Lehrbuch". Sie können im projektbezogenen Unterricht ins Energiekonzept dieses Hauses eingreifen und die Folgen ihrer Intervention – via Zugang zum zentralen Rechner – jederzeit beobachten und überprüfen.

The double gymnasium was partly dug into the ground. One can only see the encompassing ribbon of the glass façade from the outside. Thus the large building volume, which would dwarf its surroundings with its dimensions, was diminished. One can look right through the building and the roof almost seems to be a canopy. The gymnasium can be reached via a paved square on the outside that is used as a parking lot for extracurricular activities. The structure includes a small foyer, a small kitchen and stands. The school is linked to the gymnasium via a tunnel in the lower level, which is where the changing rooms are as well.

Despite the rigorous cost-cutting that was necessary, since the building was not supposed to cost more than a conventional school this size, the ecological goal of minimising energy consumption was achieved in an exemplary manner. The school house and double gymnasium do not need more energy than a single-family house. This was mainly possible due to the architectural shape that was chosen and simple technical means – low amounts of radiation-reflecting surfaces and the use of the warmth generated by the pupils in the school. Other factors were geothermics and cooling via a ventilation system installed under the forecourt. Thus high tech was not necessary. For the pupils, the house functions as a "built textbook". They can influence the energy concept of the school in their project work and observe and monitor the consequences of their intervention via access to the central computer at any time.

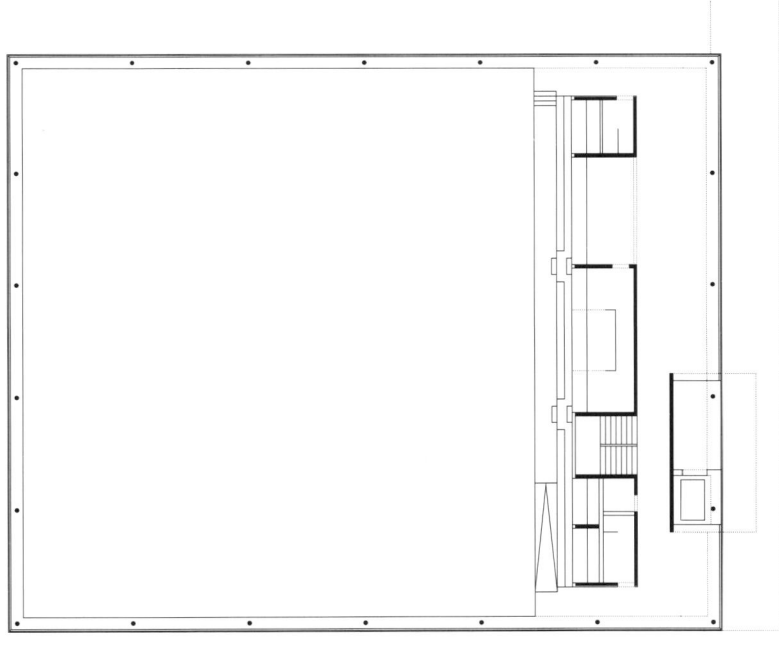

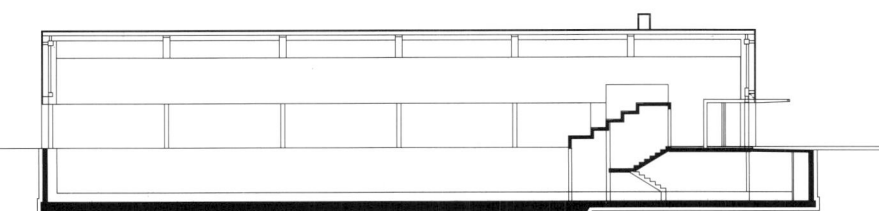

Turnhalle
Erdgeschoß
Schnitt

Gymnasium
ground floor
section

Sanierung und Erweiterung der HTL
in Bregenz, A
Refurbishment and Expansion
of the Technical School in Bregenz, Austria

Ein prominenter Standort: direkt an der Uferstraße des Bodensees. Dem Gebäude kommt schon deswegen städtebaulich eine besondere Stellung – als Tor zur Innenstadt – zu. Gefordert war **die Sanierung des Altbestandes und ein Erweiterungsbau** mit zahlreichen Klassen- und Werkräumen, Lehrerzimmern und verschiedenen Nebenräumen. Durch den Zubau wurde die Substanz fast verdoppelt.

Straßenseitig folgt das neue Gebäude dem Verlauf des Verkehrsweges, umfasst dann aber das alte L-förmige Haus so, daß eine Blocksituation mit unterschiedlichen Innenhöfen entsteht. Besonders betont: die Ecke des Blocks, die dicht an die Straße herangerückt ist. Die Torsituation wird dadurch noch verstärkt. Dazu trägt auch die Fassadenlösung des Neubaus entscheidend bei – eine Sockelzone aus schwarz eingefärbtem Beton, darüber eine Glasfassade, die von einer äußeren Haut aus horizontalen, weißen Metall-Lamellen umhüllt ist. Wichtig: die Einbettung des neuen Bauteils ins innerstädtische Umfeld. An der Fassade des ruhigen, sehr transparenten Baukörpers bildet sich ein malerisches Licht- und Schattenspiel ab, das die Dimensionen des Neubaus praktisch entmaterialisiert.

A prominent location: directly on the road along the shore of Lake Constance. This fact alone gives the building special importance in terms of urban construction, it is the gate to the inner city. What was required was **a refurbishment of the old building and the construction of an annex housing** a number of classrooms, workshops, faculty rooms and various other supplemental rooms. The total surface area of the facility was doubled with the annex.

Along the street side, the new building follows the flow of traffic. But it encompasses the old L-shaped building in a way that allowed for the creation of differing interior courtyards. Particular emphasis was given to the corner of the block, which is set close to the street. The gate location was thus given additional stress. The façade solution also made a decisive contribution to this effect – the base course is made of black stained cement with a glass façade on top that is encased in an exterior skin consisting of white metal louvers. An important feature: the new building segment is imbedded in its inner-city environment. The picturesque interplay between light and shadow on the calm, very transparent structure practically dematerialises the dimensions of the new building.

Bauherr | client **Republik Österreich** Planung | planning **Architekturbüro B & E Ziviltechniker GmbH, D.I. Norbert Schweitzer** Projektleitung | project architect **Michael Ohneberg** Statik | structural engineer **D.I. Plankel** Bebaute Fläche | built up area Erweiterung **2.650 m²**, Altbau **1.200 m²** Nutzfläche | floor area **11.400 m²** Umbauter Raum | building volume **48.200 m³** Planungsbeginn | commencement of planning Wettbewerb | competition **1990** Baubeginn | commencement of work April | April **1995** Fertigstellung | completion Februar | February **1998**

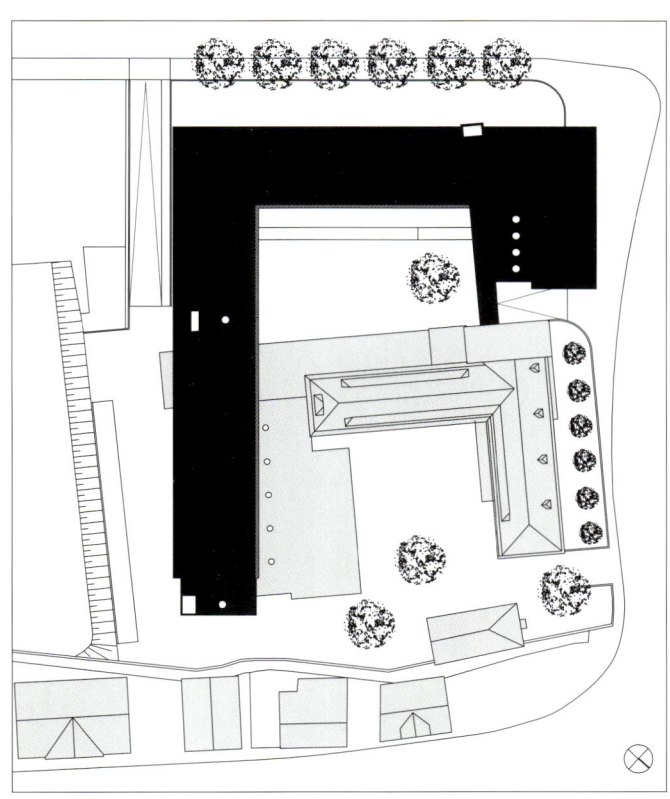

Lageplan
site plan

Die Innenhöfe sind ganz unterschiedlich ausgebildet. Wenn man das Ensemble betritt, kommt man zuerst in den südwestlich gelegenen, großen Schulhof. Er hat einen ausgesprochen kontemplativen Charakter, die rundum laufende interne Erschließung erinnert fast an einen Klostergang. Architektonisch dominiert ein kräftiger, maisgelb eingefärbter Betonraster das Bild. Er steht vor der Glasfassade und wird durch eine Sekundärstruktur aus Holzrahmen und Glasflächen bzw. die Unterteilung der Glasflächen in öffenbare, fixe und opake Elemente unterschiedlicher Größe noch in sich gegliedert. Der nordöstliche Hof (der „Auto-Hof") ist dagegen Verkehrsfläche und Anlieferungszone und wird auf der einen Seite von einer mehrgeschossigen Betonscheibe vor dem Altbauflügel begrenzt, hinter der ein neues Fluchttreppenhaus liegt; auf der gegenüberliegenden von einem nur zweigeschossigen, ebenfalls neuen Werkstattgebäude aus schwarzem Sichtbeton. Zwischen diesem Werkstätten- und dem umlaufenden Klassentrakt liegt schließlich ein weiterer, überdachter und von oben belichteter Hof. Hier schaffen zwei schmale Brücken auch eine direkte Verbindung zwischen den Klassen und den Werkstätten.

The inner courtyards were developed in different ways. When one enters the ensemble, the first space one reaches is the large school courtyard that lies on the southwestern end of the facility. It has a very contemplative character and the internal access possibilities surrounding it almost remind the visitor of a convent. The image is dominated architecturally by the intensely maize yellow-colored cement grid that stands in front of the glass façade. It is organised within itself by a secondary structure consisting of timber frames and glass surfaces. These glass surfaces are subdivided into opening, fixed and opaque elements of varying sizes. On the other hand, the courtyard to the northwest (the "car courtyard") acts as a traffic and delivery area. The border to the old building wing is defined by multi-level cement slab that conceals a new emergency escape stairway. On the other side, the courtyard is bordered by a two-story workshop building made of black unfinished cement. Between this workshop wing and the surrounding classrooms lies another covered courtyard that is lit from above. Two slender bridges create a direct connection between the classrooms and workshops.

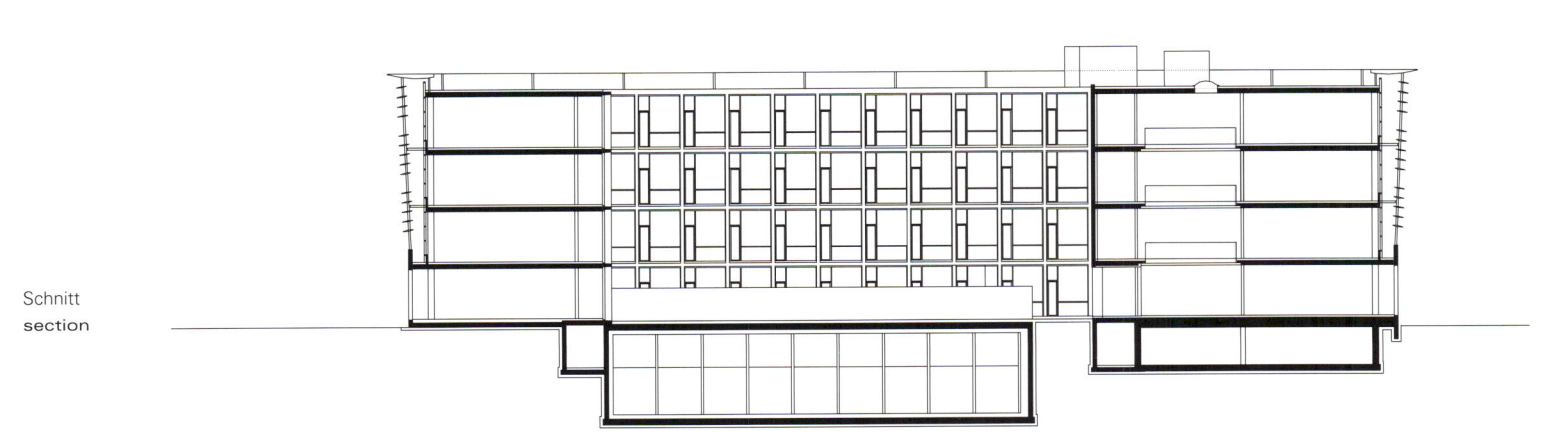

Schnitt
section

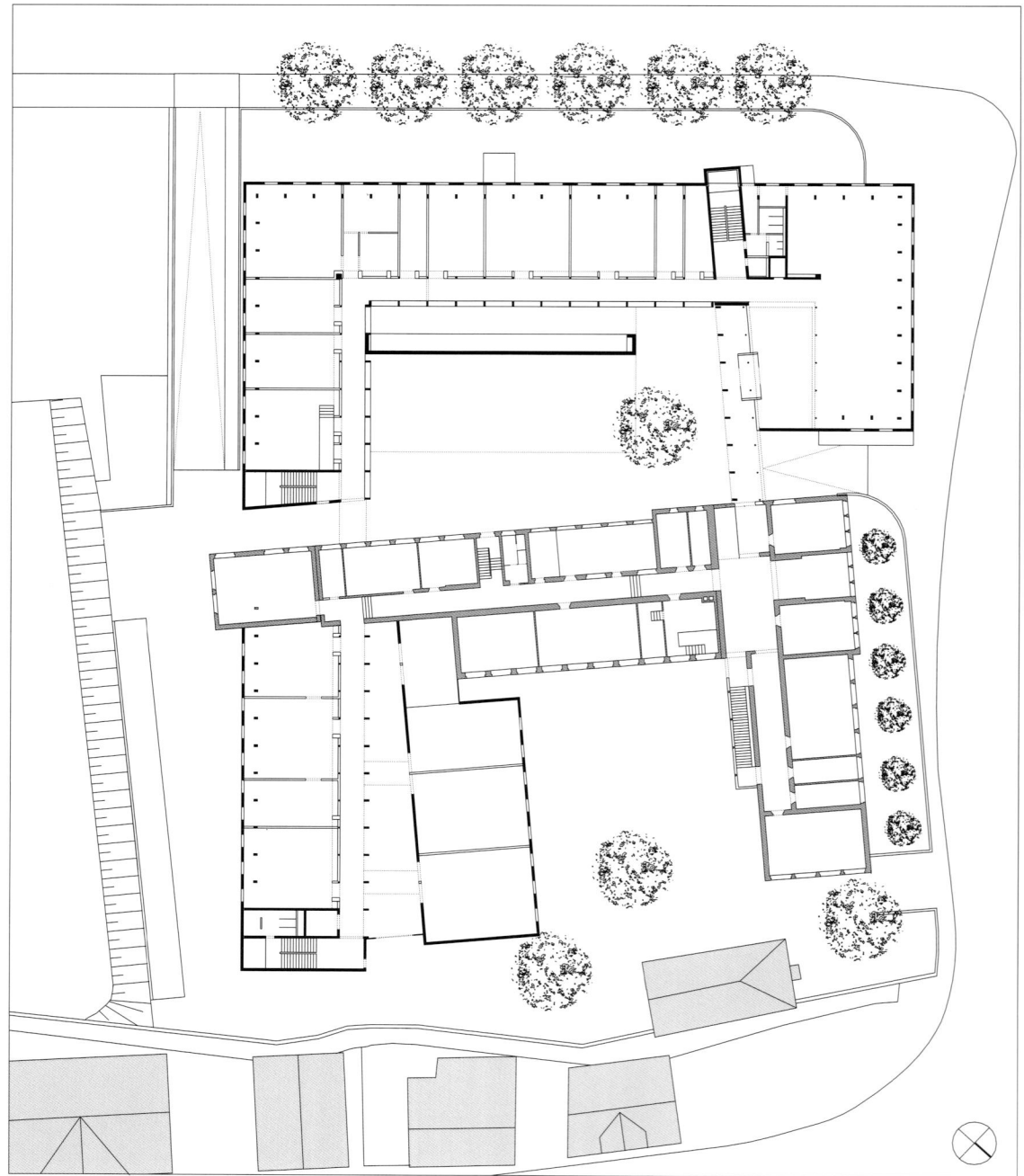

Erdgeschoß
ground floor

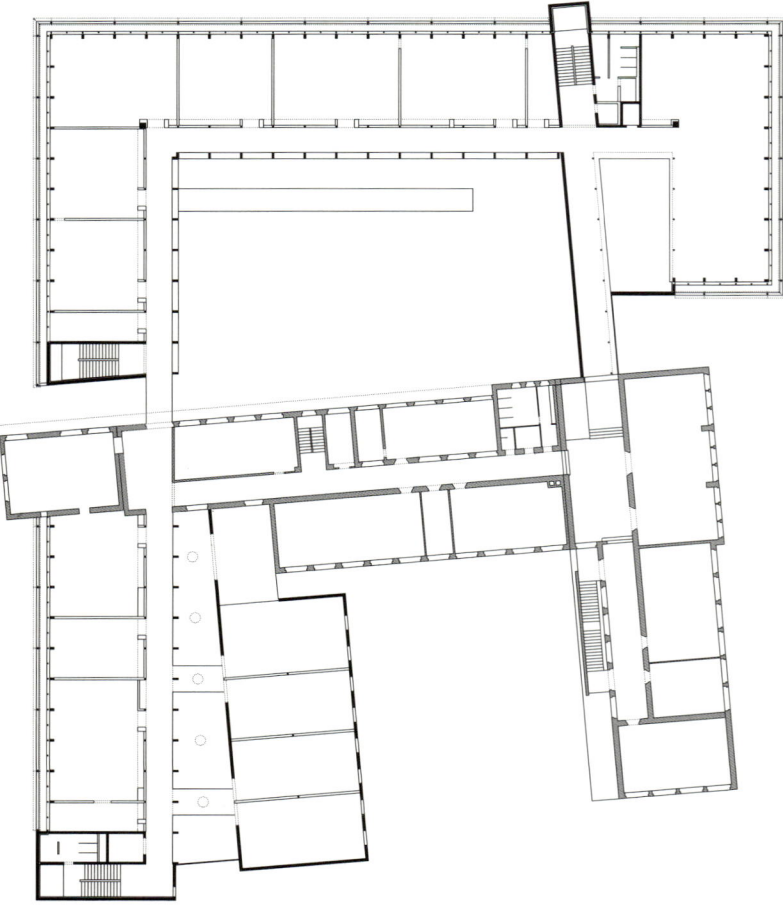

1. Obergeschoß
1st floor

Sowohl konstruktiv als auch organisatorisch haben sich B&E für **ein einfaches Konzept** entschieden. Die Tragkonstruktion des Neubaus ist ein Betonskelett, die hofseitigen Stahlstützen verschwinden in der Wand; die Gänge kragen aus; die Betonstruktur ist vorgestellt. Im Neubau bilden sich nur die Fluchtstiegenhäuser als massive Bauteile nach außen sichtbar ab. Auch organisatorisch basiert der einhüftige Neubau auf einem einfachen, trotzdem flexiblen Konzept, bietet dabei aber höchste räumliche Qualität.

B&E chose **a simple concept** with regard to construction and organisation. The supporting structure of the new building is a cement skeleton. The steel trusses disappear into the wall on the courtyard side, while the corridors project outward. The cement structure is set in front. The only elements of the new building that are delineated on the outside are the massive emergency escape stairway components. The new one-hip structure is based on a flexible concept and therefore offers the highest spatial quality.

Erweiterung der ETH in Zürich, CH
Expansion of the ETH in Zurich, Switzerland

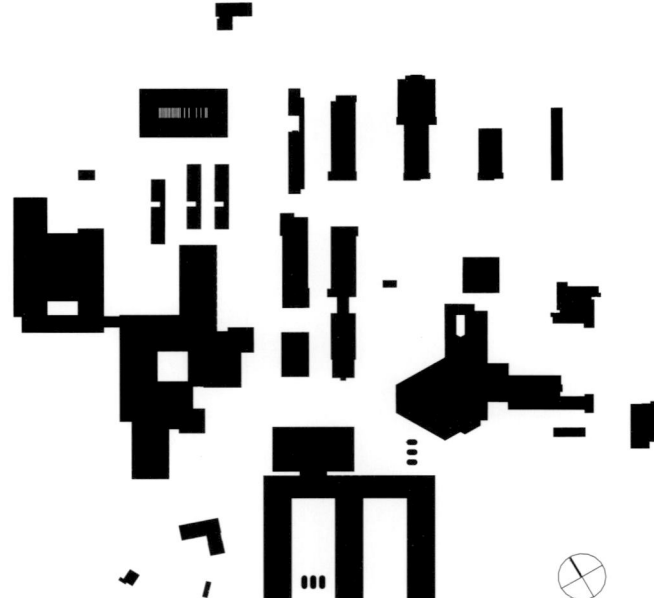

Fünf Themen – ein Gebäude (HIT)
Thema eins: Städtebau. So wie das Chemiegebäude von Mario Campi den Westabschluß der Längsachse auf dem Hönggerberg bildet, so wird das neue Informatikgebäude den Ostabschluß definieren. Wichtig dabei: die besondere Aussicht, weil der Standort gleichzeitig einen topographischen Übergang markiert, dort beginnt das Tal.
Thema zwei: Flexibilität. Es mußte ein besonders flexibles Gebäude sein, weil sich die Nutzung, speziell im Forschungsbereich, ständig und unvorhersehbar ändert. Theoretisch wäre es sogar möglich, das Gebäude in einer ferneren Zukunft völlig anders zu nutzen.
Drittes Thema: Öffentlichkeit. Ziel war ein Innenraum, der qualitativ eine vergleichbare Interpretation von Öffentlichkeit darstellt, wie sie andere Hochschulgebäude aus dem letzten Jahrhundert leisten. Deswegen die Konzentration auf die zentrale Halle – sie nimmt 40 Prozent des Gesamtvolumens in Anspruch –, in die zwar einzelne spezielle Nutzungen eingeschaltet sind, aber ohne den Raumfluß, die Kontinuität zu stören.
Viertes Thema: der Landschaftsbezug. Der Hönggerberg ist ein grüner Campus. Auf diese wesentliche Qualität des Ortes ist auch die ganze Fassade ausgerichtet, einschließlich ihrer räumlichen Schichtung.
Fünftes Thema: die energetische Optimierung. Deswegen ist es ein so kompakter Bau. Gleichzeitig wird durch die Fassadenschichtung ein hohes Maß an Selbstbeschattung erreicht, das von Ende April bis Ende September keine direkte Sonnenbestrahlung zuläßt.

Five themes – one building (HIT)
First theme: urban development, just as the chemical building by Mario Campi marks the end of the longitudinal axis to the west on Hönggerberg, the new computer sciences building will define the end to the east. Important: the special view, since the site also marks a topographical transition, the valley begins there.
Second theme: flexibility. It had to be a particularly flexible building because its use, the realm of research, is particularly prone to constant, unpredictable change. Theoretically, it would even be possible to use the building for a completely different purpose in the distant future.
Third theme: the public dimension. The objective was an interior space that represents the public aspect qualitatively, in a manner comparable to university buildings erected last century. Hence the concentration on the central hall – it occupies 40 percent of the total volume. It integrates special uses, but without disturbing the flow of space, of continuity.
Fourth theme: a relation to the setting. The Hönggerberg is a green campus. The entire façade including its spatial layering, therefore addresses this striking quality of the location.
Fifth theme: optimising energy use, that's why it is such a compact building. A high degree of shadow was created with the façade layering, since this area does not allow for direct radiation from sun from the end of April through the end of September.

Bauherr | client **ETH Zürich** Planung | planning **B & E Baumschlager-Eberle GmbH** Projektleitung | project architect **Elmar Hasler** Mitarbeiter | assistance **René Bechter** Landschaftsarchitekt | landscape architect **Vogt Landschaftsarchitekten** Haustechnik Konzept | mechanical engineer **HL Technik AG** Statik | structural engineer **D.I. Ernst Mader, D.I. Bruno Rissi** Grundstücksfläche | site area **7.000 m²** Bebaute Fläche | built up area **2.420 m²** Nutzfläche | floor area **11.810 m²** Umbauter Raum | building volume **58.600 m³** Planungsbeginn | commencement of planning März | March **2002**

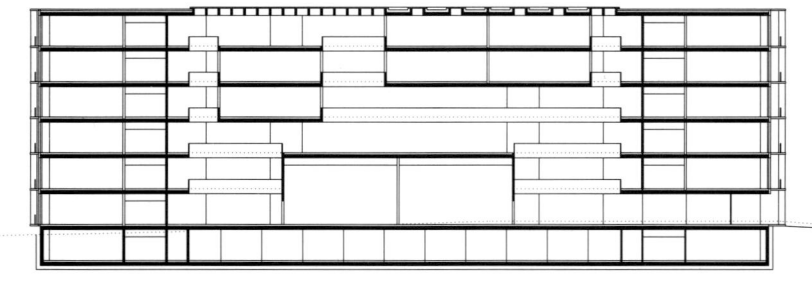
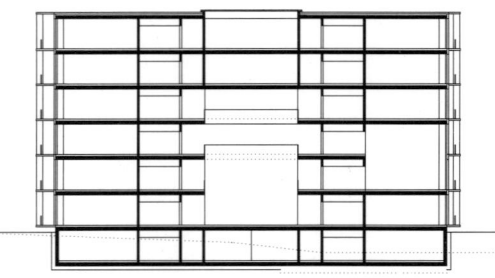

Schnitte
sections

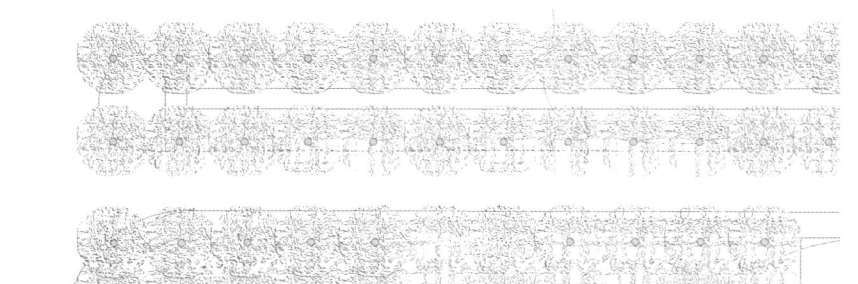
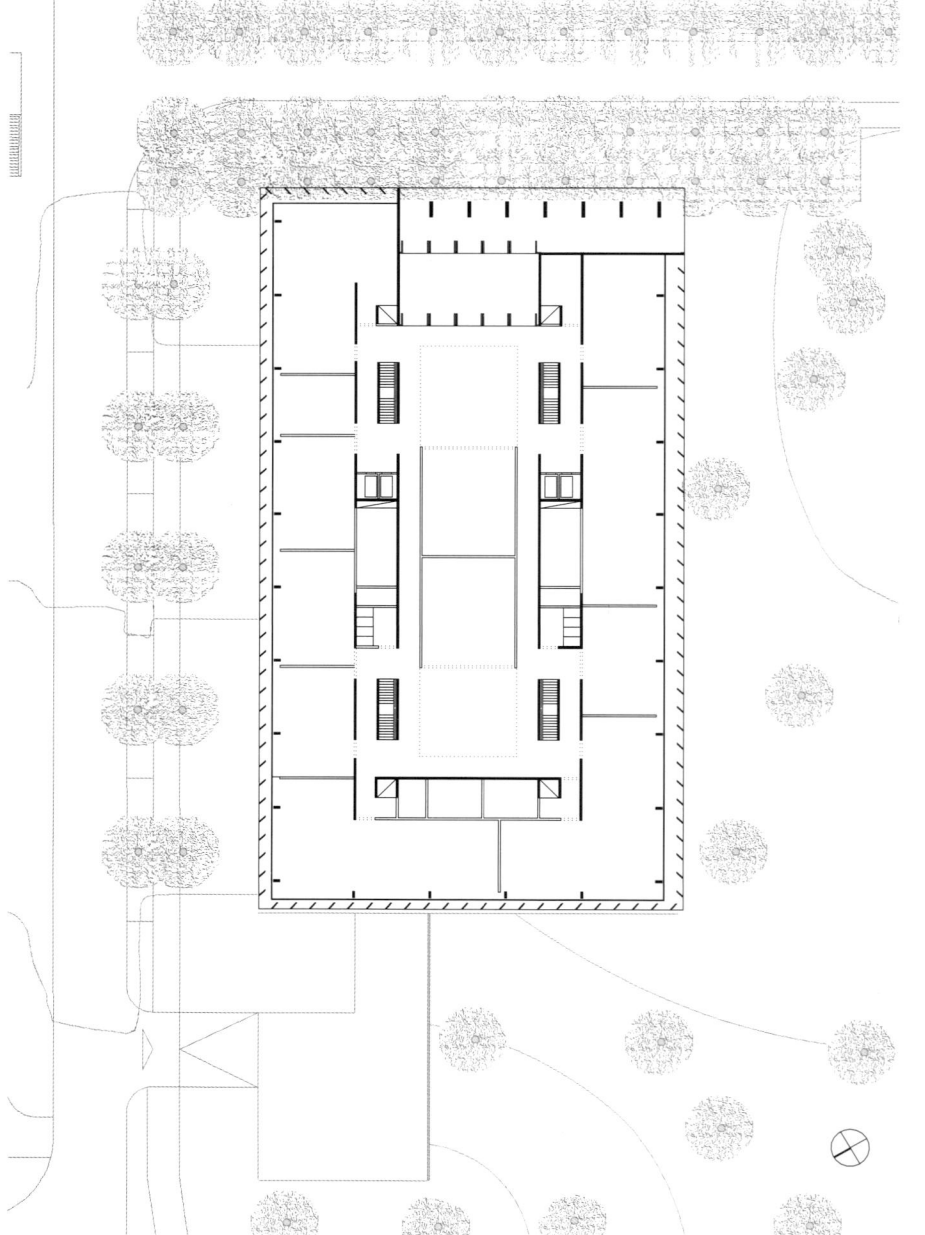
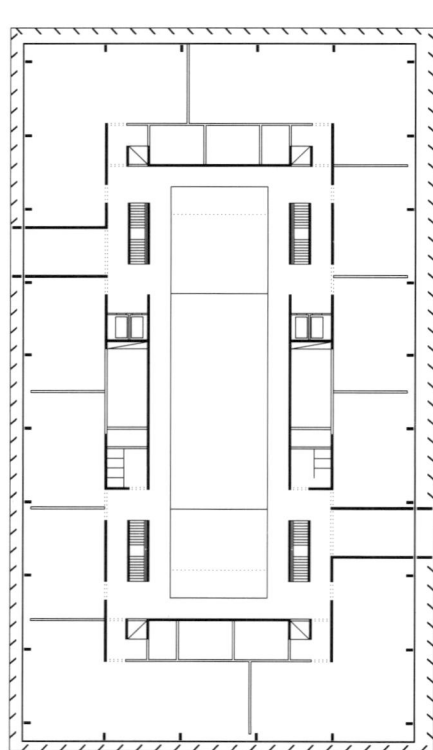

2. Obergeschoß
2nd floor

Erdgeschoß
ground floor

Zusätzlicher energetischer Aspekt: die Nachhaltigkeit des Gebäudes; seine möglichst langfristige Nutzbarkeit. Deswegen ist die Fassade, werden alle öffentlichen Bereiche in einem entsprechend haltbaren Material ausgebildet. Die Fassadenpfeiler, aber auch die gesamte innere Halle sind aus Basalt.

Additional energy factor: the sustainability of the building, the possibility of long-term use. For this reason, the façade and all public areas are built of durable materials corresponding to the need. The façade pillars, and in fact the entire hall, are made of basalt.

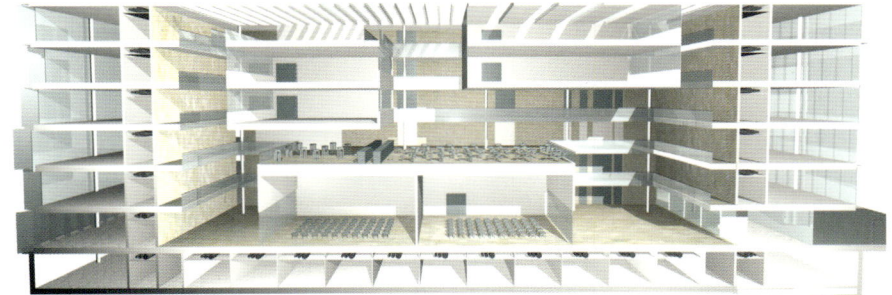

Wohnen am Lohbach in Innsbruck, A
Lohbach Residential Project in Innsbruck, Austria

Der erste Bauabschnitt einer ziemlich dichten Wohnanlage in einem schönen Grünraum. Daneben: städtebaulich und formal äußerst heterogene Wohnhäuser und ein Universitätsareal aus den sechziger Jahren.
Gefordert war eine ökonomisch und ökologisch optimierte Wohnbebauung. Daher die Entscheidung für würfelförmige Häuser mit einer innenliegenden Erschließung und einer vorgeschobenen Balkonzone, die sich durch Sonnenschutzelemente aus Kupfer nach außen abschotten lässt. Der Städtebau, der aus diesem Konzept, aus dieser Gebäudeform resultiert, ist ein scheinbar willkürliches Schachbrettmuster. Scheinbar. Denn in Wirklichkeit ist die Stellung der einzelnen Baukörper zueinander, sind die Ausblicke, die Durchsichten minutiös komponiert. Ebenso wie die Abstandsflächen zwischen den Häusern: Die Freiflächengestaltung – mit kleinen Gärten vor den Wohnungen im Erdgeschoß – läßt die Dichte der Bebauung unbedingt vergessen.

The first construction phase of a relatively densely set residential project disposed of a large green area. Next to it lie residential buildings that are heterogeneous in urban and formal terms and a university area dating back to the sixties.
Economically and ecologically optimised residential construction was required here. Thus the decision to build cube-like structures with interior access and a projecting balcony zone that can be closed off from the outside with copper sun protecting elements. The urban project that results from this concept and its cube-like shape looks similar to a random chess board pattern, seemingly. In reality the alignment of the individual structures, the views around and through the project were carefully composed. This was also the case with the spaces between the buildings: the open spaces – including small gardens in front of the ground level apartments – make it easy to forget the density of construction.

Bauherr | client **Neue Heimat Tirol, Gemeinnützige Siedlungsgesellschaft mbH** Planung | planning **Architekturbüro B & E Ziviltechniker GmbH** Projektleitung | project architect **Gerhard Zweier** Mitarbeiter | assistance **Herwig Bachmann, Reinhard Drexel, Iris Kellner, Karin Kupsky, Michael Ohneberg, Christian Tabernigg** Landschaftsarchitekt | landscape architect **Vogt Landschaftsarchitekten** Haustechnik Konzept | mechanical engineer **GMI Gasser & Messner Ingenieure** Statik | structural engineer **D.I. Wallnöfer, D.I. Fritzer, D.I. Saurwein** Grundstücksfläche | site area **14.897 m²** Bebaute Fläche | built up area **4.850 m²** Nutzfläche | floor area **22.150 m²** Umbauter Raum | building volume **112.000 m³** Planungsbeginn | commencement of planning **1997** Baubeginn | commencement of work **Oktober | October 1998** Fertigstellung | completion **Mai | May 2000**

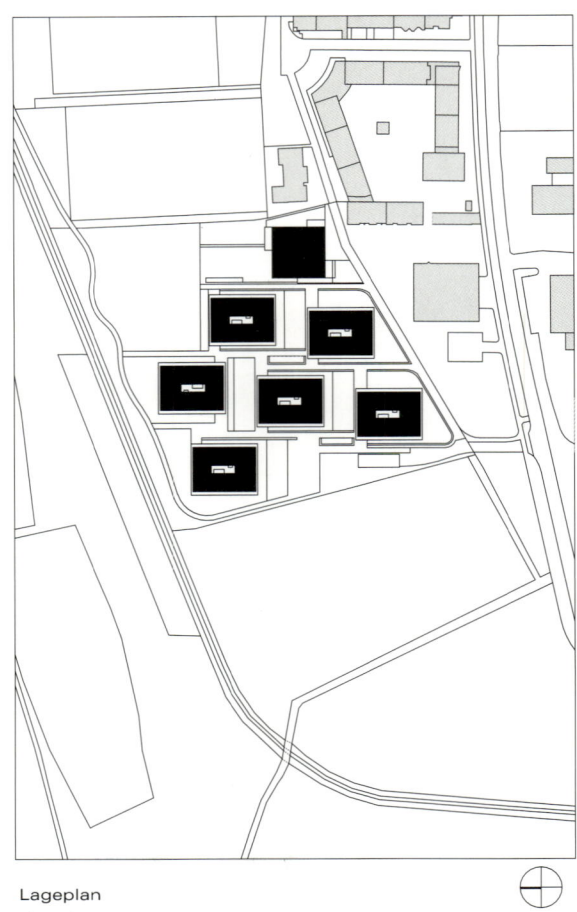

Lageplan
site plan

Die Wohnungen sind ganz unterschiedlich. Wichtig ist: Das Angebot der Sonnenschutzelemente wird von den Bewohnern voll genutzt. Sie stehen also wirklich da, diese – von den Architekten angedachten – Kuben aus Kupfer, in die nur dort, wo jemand seine Läden aufgeklappt hat, eine Öffnung eingeschnitten ist. Dieses Wechselspiel zwischen (überwiegend) geschlossen und (partiell) offen wirkt ausgesprochen reizvoll.

The apartments vary greatly. What is important is: the sun protection elements offered are used continuously by the residents. Hence the copper cubes envisioned by the architects are really there and the only openings are those created by residents who have their shutters open. This interplay between (primarily) closed and (partly) open surfaces is extremely appealing.

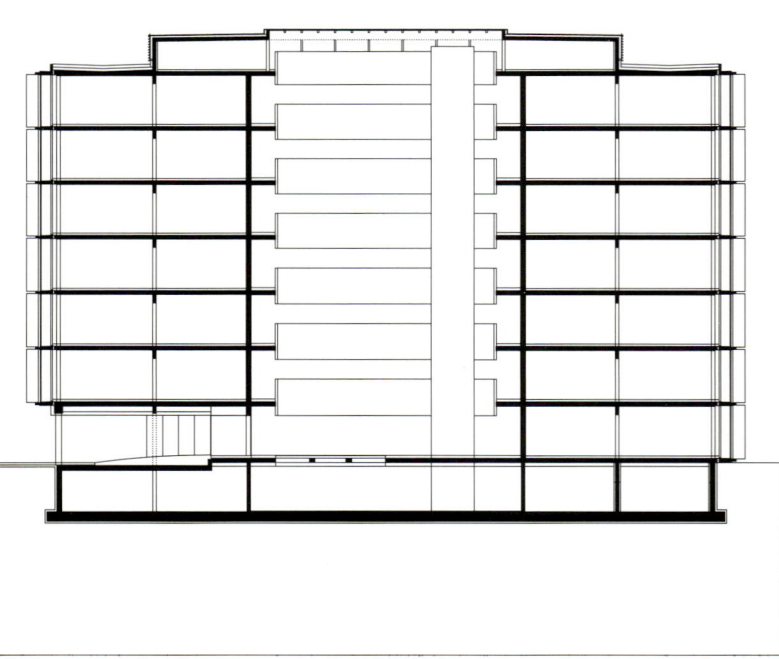

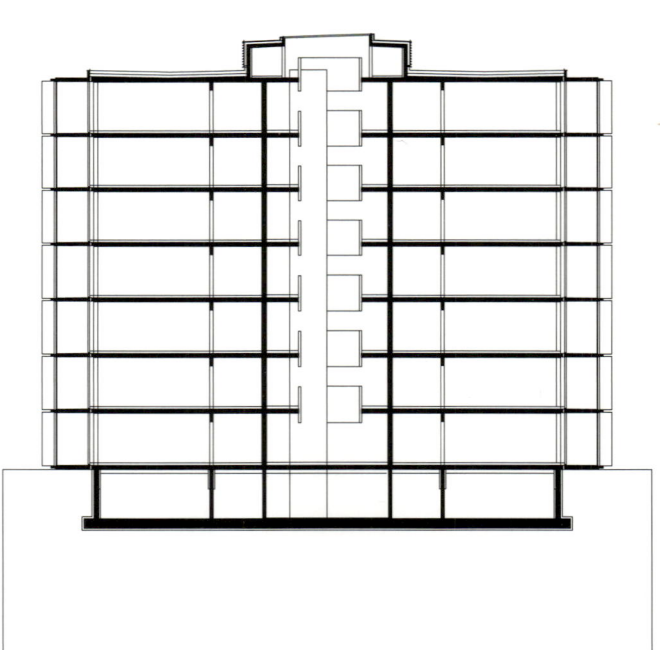

Schnitte
sections

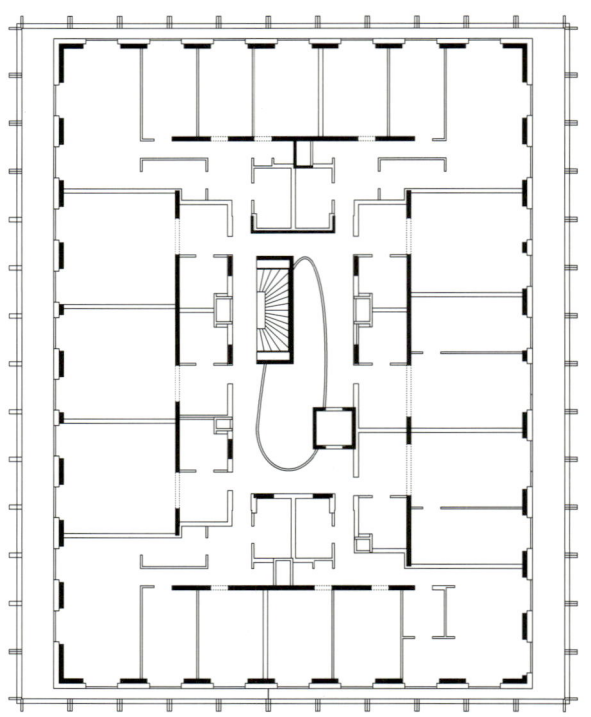

Regelgeschoß
standard floor

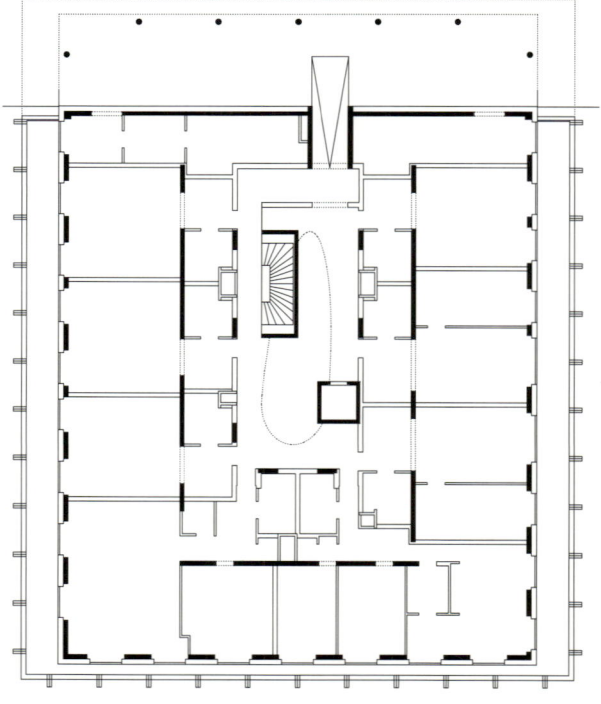

Erdgeschoß
ground floor

Etwas Zweites ist wichtig: Die Häuser sind zwar ökonomisch bis zum Äußersten optimiert, **Grundregeln des Wohnbaus** wurden dabei aber voll eingelöst. Das betrifft vor allem die Erschließung, die als wirklich attraktive, von oben natürlich belichtete – und mit einer Verglasung im Boden auch zur Tiefgarage durchlässige – Halle formuliert ist.
Schließlich das Dritte: In diesen Wohnhäusern wurden alle ökologischen Möglichkeiten, die sich heute mit einfacher Technologie nutzen lassen, angewandt. Von Sonnenkollektoren über Wärmerückgewinnung bis zur Regenwassernutzung wurde praktisch alles eingesetzt, was man – ohne High Tech – erreichen kann.
Diese Lösung wurde international prämiert. Sie steht im Verhältnis zum Quadratmeterpreis dieser Wohnungen einzigartig da. Die Nutzer wissen das zu schätzen.

There is a second important element: the houses may have been optimised as much as possible on the outside, but **the basic principles of residential construction** were adhered to completely. This is especially the case in terms of access, which was made possible by a truly attractive hall featuring natural light and glass floor paneling that allows light to reach the lower level and the subterreanean garage.
Finally, there is a third element: all the ecological possibilities allowed by today's technology were applied to these houses. These include solar energy panels, heat recovery plants and rain water use. Thus practically everything that can be achieved – without high tech – was achieved.
This solution won international awards. The price per square meter ratio is unique. The residents appreciate this fact.

B & E > Wohnen am Lohbach_A

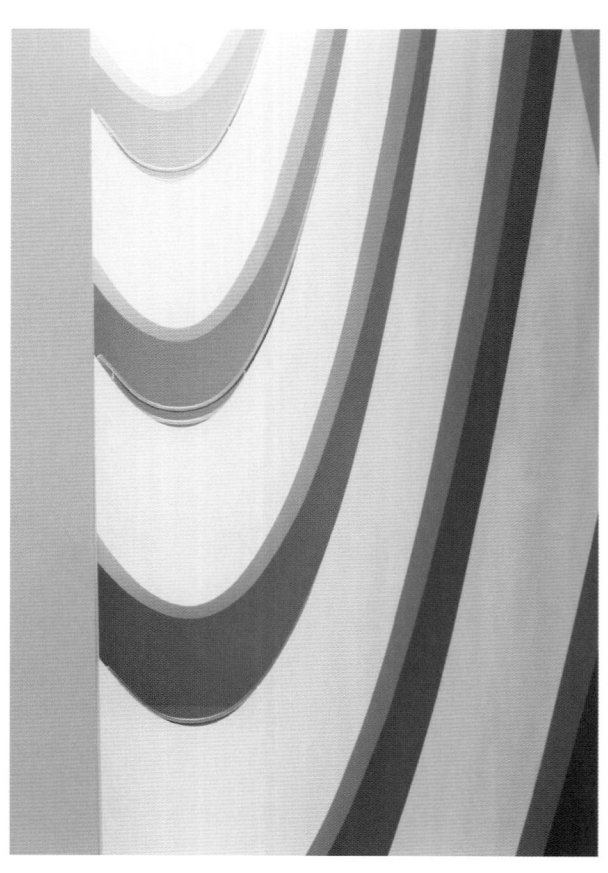

Wohnanlage Sebastianstraße in Dornbirn, A
Sebastianstrasse Residential Project in Dornbirn, Austria

Wohnen an der Abstandsgrenze. **Die Situation:** ein altes Wohnhaus mit Scheune straßenseitig, im dichten Stadtgebiet, dahinter der Bauplatz. Der Altbestand nun renoviert, die Scheune erneuert, der relativ teure Bauplatz bis an die Abstandsgrenze ausgenutzt und mit einem Wohnhaus besetzt.

Eine weiße, gläserne Gebäudekonfiguration, die je nach Wetterlage, Tageszeit und Wochentag ein unterschiedliches Fassadenbild präsentiert. Oft geschlossen, manchmal natürlich auch offen, je nach der Befindlichkeit der Nutzer jeder einzelnen Wohnung. Daß die im eigenen Interesse von innen nach außen denken, ist ganz normal. Daß die Architekten die öffentlich maßgeblichen Folgen dieses Denkens zur Grundlage ihrer Strategie machen, ist ein Mehrwert. Hier ging es darum, vereinheitlichende Maßnahmen umzusetzen.

Es ist ein Leichtbau. Eine isolierte Holzkonstruktion mit einer Wetterschutzplatte außen. Davor: eine Schiebeanlage, die technisch gesehen ein Massenprodukt ist. Glasscheiben, die mit einem Siebdruck belegt sind. Effekt: Von draußen sieht man nicht nach drinnen, aber von drinnen nach draußen. Zweiter Effekt: Es ist steuerbar, wieviel man von draußen sieht; die Scheiben übereinander geschoben ergeben eine fast undurchsichtige (Glas)Wand.

Living on edge. **The location:** an old residential building with a barn facing the street in a dense urban area; the construction site lies behind it. The existing building was refurbished and the barn was renovated. The relatively expensive plot was used right up to the bordering edge for the construction of a residential building.

A white, glass building configuration that presents a different façade according to the weather conditions, the hour of the day and the day of the week. It is often closed, although it is also opened from time to time, according to the user's mood in each individual apartment. It is absolutely normal for the residents to think from the inside to the outside. But the fact that the architects made the extensive effects of this thinking the foundation of their strategy represents an additional value. This project was about implementing unifying measures.

It is a lightweight structure. A timber construction with protective weather boarding on the outside. In front lies a mass-produced sliding mechanism. Glass panels that feature silk screens create the following effect: A person outside cannot look inside, but a person on the inside can see the goings on outside. This leads to a second effect: it is possible to adjust what can be seen from the outside; layering the panels over one another results in a visually almost impenetrable glass wall.

Bauherr | client **I+R Schertler Ges.mbH** Planung | planning **B & E Baumschlager-Eberle GmbH** Projektleitung | project architect **D.I. Nasahl, I+R Schertler Ges.mbH** Mitarbeiter | assistance **Christine Falkner** Landschaftsarchitekt | landscape architect **Vogt Landschaftsarchitekten** Haustechnik Konzept | mechanical engineer **Ingenieurbüro Diem** Statik | structural engineer **Rüsch, Diem, Schuler - Eric Hämmerle** Grundstücksfläche | site area **1.302 m²** Bebaute Fläche | built up area **391 m²** Nutzfläche | floor area **692 m²** Umbauter Raum | building volume **5.258 m³** Planungsbeginn | commencement of planning Juni | June **1999** Baubeginn | commencement of work Juni | June **2000** Fertigstellung | completion November | November **2001**

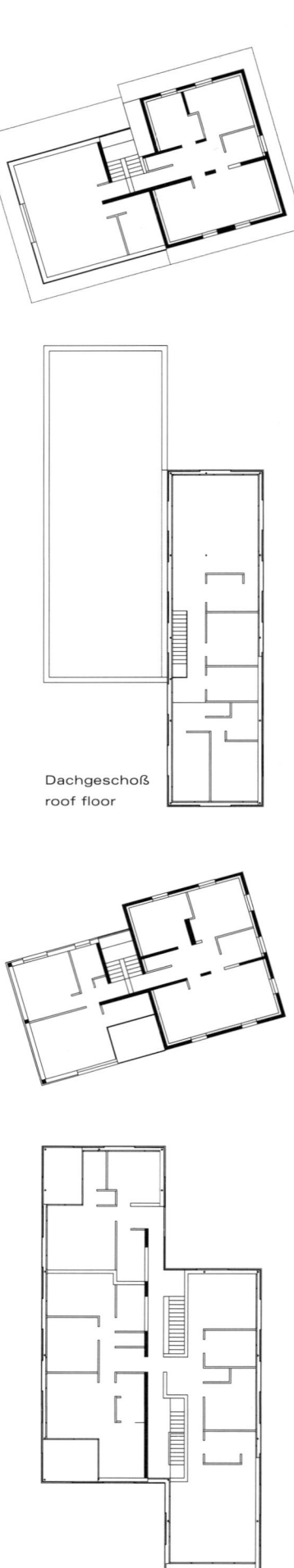
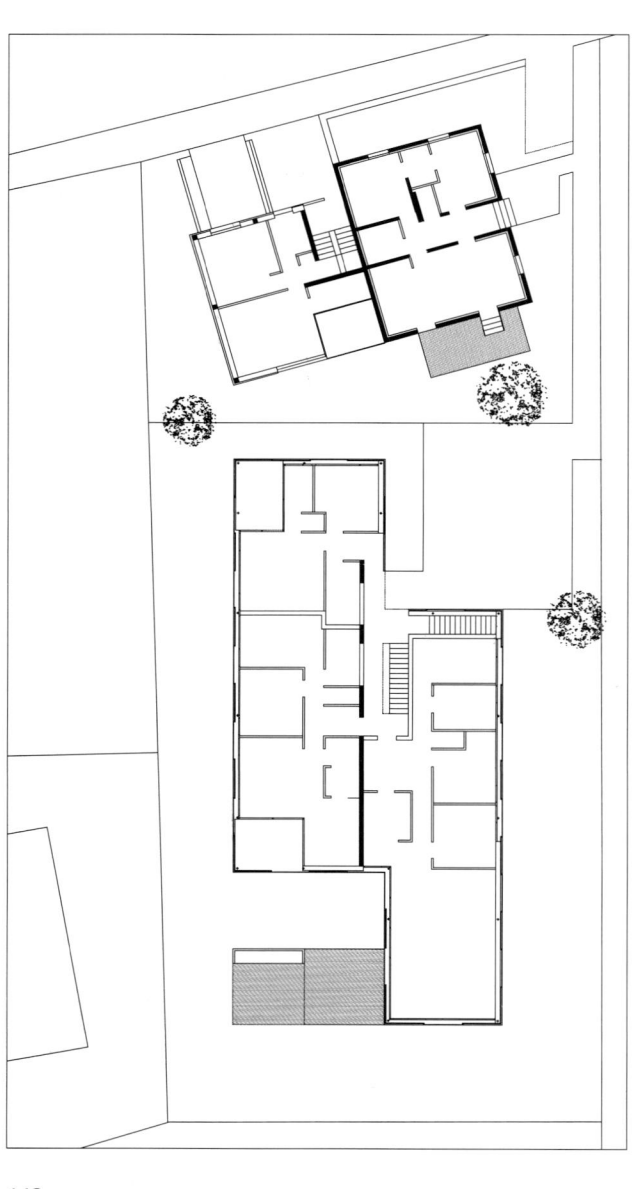

Dachgeschoß
roof floor

Erdgeschoß
ground floor

1. Obergeschoß
1st floor

B & E > Wohnanlage Sebastianstraße_A

Das Thema war: Individuelles Wohnen – und das schließt ein, daß sich jeder aussuchen kann, wo er seine Fenster hat, und daß er selbst regulieren kann, ob und wieweit er auf Abstand zu seiner Umgebung geht. Hier braucht keiner Vorhänge oder Rollos. Denn selbst wenn die Glashaut auch dort geschlossen ist, wo Loggien angesiedelt sind, bleibt subjektiv der Eindruck des Freiraumes erhalten.
Das Konzept funktioniert ohne Abstriche. Die Bewohner nutzen die Möglichkeiten ganz im Sinn der Architekten. Und die Geometrie der zweiten Fassade, der Glashaut, ist ein visuell spannender Beitrag zum Umfeld.

The theme was: individual living, and that includes allowing everyone to choose how many windows they want to have, where they want them to be and how much distance they require from their environment. Nobody needs curtains or blinds here, since the subjective impression of being in an open space remains, even when the loggia spaces are closed.
The concept works without any shortcomings. The residents use these possibilities the way the architects intended them to. And the geometry of the second façade is an exciting addition to the surroundings.

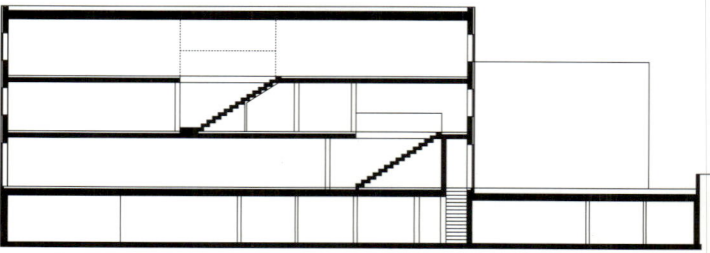

Schnitt
section

Wohnanlage Achslengut,
zweiter Bauabschnitt, in St. Gallen, CH
Achslengut Residential Project,
Second Segment in St. Gallen, Switzerland

Eine sehr spezifische Projektgeschichte: B&E wurden im nachhinein, nach einem Wettbewerb, den ein Schweizer Büro gewonnen hatte, aufgefordert, in die Planung einzusteigen. Zu diesem Zeitpunkt war der Bebauungsplan für die gesamte Anlage bereits beschlossen. Daher die Zeilenbebauung – mit vorgegebener Trakttiefe und Gebäudelänge – des ersten Bauabschnittes. In der Folge wurde schließlich doch eine Änderung des Bebauungsplanes erreicht. **Der zweite Bauabschnitt** präsentiert sich daher mit einem radikal anderen, wesentlich sinnvolleren Städtebau. Es sind Punkthäuser, kompakte Baukörper mit innenliegender Erschließung und einer vorgeschalteten Balkonzone. Wichtig die Situierung der Baukörper: Sie ist im Hinblick auf den Ausblick zum Bodensee komponiert.

Den Wohnungen vorgelagert: **Schiebeelemente aus Glas**, die zum Teil transparent, zum Teil nicht transparent sind. So läßt sich zweierlei optimal regulieren: das Abstands- und Einsichtproblem zwischen den Wohnbauten – wenn jemand z.B. zwei solche Scheiben vor das Schlafzimmer stellt, sieht niemand mehr hinein, die Privatsphäre ist geschützt; andererseits werden aber auch die individuellen Nutzungsturbulenzen, die sich auf den Balkonen abspielen können und für die Qualität des öffentlichen Raumes oft so störend sind, unsichtbar. Auf diese eigentlich einfache Weise ist also eine klare Entflechtung zwischen öffentlichen und privaten Interessen erreicht.

This project is characterised by a very specific history: B&E were asked to participate in the planning after the project had already been awarded to a Swiss architecture office. However, the construction plan for the entire project had been defined by this time. Therefore, the first construction segment was completed according to previously established wing depth and length parametres. Finally, a change in the construction plans was agreed on after all. Hence the **second segment** is a radically different, much more useful urban structure. They are housing "dots", compact structures with interior access and projecting balcony zones. The placement of the buildings is important: it is a composition based on the view of Lake Constance.
Glass sliding elements are located in front of the apartments, some are transparent, some aren't. This allows for ideal regulation of two things: spacing and interior view problems between the residential buildings. If, for example, someone slides two such panels in front of the bedroom, nobody can look inside, the tenant's privacy is protected. On the other hand, the individual turbulences of use on the balconies that often disturb public spaces are concealed this way. Thus a clear separation between public and private interests was achieved with these simple means.

Bauherr | client **Pensionskasse der Credit Suisse Gallintra AG co UBS Fund Management AG Ortsbürgergemeinde St. Gallen** Generalunternehmer | general contractor **SENN BPM AG** Planung | planning **B & E Baumschlager-Eberle GmbH, SENN Architektur AG** Projektleitung | project architect **Hanspeter Stacher** Mitarbeiter | assistance **Stephan Moor, Christian Rusch** Landschaftsarchitekt | landscape architect **Vogt Landschaftsarchitekten** Haustechnik Konzept | mechanical engineer **Bühler + Scherler AG** Statik | structural engineer **NÄF + Partner** Grundstücksfläche | site area **21.702 m²** Bebaute Fläche | built up area **4.625 m²** Nutzfläche | floor area **14.700 m²** Umbauter Raum | building volume **87.040 m³** Planungsbeginn | commencement of planning Frühjahr | Spring **1998** Baubeginn | commencement of work Frühjahr | Spring **2000** Fertigstellung | completion Herbst | Autumn **2002**

B & E > Wohnanlage Achslengut 2_CH

Die Bewohner gehen mit den Möglichkeiten, die diese Fassadenlösung bietet, sehr selbstverständlich um. Wobei sich an der spezifischen **Geometrie des Erscheinungsbildes** dieser Wohnhäuser durch die individuellen Verhaltensweisen nicht wirklich etwas ändert. Sie sind eben nie ganz geschlossen, nie ganz offen. So war es von vornherein gedacht. Und das ist es auch, was diesen architektonischen Entwurf so besonders macht. Irgendwie hält er die ganz gewöhnliche, die alltägliche Nutzung locker aus.

The residents make use of the possibilities this façade solution offers in a very matter-of-fact fashion. It should be noted that the **specific geometric appearance** of these residential buildings is not affected by the individual behavioural patterns of the tenants. They are never really closed nor ever really open. This was intended from the beginning and it is what makes this project's architectural design so special. Somehow, it stands up to everyday use with complete ease.

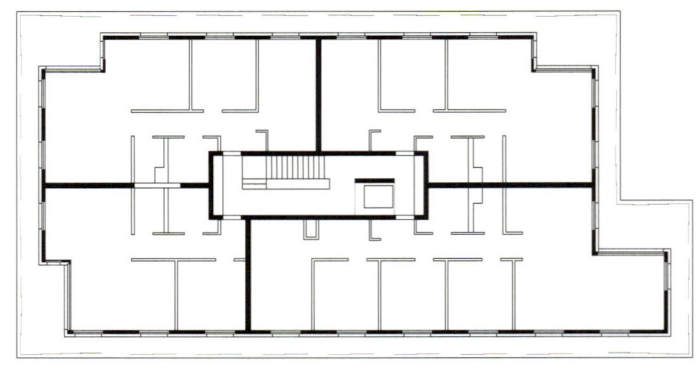

Schnitt
section

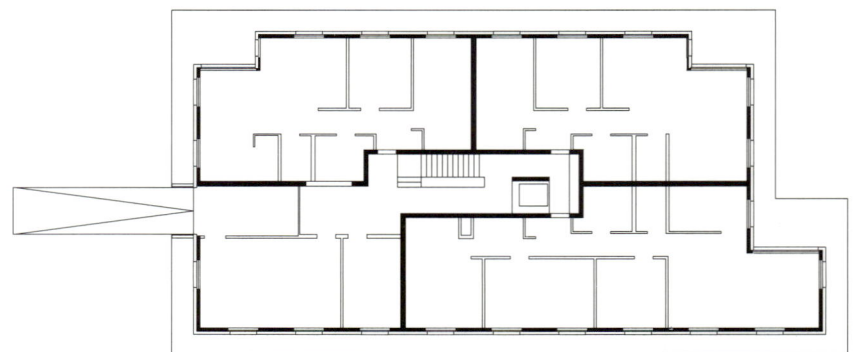

1. Obergeschoß
1st floor

Erdgeschoß
ground floor

Projekt für ein 1.000-Betten-
Krankenhaus in Kortrijk, B
1.000-Bed Hospital Project
in Kortrijk, Belgium

Der Planungsauftrag erging nach einem Präsentationsverfahren, bei dem die Geladenen aufgefordert waren, einen spezifischen Fragenkatalog zu beantworten. Der Vorschlag, den die Büros B&E und Itten+Brechbühl bei dieser Gelegenheit vorstellten, basiert auf einer uralten, traditionellen Typologie – einer Hofstruktur.
Dafür gibt es gute Gründe: Ziel war sicher, trotz der Größe des Projektes (ca. 140.000 m²), städtebaulich eine Integration in die Bebauung der Umgebung zu erreichen; Ziel war aber vor allem, architektonische Identifikationsmomente innerhalb einer so großen Anlage zu schaffen. Mit der **Hofstruktur** kann ein solches Anliegen umsetzbar sein, weil es ganz unterschiedliche Atmosphären zuläßt, die der Gefahr der Anonymisierung wirksam entgegentreten.
Organisatorisch geht es in einem eher niedrigen, flächig angelegten Krankenhaus vor allem um kurze Wege. Das wird durch die zentrale Anordnung der Hauptfunktionen (Operationssäle, Intensivstationen etc.) und den direkten Zugang beispielsweise im Notfallbereich garantiert. Das Gelände ist nicht ganz eben, man geht auf der Hanggeschoßebene (EG) hinein, die Ebene darunter (1.UG) ist aber ein Vollgeschoß, das neben wichtigen patientenorientierten Funktionen auch die gesamte Logistik enthält.

The planning contract was awarded after a presentation process in which the participants were requested to answer an array of specific questions.
The joint project proposed by the offices of B&E and Itten+Brechbühl in this case, was based on an age-old, traditional typology: a courtyard structure.
There were good reasons for this: the goal was to achieve an integration of the development within its surroundings despite its size (approx. ca. 140.000 m²). Nonetheless, the main objective was to create moments of architectural identification within such a large complex. **The courtyard structure** made it possible to address this need since it allows for vastly differing atmospheres, which effectively counter the danger of anonymity.
In organisational terms, the most important elements are short distances in a low-slung, flat-level hospital design. This is guaranteed by the central alignment of its main functions (operation rooms, intensive care wards etc.) and the direct access to the emergency area, for example. The terrain is not entirely level, the ground floor begins on the incline of the slope, but the lower level beneath is also a fully operational floor that features patient-oriented functions and the entire unit's logistics.

Bauherr I client „A.Z. Groeninge" v.z.w. Kortrijk Planung I planning **B & E Baumschlager-Eberle GmbH, FDA architecten & ingenieurs nv, Itten + Brechbühl AG** Projektleitung I project architect **Baumschlager-Eberle GmbH, FDA architecten & ingenieurs nv** Mitarbeiter I assistance **Elmar Hasler, Christian Tabernigg** Landschaftsarchitekt I landscape architect **Vogt Landschaftsarchitekten** Haustechnik Konzept I mechanical engineer **Sorane SA, Lenum, AG** Grundstücksfläche I site area **135.000 m²** Bebaute Fläche I built up area **21.120 m²** Nutzfläche I floor area **84.482 m²** Umbauter Raum I building volume **370.000 m³** Planungsbeginn I commencement of planning Juni I June **2000** Baubeginn I commencement of work Juni I June **2004** Fertigstellung I completion Juni I June **2018**

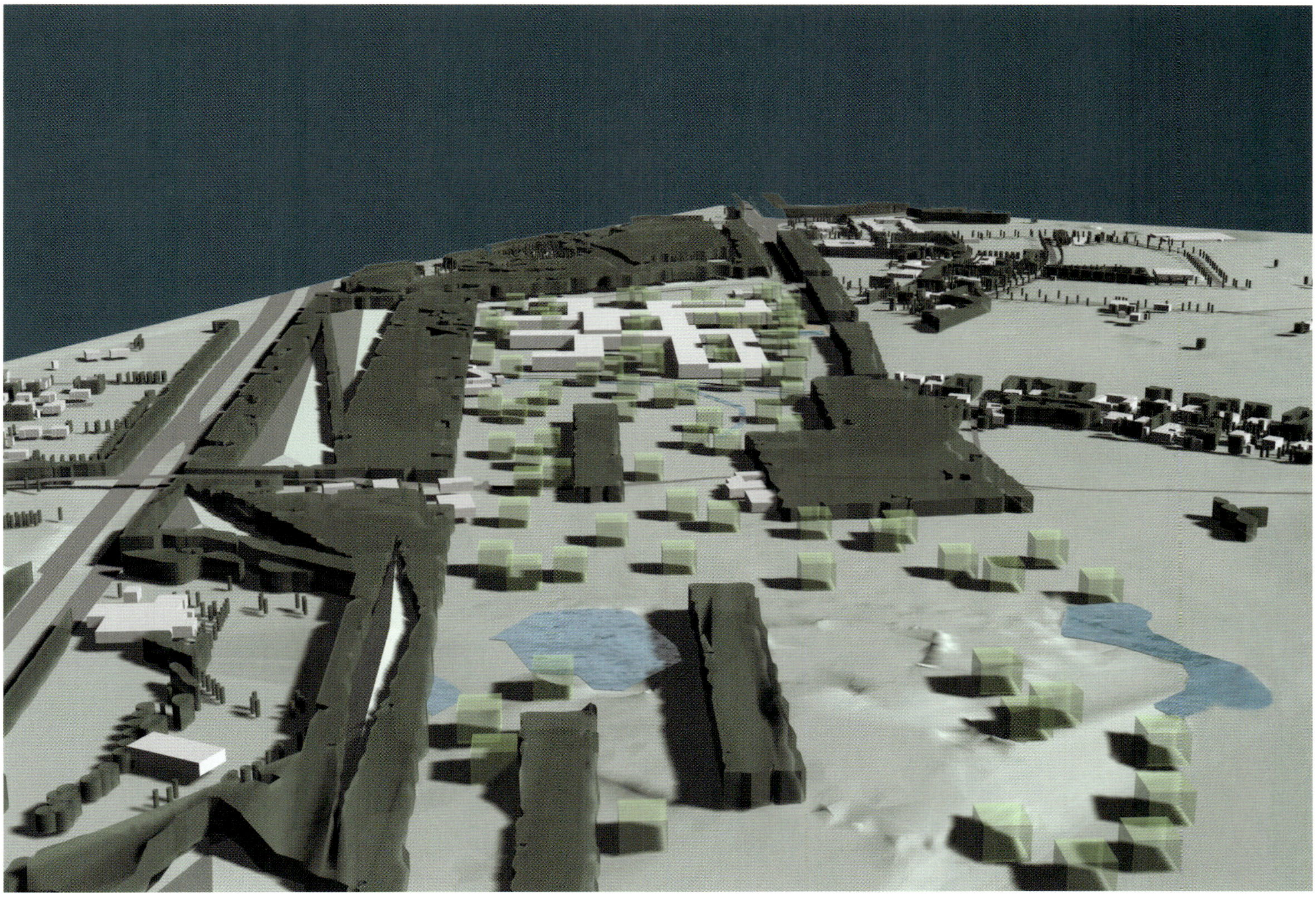

Alleys
Water
Groups of trees
Ways
Topografic
Forest
Leenbos
K3
K8
A14
Kennedypark
Arme Leute
Klarenhoek
K 45
N43
A17
Don Bosco
Rollegemknok

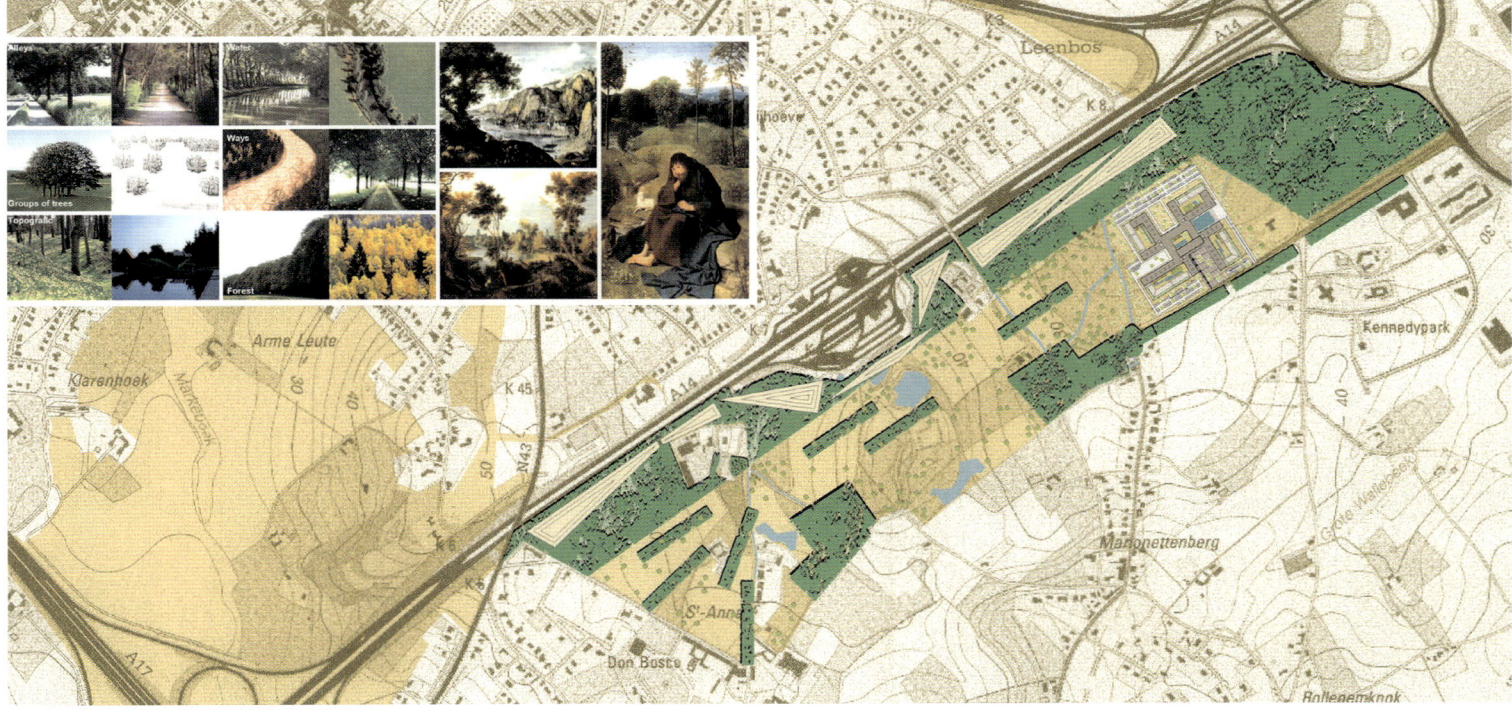

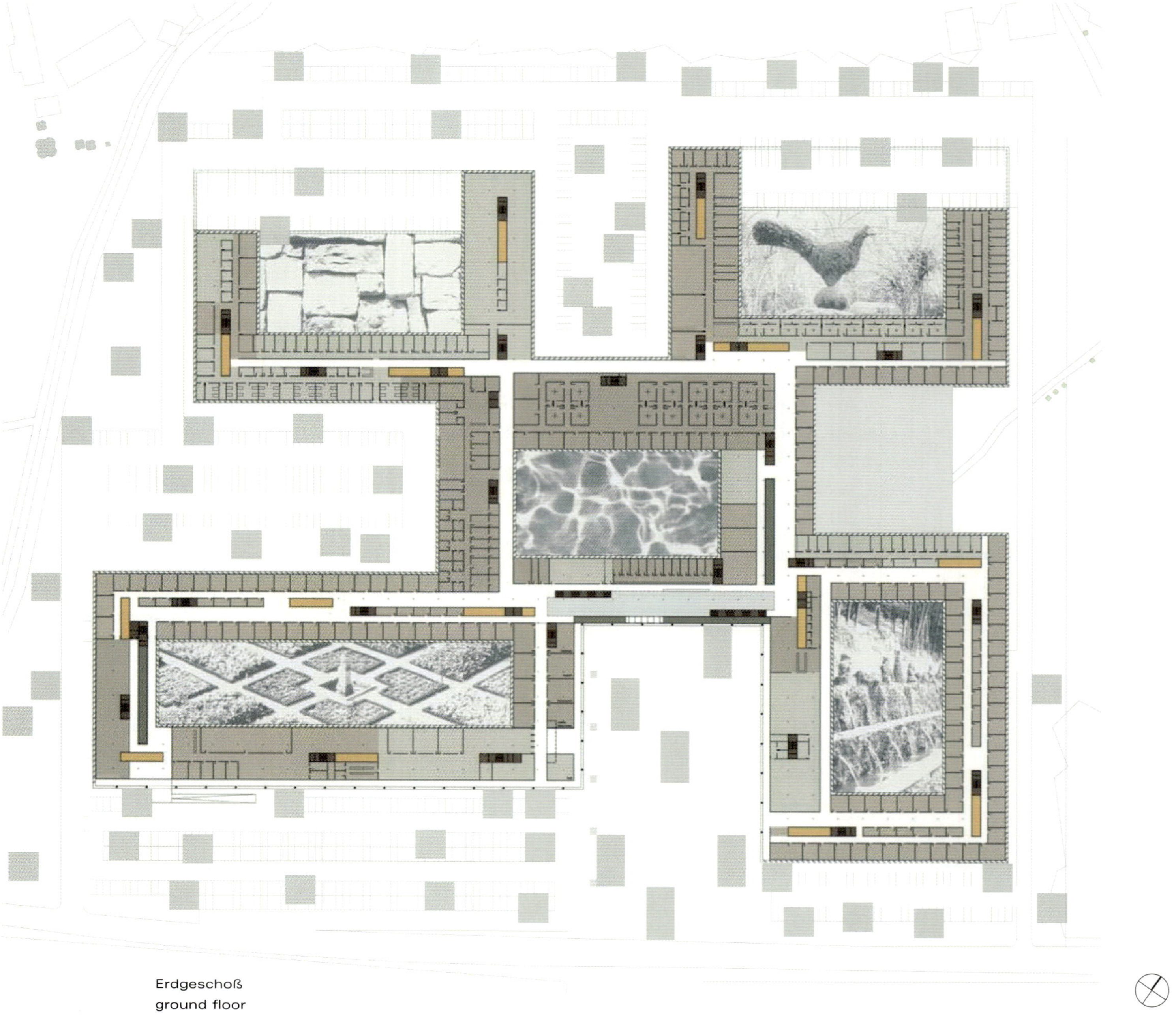

Erdgeschoß
ground floor

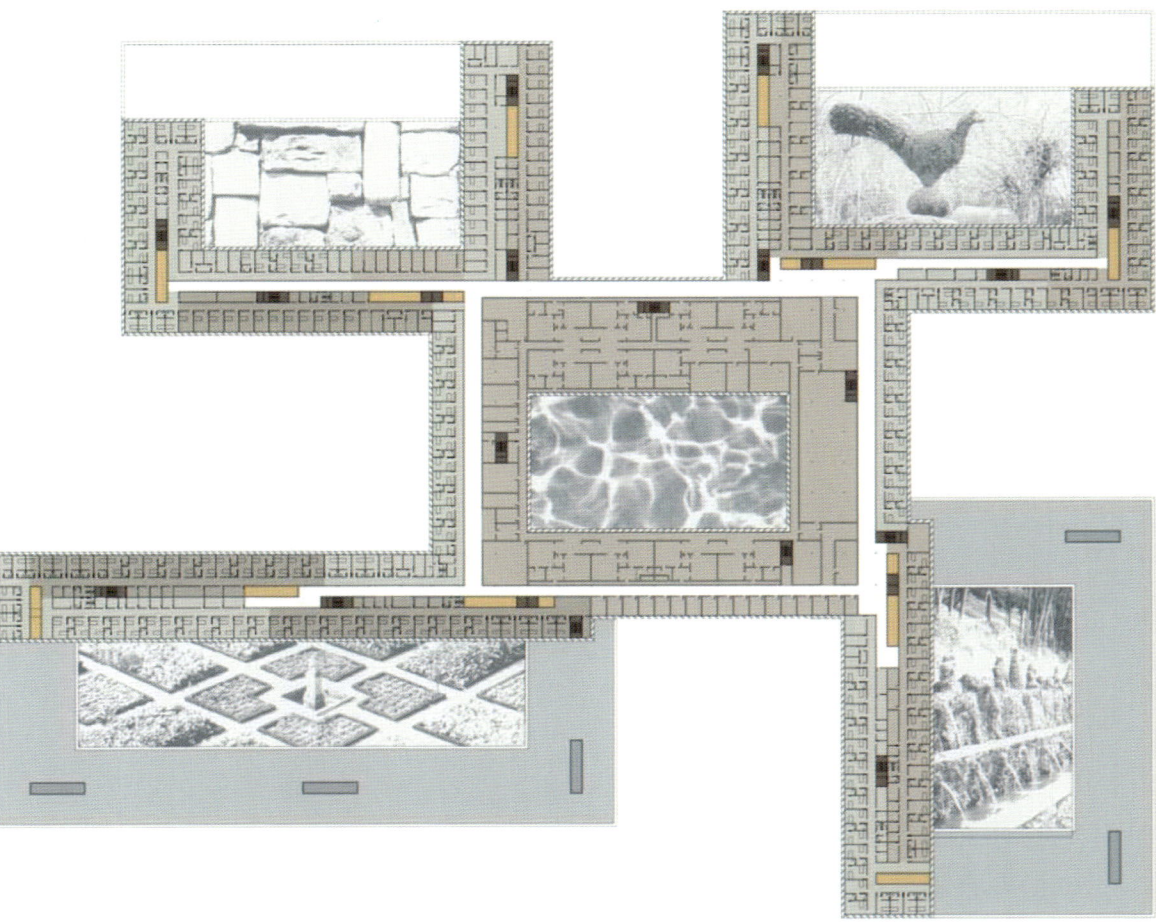

2. Obergeschoß
2nd floor

Zwei Themen waren für den Entwurf ausschlaggebend: Die Entwicklung im Krankenhausbereich befindet sich – medizintechnisch, finanztechnisch, politisch, personell – in einem kontinuierlichen Prozess. Ebensowenig weiß man, welche Konsequenzen die Fortschritte in der Gentechnik oder in der chemischen, medikamentösen Behandlung in Zukunft machen. Darauf muß die Architektur mit Flexibilität reagieren – alle Gebäude sind daher auch ganz anders, etwa als Hotel oder Bürohaus, selbst als Dienstleistungsunternehmen nutzbar.

Krankenhausatmosphäre kontra Hotelflair: Von vornherein ging es darum, ein möglichst hohes Maß an Normalität zu erzielen. Tageslicht, Raumhöhe, Materialisierung, Oberflächen, die Beziehung nach außen – das sind die konstituierenden Fragen, auf die bei der plastischen Ausbildung dieser riesigen Figur Wert gelegt wurde.
Bei der Fassade wurde eine Lösung gewählt, die zumindest teilweise den lokalen Bautraditionen entspricht: gemauerte Klinkerpfeiler in der Vertikalen, Betonfertigteile in der Horizontalen (in die ist die Gebäudetechnik integriert, sodaß die Neutralität der Flächen innen gewährleistet ist). Und gerichtete Glasscheiben, die sich nach dem Sonnenstand orientieren, die für Beschattung sorgen, aber einen ungehinderten Blick nach draußen ermöglichen.

Two themes were decisive factors for the design: developments in the hospital sector are the result of fluid processes in terms of technical medical equipment, financing, politically and with regard to human resources. It also isn't clear which consequences the advances in genetic technology or in chemical/medication-based treatment will have in the future. Architecture has to react flexibly to these conditions – all buildings are thus usable for entirely different purposes, as hotels or office buildings, even as service company structures.

Hospital atmosphere versus hotel flair: from the very beginning, it was important to achieve a high degree of normality. Daylight, room height, materialisation, surfaces, and the relationship to the outside – those were the decisive questions that had priority in designing the actual three-dimensional form of this enormous figure.
A solution was chosen for the façade that corresponds with the local construction traditions to a degree: clinker brick masonry was used vertically, while pre-fabricated cement components were used on the horizontal elements (the buildings technical lines are integrated in these segments to guarantee the neutrality of the surfaces on the inside). The windows are mounted in compliance with the levels of the sun, they provide shadow, but also allow for an unimpeded view of the outside.

Schnitte
sections

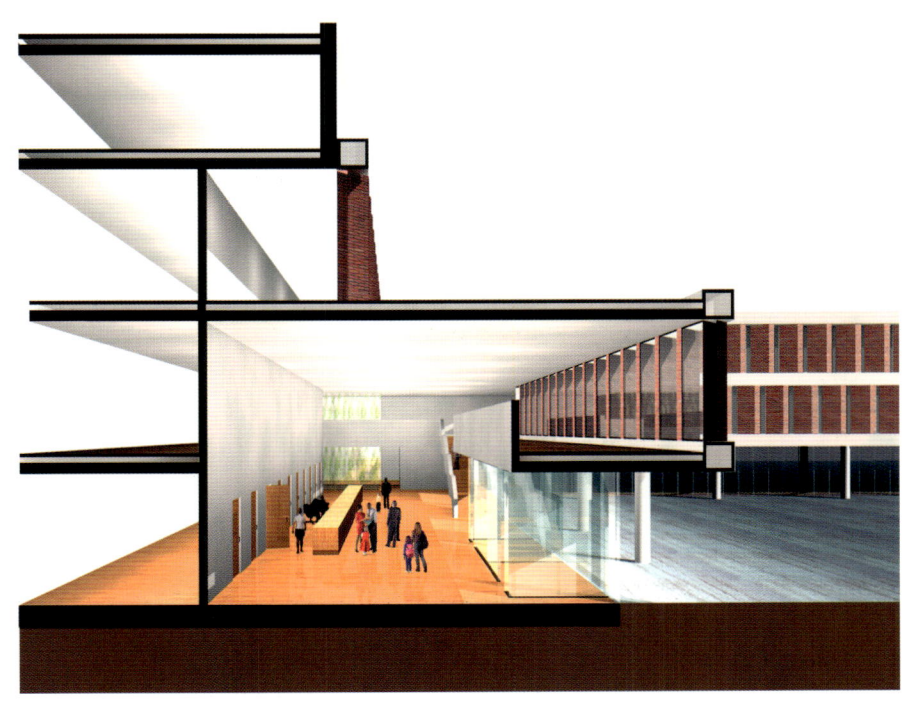

Wettbewerbe
Competitions

Move TO, Projekt
für die Porta Susa in Turin, I
Move TO, Project
for the Porta Susa in Turin, Italy

Mitten in der Stadt. Eigentlich die Hauptachse durch die Stadt. Das Bahnhofsgelände unterirdisch, eine sehr, sehr breite Straße als Barriere. Hier werden durch eine Reduzierung des Bahnhofsgeländes und Gleisverlegungen Areale frei. Gefordert: ein neuer Zugang zum Bahnhof und Zusatznutzungen (Hotel, Büros). Vorschlag von B&E: eine große Wasserfläche, eine Art künstlicher (urbaner) See, in den die Abgänge zum unterirdischen Bahnhof wie Trichter hineinstossen (übrigens ein reizvolles Pendant zum großen Park nebenan). Städtebaulicher Abschluß und architektonisches Highlight dieses zentralen Raums für Turin: ein Doppelturm mit Hotel- und Büronutzung. Der Vorschlag verhält sich kontrapunktisch zu den Vorstellungen des Bauherrn, der dort eigentlich eine niedrige – ein- bis zweigeschossige – Bebauung angedacht hatte.

In the middle of the city, actually on the main axis through the city, the train station site is located underground with a very, very wide road as a barrier bordering it. Spaces are made free by reducing the size of the train station site and moving tracks. Required: a new form of access to the station with additional uses (hotel, offices). B&E's proposal: a large water surface, a form of artificial urban lake from which the downward access ways funnel down into the subterranean station (which is also an appealing counterpart to the park alongside). The culminating urban planning element and the architectural highlight of this central area of Turin: a pair of towers for hotel and office use. The proposal is a counterpoint to the client's considerations, one to two-storey buildings were supposed to stand on the projected site.

Bauherr I client **Ferrovie dello Stato, Italia** Planung I planning **B & E Baumschlager-Eberle GmbH, Architekturbüro Hartmut Grabowski, Itten+Brechbühl AG** Projektleitung I project architect **Hans Ullrich Grassmann** Mitarbeiter I assistance **Stefan Beck, Guido Drocco, Valentina Drocco, Davide Dutto, Joanna Janiec, Mateusz Kropop** Landschaftsarchitekt I landscape architect **Vogt Landschaftsarchitekten** Haustechnik Konzept I mechanical engineer **Cesare Boffa, Acta S.r.l., Franco Rubini** Statik I structural engineer **D.I. Ernst Mader, Innocente Porrone** Sicherheit I security **Gian Carlo Gramoni** Verkehrsplanung I traffic planning **Michele Galatola** Nutzfläche Bahnhof I built up area station **15.000 m²** Nutzfläche Turm I built up area tower **34.000 m²** Wettbewerb I competition **2001**

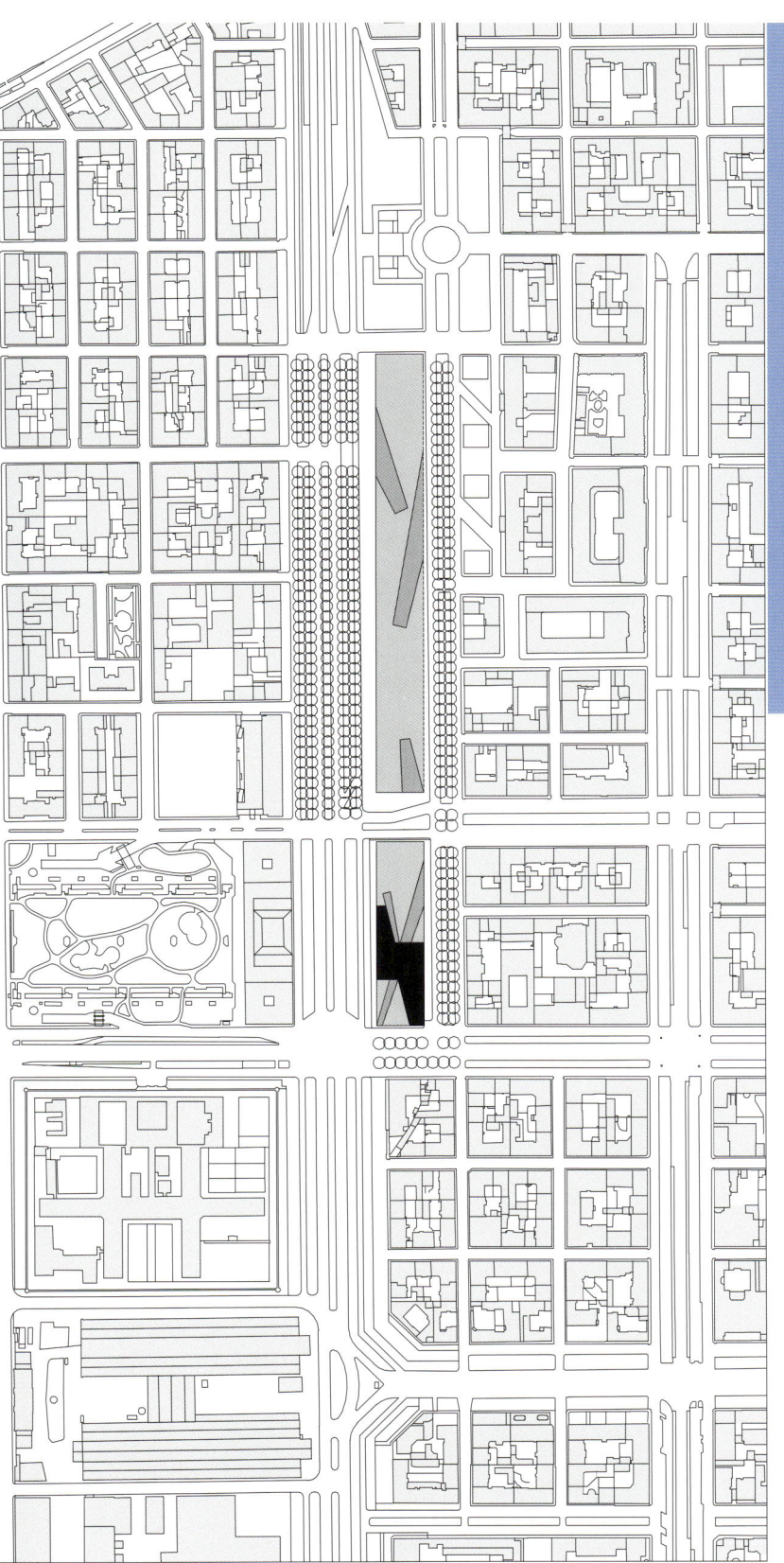

Bürohochhaus Räffel Park in Zürich, CH
Räffel Park High-Rise Office Building in Zurich, Switzerland

Ein sensibles Stadtgefüge: auf der einen Seite ein ostwestlich verlaufender Grüngürtel, auf der anderen die Räffelstraße. Unmittelbar daneben: Zeilenbebauung. Das Projekt gliedert sich mit seinen zwei Bauteilen Richtung Ost und West (siebengeschossig) und dem Nordflügel (zwölfgeschossig) schon durch die Höhenstaffelung ein. Außerdem wurde dem Erdgeschoß durch eine Überhöhung und die teilweise Auflösung des Stützenrasters eine spezielle Bedeutung zugeordnet, ebenso der Zugangssituation, die durch eine hofartige Vorzone formuliert ist.

Ausgangspunkt der Überlegungen war das generelle Problem des Außenbezugs im heutigen Bürohausbau. Die angebotene Lösung: große (begrünte) Lufträume, in die Büroboxen eingeklinkt sind. So entsteht eine Verräumlichung der Bürolandschaft in die Vertikale, die zwar sicher artifizieller ist als die natürliche Landschaft – sie verläuft ja doch immer horizontal –, die aber grundsätzlich wie der übliche Übergang zwischen natürlicher und „künstlicher" Landschaft (Garten, Hof) etwa im Wohnbau im Grünen funktioniert.

Das Konzept potenziert die Arbeitsqualität in den Büros. Es geht hier allerdings nicht um die Addition von Einzelbüros, sondern um ein kommunikativeres Konzept. Der Mehrwert: Trotz des beachtlichen Anteils an Großraumbüros kommt es zu keiner Anonymisierung des Gebäudes, die übliche Monotonie wird zugunsten der Diversifizierung räumlicher Zusammenhänge im Bürohausbau vermieden.

An area characterised by sensitive urban structuring: on one side a green belt running east-west, and Räffelstrasse on the other. And immediately next to the site: row housing. The property's staggered height and structure in two construction segments to the east and west (seven-storey buildings) and the North Wing (twelve-storey) help integrate it in its surroundings. Aside from this, the pronounced height and partial dissolution of the support grid give the ground floor special importance. This is also the case with the access situation, whose formulation was accentuated with a courtyard-like zone on the front.

Considerations on the general problem of outside access in contemporary office construction framed the beginning of the project. The solution offered: large, airy spaces featuring greenery with integrated office boxes. This gives the office environment's spatial relations a vertical sense that though certainly more artificial than a natural landscape – that always follows a horizontal course – essentially works as the usual transition between natural and 'artificial' landscapes (garden, courtyard) as is the case in residential construction in green areas.

The concept increases the quality of working in the offices exponentially. In this case, however, it isn't merely an addition of individual offices. Instead it is a communication concept. The added value: despite the considerable amount of large-area offices, the building isn't anonymous, the usual monotony was avoided in favour of diversifying spatial relations in office building construction.

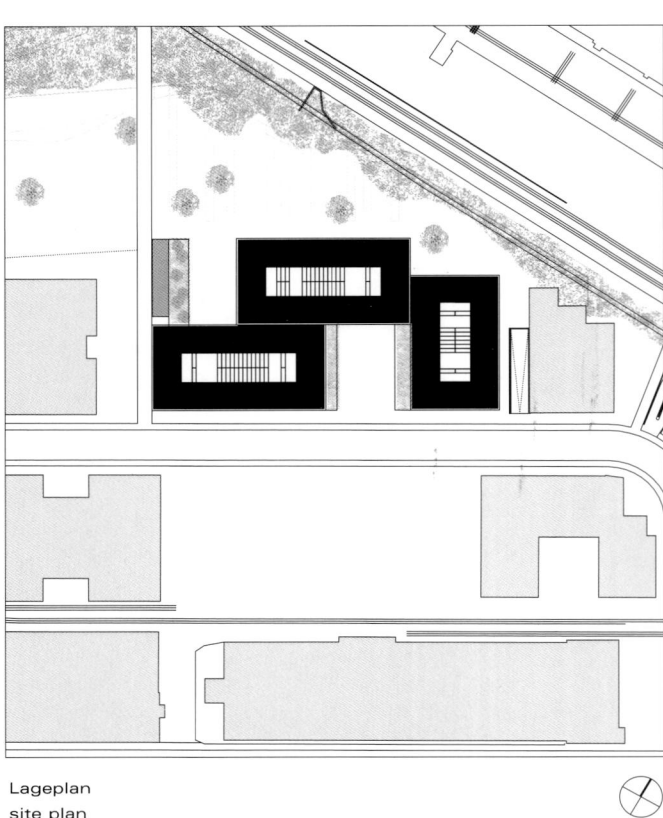

Lageplan
site plan

Bauherr | client **Rentenanstalt Swiss Life** Generalunternehmer | general contractor **Zschokke GU. AG** Planung | planning **Baumschlager Eberle Anstalt** Projektleitung | project architect **Christian Tabernigg** Mitarbeiter | assistance **Alexia Monauni, Marlies Sofia** Landschaftsarchitekt | landscape architect **Vogt Landschaftsarchitekten** Haustechnik Konzept | mechanical engineer **Robert Aerni Ingenieur AG** Statik | structural engineer **Edi Toscano AG** Grundstücksfläche | site area **5.121 m²** Bebaute Fläche | built up area **4.400 m²** Nutzfläche | floor area **41.737 m²** Umbauter Raum | building volume **128.138 m³** Planungsbeginn | commencement of planning Januar | January 2002

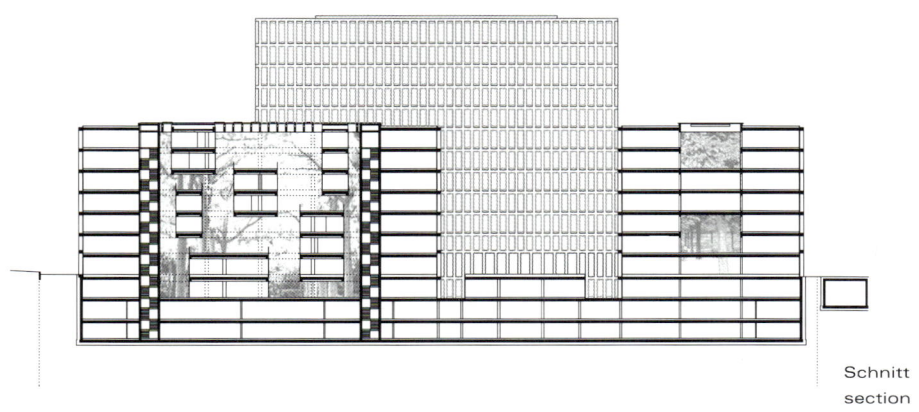

Schnitt
section

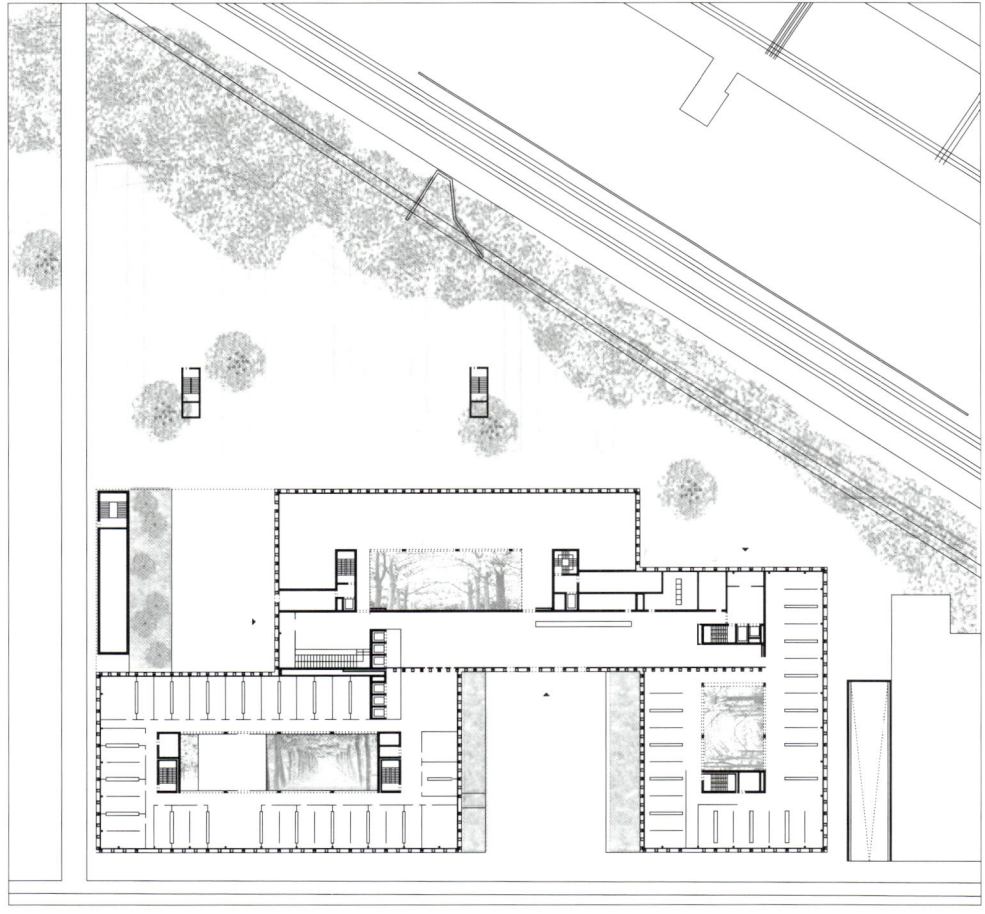

Erdgeschoß
ground floor

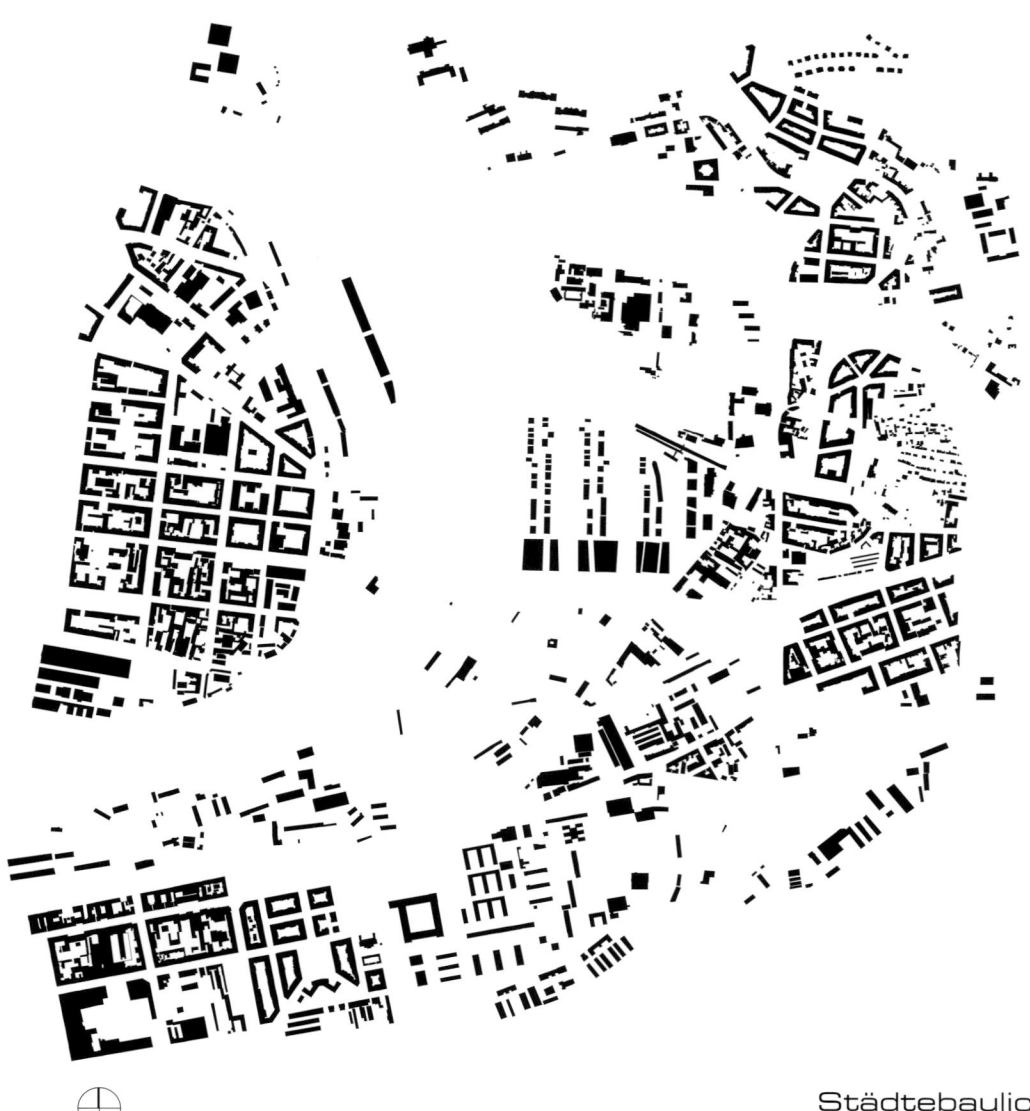

Städtebauliche Planung für die Docks Prag 8, CZ
Urban Planning Project for the Prag 8 Docks, Czech Republic

Überspitzt formuliert: Venedig an der Moldau, nur nicht so angenagt vom Zahn der Zeit, sondern zeitgenössischer Wohnbau vom Feinsten. Ein gründerzeitliches Industrieareal, abgewirtschaftet, aber mit einem unbezahlbaren Entwicklungspotential – die Industriebauten braucht keiner mehr, dafür ist der Zugang zum Wasser umso attraktiver. Landzungen bilden hier eine wundervolle Docklandschaft, es gibt eine bestehende Brückenverbindung zum „Festland", die möglichen Freizeitqualitäten sind einzigartig. Städtebaulicher Vorschlag von B&E: entlang der Hauptstraße urbane Dichte, entsprechend hoch und jeweils als Doppelspange – Büros und Wohnungen – organisiert, dahinter eine kleinteilige Wohnbebauung, im Grund ein Villenviertel – Reihenhäuser, Einfamilienhäuser, kleine Wohngebäude mit hohem Grünanteil, Bootsanlegestellen und einem garantierten Sicherheitsanspruch.

In exaggerated terms: Venice on the Vitava, just not as eroded by time, instead it offers contemporary residential buildings of the finest quality. An industrial estate dating back to the early days, run-down, but still of invaluable potential – nobody needs the industrial buildings anymore, but the body of water access is an attractive feature. Headland projections create a wonderful dock landscape, and a bridge connects it to the 'mainland'. The recreational possibilities are unique. B&E's urban planning proposal: urban density along the main road of the necessary height and aligned as double braces – offices and apartments. Behind these elements lie small-scale residential units, a villa area, terraced housing, single-family houses and small residential buildings with a high degree of green areas as well as docking opportunities and guaranteed security.

Bauherr | client **Real Estate Karlin Group** Planung | planning **B & E Baumschlager-Eberle GmbH** Projektleitung | project architect **Ullrich Grassmann** Mitarbeiter | assistance **Mateusz Kropop, Joanna Janiec** Nutzfläche | floor area **151.749 m²** Wettbewerb | competition **2002**

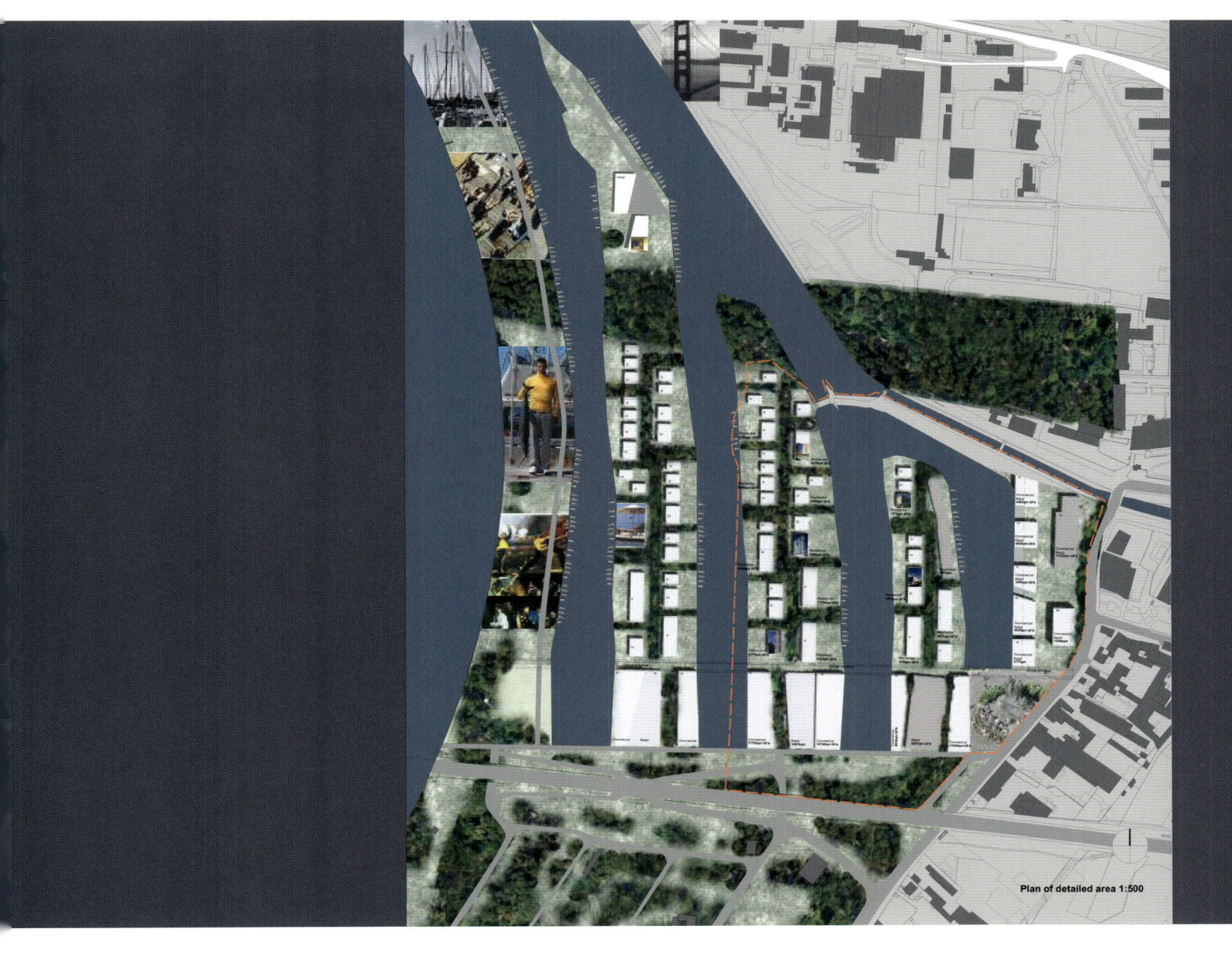

Plan of detailed area 1:500

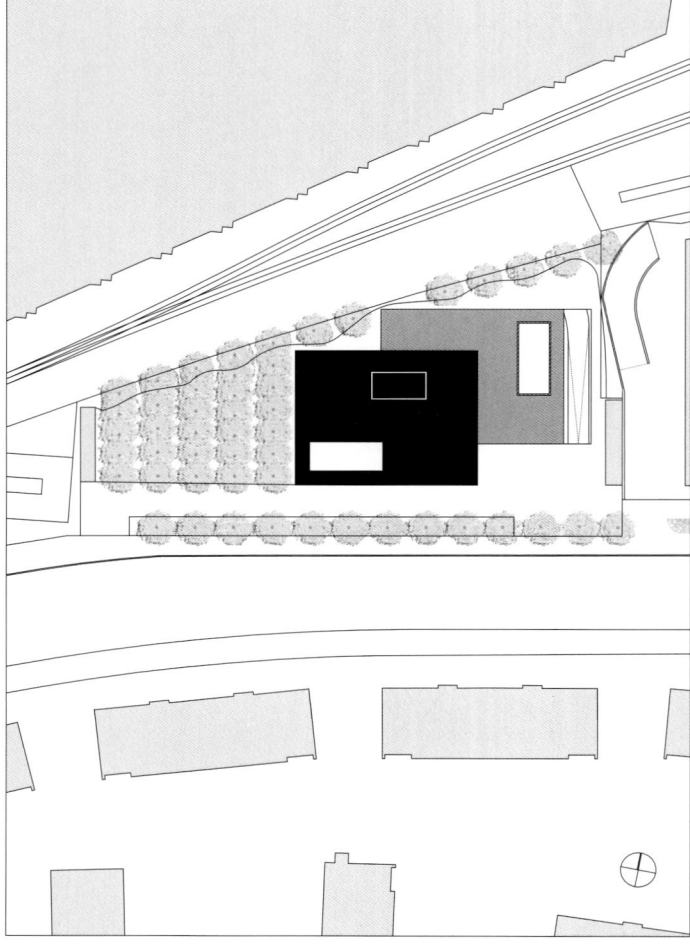

Lageplan
site plan

Bürohochhaus Hohlstraße in Zürich, CH
Hohlstrasse High-Rise Office Building in Zurich, Switzerland

Das Projekt definiert städtebaulich den Abschluß einer Dienstleistungsachse, die sich entlang eines Gleisfeldes – der Bahnhof ist nur 500 Meter entfernt, die Anbindung durch öffentliche Verkehrsmittel sehr gut – und dem Straßenbereich entwickelt. Das Haus steht genau an dem Punkt, wo sich Straße und Bahngelände am nächsten kommen, städtebaulich definiert es eine Torsituation. In Relation zu seiner Höhe (knapp 60 Meter) ist das Gebäude ziemlich schlank, in der Sockelzone mit Café, Seminarräumen und Ausstellungsbereich, vorgeschoben ein kleiner Park.
Darüber: flexible Bürogeschosse, großteils mit Aussicht auf das riesige Gleisfeld als Freiraum. Die zweischalige Fassade dient sowohl als energetische Maßnahme (Sonneneinstrahlung, Winddruck) als auch als Schallschutz. In der eigentlichen thermischen Haut sitzen im Abstand von 1,20 Metern öffenbare Fenster.

At an urban planning level, the building defines the final service segment of the project. It is located along a set of railway tracks – the train station is only 500 metres away, which makes for very good public transportation connections – helps develop the road section of the site. The building stands at the point where the road and station grounds come closest to each other, serving as a gate in an urban planning context. The building is slender in relation to its height (almost 60 metres tall) and it features a café, seminar rooms and an exhibition space with a small forecourt park in the base course zone.
On top: flexible office floors, most of them feature a view of the huge track yard as an open space. The double façade serves as both an energy measure (sunlight, wind pressure) and as protective sound insulation. Operable windows were placed in the actual thermic skin of the building in 1.20 metre intervals.

Bauherr l client **Senn BPM AG** Generalunternehmer l general contractor **Senn BPM AG** Planung l planning **Baumschlager Eberle Anstalt** Projektleitung l project architect **Christian Tabernigg, Gerhard Zweier** Mitarbeiter l assistance **Stefan Beck, Marc Fisler, Marlies Sofia** Landschaftsarchitekt l landscape architect **Vogt Landschaftsarchitekten** Haustechnik Konzept l mechanical engineer **Helbling Ingenieurunternehmung AG** Statik l structural engineer **Wismer + Partner** Grundstücksfläche l site area **2.280 m²** Bebaute Fläche l built up area **767 m²** Nutzfläche l floor area **6.650 m²** Umbauter Raum l building volume **37.000 m³** Planungsbeginn l commencement of planning August l August **2001** Baubeginn l commencement of work September l September **2002** Fertigstellung l completion Dezember l December **2003**

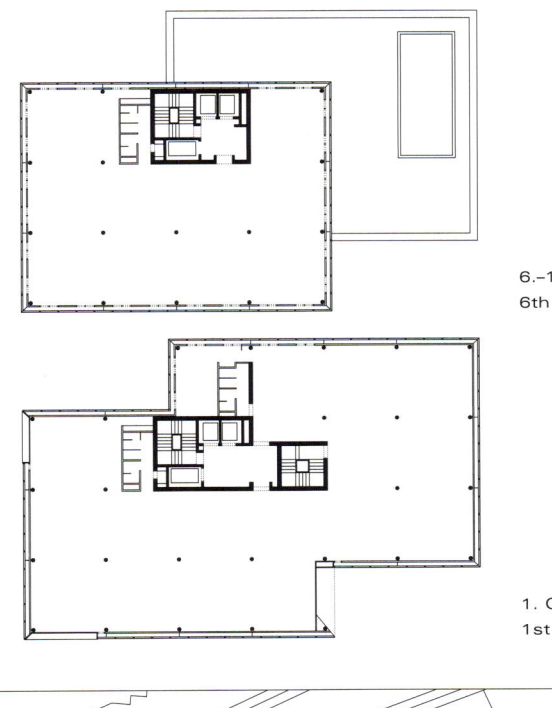

6.–13. Obergeschoß
6th–13th floor

1. Obergeschoß
1st floor

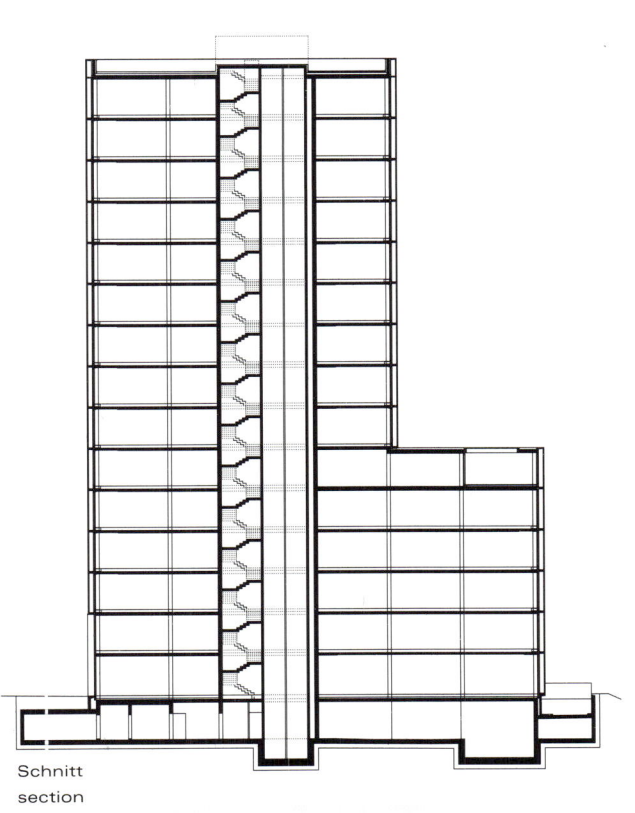

Schnitt
section

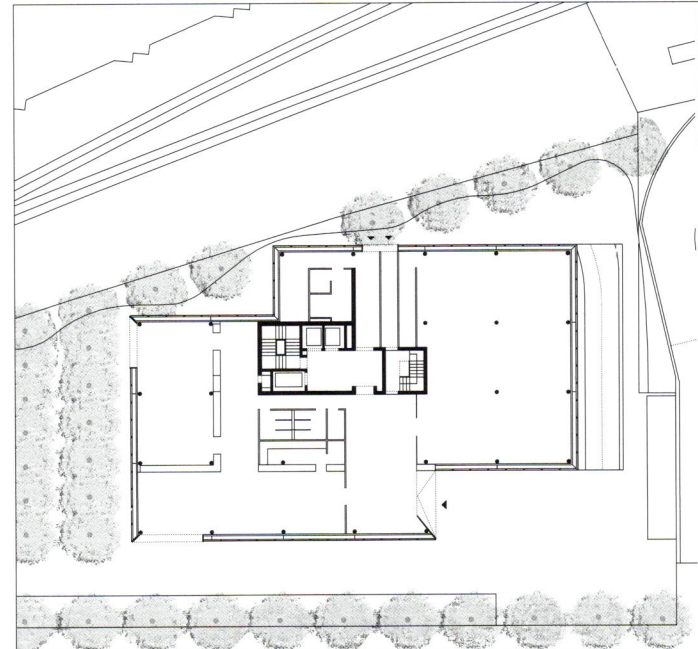

Erdgeschoß
ground floor

Mega Hall für Peking, China
Mega Hall for Beijing, China

Gefordert: drei Hochhäuser von großer städtischer Dichte, die an einem neuen Verkehrsknotenpunkt, am Rand der Innenstadt von Peking errichtet werden. Das Areal umfaßt eine ganze Reihe von Neubauten. Die drei Türme von B&E – höhenmäßig differenziert von knapp 100 bis knapp 80 Meter – beinhalten in einer horizontal geschichteten Zone Shopping und Dienstleistungen, darüber Wohnungen. Besonderes Augenmerk wurde der Gebäudetechnologie gewidmet. Peking leidet unvergleichbar stärker unter der Umweltbelastung als jede europäische Stadt. Darauf wurde bei der Planung besonders geachtet – diese spezifische Qualifikation des Büros war wohl auch ein Grund für die Beauftragung von B&E.

Program: three high-rise buildings providing great urban density are to be built for a new traffic hub at the edge of Beijing's inner city. The space comprises a number of new buildings. The three B&E towers, of differing heights (approx 100 to 80 metres tall) offer horizontally layered shopping zones and service areas with apartments above these sections. Special attention was given to the building equipment and technology. Beijing is under a much greater environmental strain than any European city. This aspect was given particular importance during planning – this specific qualification was also presumably the reason for which B&E was hired.

Lageplan
site plan

Bauherr | client **Beijing Modern Hong Yun Real Estate Dev. Co, Ltd** Planung | planning **Baumschlager Eberle Anstalt** Projektleitung | project architect **Christian Tabernigg** Mitarbeiter | assistance **Stefan Beck, Sabrina Contratto, Marc Fisler, Alexia Monauni, Marlies Sofia** Haustechnik Konzept | mechanical engineer **KellerTechnologies** Grundstücksfläche | site area **10.240 m²** Bebaute Fläche | built up area **4.430 m²** Nutzfläche | floor area **100.000 m²** Umbauter Raum | building volume **260.000 m³** Planungsbeginn | commencement of planning Juli | July **2002** Baubeginn | commencement of work Juni | June **2003** Fertigstellung | completion Juni | June **2005**

B & E > Wettbewerbe | Competitions

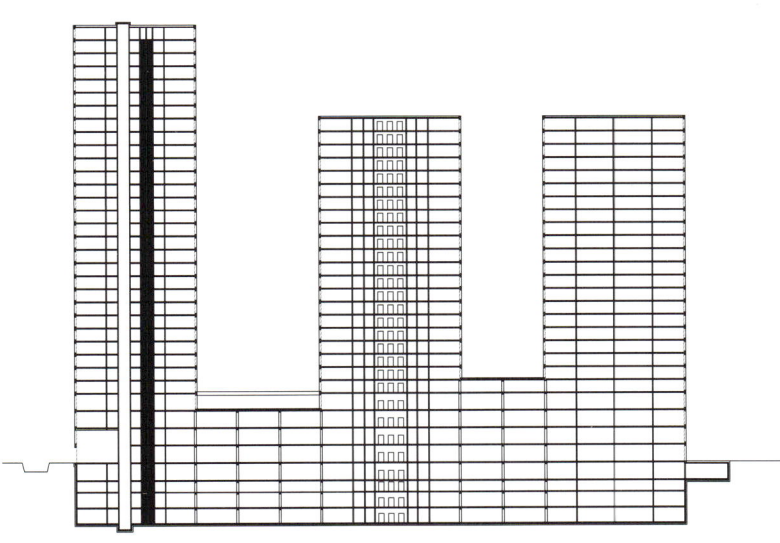

Schnitt
section

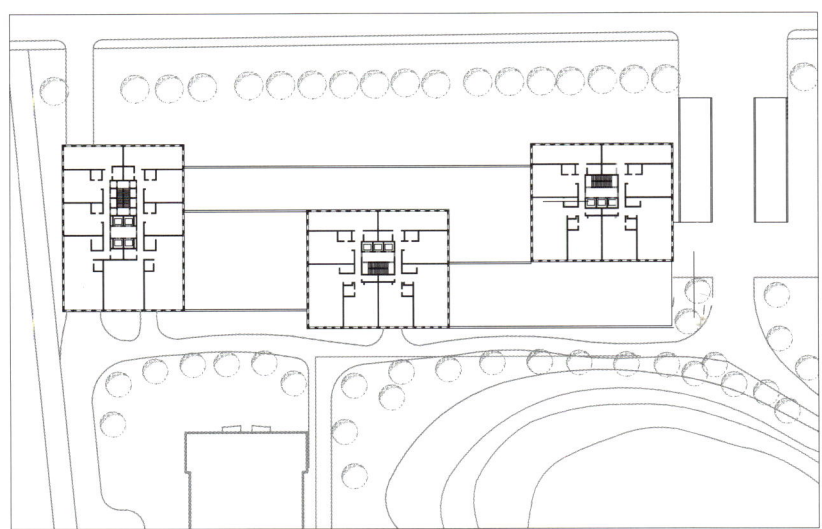

Erdgeschoß
ground floor

Plot 1

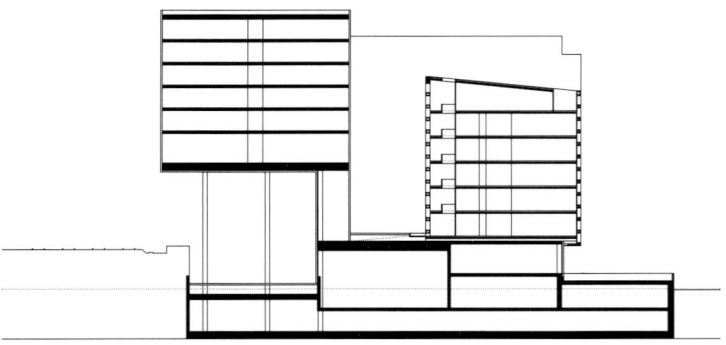

Schnitt
section

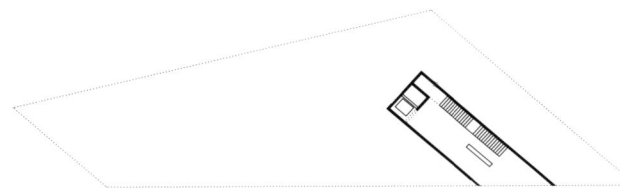

Erdgeschoß
ground floor

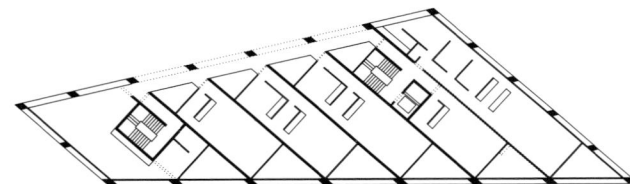

Regelgeschoß
standard floor

Bauherr | client **OOA Oosterdokseiland Ontwikkeling Amsterdam Cv** Planung | planning **B & E Baumschlager-Eberle GmbH** Projektleitung | project architect **Willem Bruijn** Mitarbeiter | assistance **René Bechter, Torsten Guder, Joanna Janiec, Philipp Raupach** Landschaftsarchitekt | landscape architect **Agence Ter** Haustechnik Konzept | mechanical engineer **Deems** Statik | structural engineer **Arcadis** Grundstücksfläche | site area **650 m²** Bebaute Fläche | built up area **5.900 m²** Nutzfläche | floor area **3.675 m²** Umbauter Raum | building volume **18.850 m³** Planungsbeginn | commencement of planning September | September **2001** Baubeginn | commencement of work Mai | May **2003** Fertigstellung | completion Juni | June **2007**

Projekt Oosterdokseiland in Amsterdam, NL
Oosterdokseiland Project in Amsterdam, The Netherlands

Auch von der Vorgangsweise ein interessantes Entwicklungsvorhaben. Der holländische Entwickler MAB lud für das hauptsächlich von Bahn und Post besetzte Areal eine Reihe internationaler Architekten ein, die einen vorgegebenen Fragenkatalog zu beantworten hatten. Es ging dabei aber nicht um die Entwicklung eines konkreten Projektes. Es ging darum, eine Dialogbasis mit den Architekten zu finden. Gesprächsthema: die Reduzierung der Bahn, der Abriß der Post, ein städtebauliches Konzept für Büros und Wohnbau, für ein Hotel und das sogenannte „Network Facility Center", ein Handelszentrum für den asiatischen Raum. Die Besetzung ist international: von David Chipperfield bis Toyo Ito, von Cruz & Ortiz bis B&E. Den städtebaulichen Zuschlag erhielt Erick van Egeraat mit einem allerdings ziemlich komplizierten Projekt. Denn die einzelnen Bauvorhaben – B&E sind mit drei Objekten betraut –, sind nicht an Parzellen festgemacht, sie überlagern, überlappen einander. Das hat gravierende konstruktive, statische Probleme zur Folge. Wenn die Umsetzung trotzdem gelänge, wäre das ein wichtiger Schritt. Dann hätte eine neue planerische Zukunft auf der Basis ganz neuer Möglichkeiten der Zusammenarbeit begonnen.

Übrigens präsentierte Erick van Egeraat das Gesamtprojekt in Venedig bei der Architekturbiennale 2002 im niederländischen Pavillon.

Yet another interesting approach to a development project. The Dutch developer MAB invited a number of internationally acclaimed architects to submit proposals in accordance with a catalogue of demands for the site, which was intended for postal and railway services. However, the objective wasn't to discuss an actual project but to establish a basis for dialogue. The intent: the reduction of the railway and tearing down the postal services, and an urban development concept for offices and residential units, as well as a hotel and the so-called 'Network Facility Center', a trade centre for the Asian region. The list of participants is international: from David Chipperfield to Toyo Ito, Cruz & Ortiz and B&E. Erick van Egeraat was awarded the urban planning contract for the project for a rather complicated solution. The individual buildings – B&E was entrusted with three – are not on specific plots, instead they are layered and overlap one another. This leads to major construction and structural engineering problems. The realisation of the project despite these difficulties would be an important step. If so, it would mark the beginning of a new future in planning on the basis of thoroughly new cooperation possibilities.

By the way: Erick van Egeraat presented the complete project at the Dutch Pavilion of the 2002 Architecture Biennial in Venice.

Plot 2

Plot 6

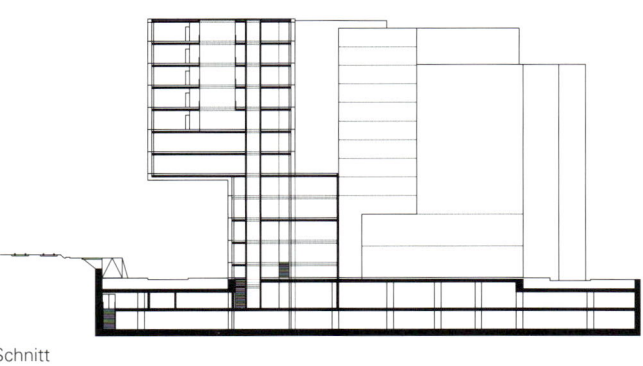

Schnitt
section

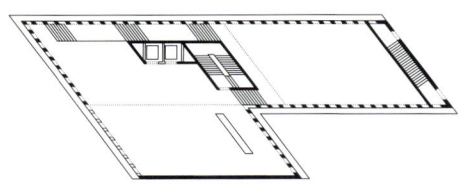

Erdgeschoß
ground floor

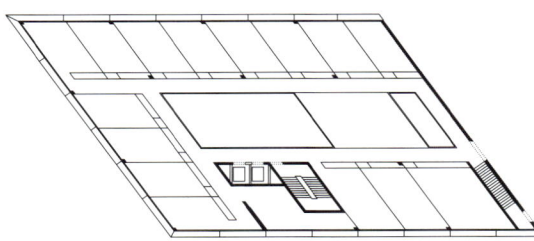

Regelgeschoß
standard floor

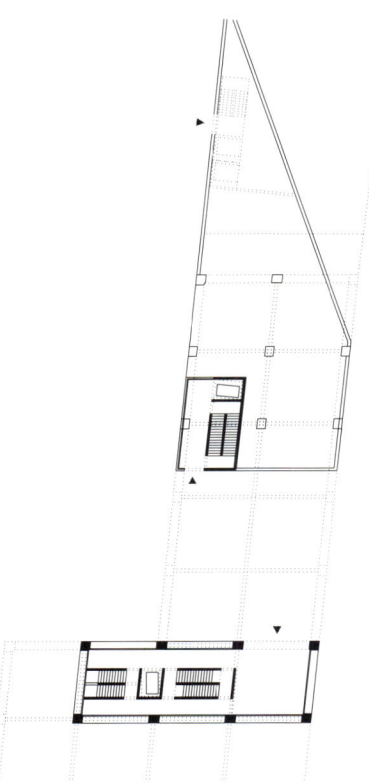

Erdgeschoß
ground floor

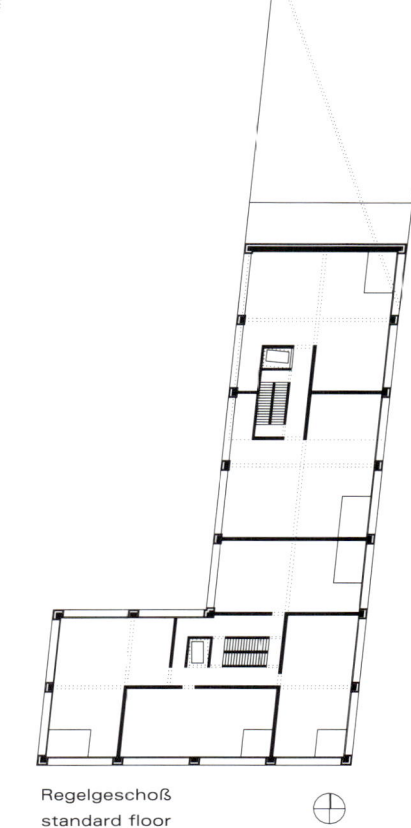

Regelgeschoß
standard floor

Statik | structural engineer **Arcadis** Grundstücksfläche | site area **500 m²** Bebaute Fläche | built up area **9.000 m²** Nutzfläche | floor area **6.500m²** Umbauter Raum | building volume **32.400 m³** Planungsbeginn | commencement of planning September | September **2001** Baubeginn | commencement of work Mai | May **2003** Fertigstellung | completion Juni | June **2007**

Statik | structural engineer **Aronsohn** Grundstücksfläche | site area **1.000 m²** Bebaute Fläche | built up area **8.700 m²** Nutzfläche | floor area **6.750m²** Umbauter Raum | building volume **27.000 m³** Planungsbeginn | commencement of planning September | September **2001** Baubeginn | commencement of work Mai | May **2005** Fertigstellung | completion Juni | June **2009**

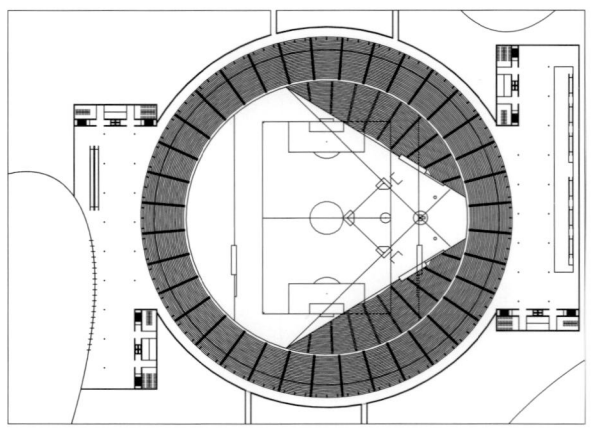

Fußball- und Baseballstadion in Sapporo, J
Football and Baseball Stadium in Sapporo, Japan

Trotz Randlage ein städtebaulich bedeutsamer Standort: an einer großen Einfallstraße nach Sapporo, auf einer ausgedehnten unbebauten Fläche, die als Sport- und Kulturbereich entwickelt werden soll. Und eine extreme Aufgabenstellung: Denn ein Fußballstadion ist flächig organisiert, ein Baseballstadion funktioniert über die Höhe; außerdem ist in beiden Fällen die Tribünenanordnung unterschiedlich; der Umbau von einer Nutzung zur anderen mußte aber in kürzester Zeit möglich sein. Zusätzlich gefragt: eine Verkehrslösung, Parkflächen, eine Sporthochschule, ein Fitness-Großbereich.

Die Idee: eine riesige, teilweise ins Gelände eingegrabene Halle, ab Tribünenhöhe – bis hinauf zum Dach – aus Glas. Sie ist praktisch stützenfrei, denn es gibt nur vier tragende Kerne, in denen die gesamte Erschließung untergebracht ist. Darüber ein Dachaufbau mit den diversen, besonders umfangreichen Zusatzfunktionen. Der Rasen für das Fußballfeld ist ins Freie, auf das Dach hochgezogen und wird im Bedarfsfall heruntergefahren und auf dem Boden installiert. Wenn der Rasen unten ist: Durchblicke nach oben. Ein Indoor-Konzept also, das den Charakter eines überdachten Außenraumes hat, nicht eines geschlossenen Innenraumes.

Es war ein weltweiter Wettbewerb. Auf den ersten drei Plätzen landeten japanische Architekturbüros. An vierter Stelle: B&E.

Despite its location on an edge, the site is important in terms of urban construction. It is located on one of the Sapporo access roads on a large undeveloped plot that will be developed as a sports and cultural centre. The task was also extreme since a football stadium is organised in terms of surface and a baseball stadium requires height. The alignment of the stands for both sports also differs, so it was necessary to be able to reconfigure the stadium in the shortest possible period of time. A traffic solution that would comprise parking areas, a sports school and a large fitness area was also necessary.

The idea: a huge glass dome, partly dug into the ground from the level of the stands to the roof. It requires practically no supports. Instead, it relies on four load-bearing cores which contain all installations and access possibilites. Above them is the roof structure with all the various, comprehensive additional functions. The football pitch can be pulled up and outside on to the roof and can be lowered and installed on the floor when needed. Views up and to the outside are possibe when the turf is set. Thus this is an indoor concept with the character of a protected outer space and not that of an enclosed inside space.

It was a worldwide competition.
Projects from Japanese architecture offices won the first three spots. B&E took fourth place.

Bauherr I client **Stadt Sapporo** Planung I planning **Architekturbüro B & E Ziviltechniker GmbH** Projektleitung I project architect **Carlo Baumschlager, Dietmar Eberle** Mitarbeiter I assistance **Nori Sasaki, Christian Tabernigg** Landschaftsarchitekt I landscape architect **Vogt Landschaftsarchitekten** Statik I structural engineer **D.I. Ernst Mader** weltweiter Wettbewerb I worldwide competition **1996, 4. Platz** I 4th place

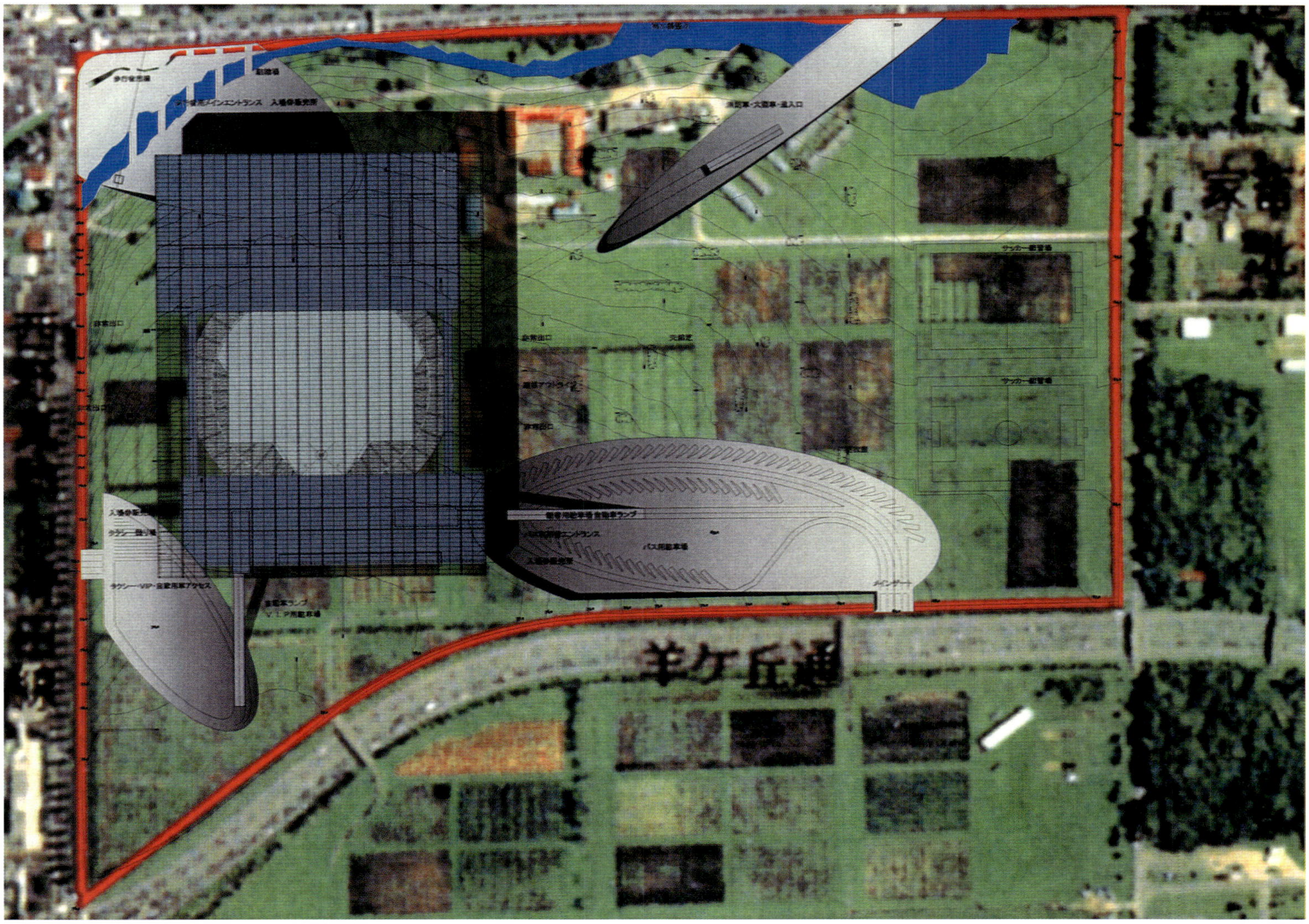

Werkverzeichnis
List of Projects

Wohnanlage Rieden
Bregenz
Projekt 2002

Gewerbebau Rhomberg-Areal
Bregenz
Projekt 2002

Wohnanlage Karmeliter-Kloster
Innsbruck
Projekt 2002

Wohnanlage V100 AH
Frastanz
Projekt 2002

Wohnanlage Velux
Malchen (D)
Studie 2002

Einfamilienhaus Alge
Dornbirn
Realisierung 2002

Einfamilienhaus Böhler
Schwarzach
Realisierung 2002

Arztpraxis Pechlaner
Bregenz
Realisierung 2002

Finanzamt
Bregenz
Realisierung 2002–2003

ETH Neubau HIT
Zürich (CH)
Projekt 2002

Verwaltungsbebäude OMS/Onusida
Genf (CH)
Projekt 2002

Flughafen
Antwerpen (B)
Projekt 2002

Mega Hall – 3 Wohnhochhäuser
Peking (China)
Realisierung 2002 –

Verwaltungsgebäude Saeco Erweiterung
Lustenau
Realisierung 2002

Schulgebäude GBS Sanierung
Bregenz
Realisierung 2002–2003

Wohnanlage Verwalter
Dornbirn
Realisierung 2002–2003

Wohnanlage Lehmweg
Hamburg (D)
Realisierung 2002–2003

Krankenhaus
Hohenems
Realisierung 2002–2005

Flughafen
Wien-Schwechat
Realisierung 2002–

Einfamilenhaus Amann
Altach
Realisierung 2002

Gewerbebau LTW Erweiterung
Wolfurt
Realisierung 2002–2003

Gewerbebau Elektro Graf Erweiterung
Dornbirn
Realisierung 2002–2003

Städtebau
Dorfzentrum Lochau
Realisierung 2002–2003

Wohnanlage Hötting West (Lohbach) 2. Baustufe
Innsbruck
Realisierung 2002–2003

Restaurant Caruso
Dornbirn
Realisierung 2001–2002

Wohnanlage Weissenreute
Bregenz
Studie 2001

Gewerbebau Achpark Erweiterung
Lauterach
Projekt 2001

Wohnanlage Eschlestraße
Hard
Realisierung 2001–2003

Bürohochhaus Hohlstraße
Zürich (CH)
Projekt 2001

Hotel
Krems
Projekt 2001

Wohnanlage
Hohenweiler
Projekt 2001

Wohnbau ODE Plot 1
Amsterdam (NL)
Projekt 2001

Handelszentrum ODE Plot 2 NFC
Amsterdam (NL)
Projekt 2001

Wohnbau ODE Plot 6
Amsterdam (NL)
Projekt 2001

Einfamilenhaus Schram
St. Gilgen
Projekt 2001

Hotel
Wien-Schwechat
Projekt 2001

Bürohochhaus Räffel Park
Zürich (CH)
Projekt 2001

Landesmuseum
Bregenz
Realisierung 2001

Wohnanlage Langgasse
Rankweil
Realisierung 2001–2002

Geschäft Sagmeister
Bregenz
Realisierung 2001

Gewerbebau Zumtobel AG Werk 1
Dornbirn
Realisierung 2001

Geschäft Sagmeister
Vaduz (FL)
Realisierung 2001

IT Data Center Zumtobel
Dornbirn
Realisierung 2001–2002

Bürohaus
Wien-Schwechat
Realisierung 2001

Wohnanlage Dammstraße
Lauterach
Realisierung 2001–2002

Wohnanlage Bildsteinerstraße
Wolfurt
Realisierung 2001–2002

Gasthaus Adler
Hohenems
Realisierung 2001

Landeskrankenhaus
Bregenz
Realisierung 2000–2005

Wohnanlage Nofels
Feldkirch
Studie 2000

Wohnanlage Wallenmahd
Dornbirn
Studie 2000

Wohnanlage Belruptstraße
Bregenz
Studie 2000

Hotel
Prag (Cz)
Studie 2000

Wohnanlage Lochau-Süd
Lochau
Studie 2000

Wohnanlage Zollgasse
Dornbirn
Projekt 2000

Wohnanlage Heinzenbeer
Dornbirn
Projekt 2000

Gewerbebau Schwefel
Dornbirn
Projekt 2000

Wohnanlage Alte Landstraße
Bludenz
Projekt 2000

Wohnanlage Krems-Wieden
Krems
Studie 2000

Wohnanlage Falkenried
Hamburg (D)
Projekt 2000

Wohnanlage Vogelherd
St. Gallen (CH)
Projekt 2000

Wohnanlage B31
Friedrichshafen (D)
Projekt 2000

Einfamilienhaus Witt
Hamburg (D)
Projekt 2000

Bürohaus Luxmate Controls
Dornbirn
Realisierung 2000

HTL Michael Felder Straße
Bregenz
Projekt 2000

Wohnanlage Krone
Lustenau
Realisierung 2000–2002

Wohnanlage Sebastianstraße
Dornbirn
Realisierung 2000–2001

Wohnanlage Gratkorn
Graz
Realisierung 2000–2001

Wohnanlage Herrenried
Hohenems
Realisierung 2000–2003

Wohnanlage McNair
Berlin (D)
Realisierung 2000–2002

Wohnanlage Lachen
St. Gallen (CH)
Realisierung 2000–2001

Einkaufszentrum Ambergpark
Feldkirch
Realisierung 2000–2001

Hafengebäude Rohner
Fussach
Realisierung 2000

Gewerbebau Bauhof
Bregenz
Realisierung 2000–2001

Wohnanlage Bildsteinerstraße
Wolfurt
Realisierung 2000–2003

Wohnanlage Stüdler Mahd
Mäder
Projekt 1999

Wohnanlage Sohmgründe
Lauterach
Projekt 1999

Wohnanlage Beck-Areal
Hohenems
Projekt 1999

Gewerbebau
Traun
Projekt 1999

Wohnanlage Gehren II
Lochau
Projekt 1999

Wohnanlage V88 AH
Fussach
Realisierung 1999–2000

Gewerbebau Rhomberg Center II
Lochau
Projekt 1999

Wohnanlage V85 AH
Lustenau
Projekt 1999

Büro- und Gewerbebau Ospelt
Vaduz (FL)
Realisierung 1999–2001

Einfamilienhaus Flatz
Schaan (FL)
Realisierung 1999–2000

Wohnanlage Ostufer
St. Pölten
Studie 1999

Gewerbebau Doppelmayr
Wolfurt
Projekt 1999

Einkaufszentrum
Bregenz
Projekt 1999

Gewerbebau Zumtobel AG Werk 2
Dornbirn
Realisierung 1998–1999

Einfamilenhaus
Engenberg (D)
Realisierung 1998–2000

Sanierung Arlbergstraße
Bregenz
Realisierung 1998

Wohnanlage Achslengut 2. Baustufe
St. Gallen (CH)
Realisierung 1998–2002

Zubau Helbock
Koblach
Realisierung 1998

Technische Hochschule
Kuwait
Studie 1998

Wohnanlage Köpenick
Berlin (D)
Projekt 1998

Wohnanlage AH Lustenau
Lustenau
Realisierung 1998–1998

Gewerbebau Sirch
Böhen (D)
Realisierung 1998

Wohnanlage Hötting West (Lohbach)
Innsbruck
Realisierung 1998–2000

Wohnanlage Klosterwiesenweg
Schwarzach
Realisierung 1998–2000

Wohnanlage V78 AH
Bludenz
Realisierung 1997–1998

Mehrfamilienhaus Giesinger
Altach
Realisierung 1997–1998

Betriebsgebäude Saeco
Lustenau
Realisierung 1997–1998

Gewerbebau Achpark
Lauterach
Realisierung 1997–1998

Werbeagentur Baschnegger
Sanierung und Zubau
Dornbirn
Realisierung 1997–1998

Bankgebäude BTV
Wolfurt
Realisierung 1997–1998

Gewerbebau Doppelmayr
China
Projekt 1997

Einfamilienhaus Dotter
Wolfurt
Projekt 1997

Büro- und Wohnhaus Groß + Groß
Schweiz
Projekt 1997

Wohnanlage Mitterweg
Innsbruck
Realisierung 1997

Wohnanlage Rhomberg
Hard
Projekt 1997

Verwaltungsgebäude Rhomberg
Bregenz
Projekt 1997

Umbau Sagmeister
Dornbirn
Realisierung 1997

Wohnanlage Schertler
Lech
Realisierung 1997–1999

Wohnanlage Schertler
Schwarzach
Projekt 1997

Wohnanlage Mildenberg
Bregenz
Realisierung 1997–1999

Wohnanlage
St. Pölten
Realisierung 1997–1998

Umbau Ullmann
Berlin (D)
Realisierung 1997

Einfamilienhaus Ulmer
Schwarzach
Realisierung 1997–1998

Wohnanlage
Dorfzentrum Lochau
Realisierung 1997–2000

Wohnanlage V78
Bludenz
Realisierung 1997–1998

Wohnanlage Achslengut
St. Gallen (CH)
Realisierung 1993–1998

Einfamilienhaus Böhler-Jutz
Dornbirn
Realisierung 1996–1998

Vereinshütte Deutscher Alpenverein
Schattwald (D)
Realisierung 1996–1997

Öko-Hauptschule
Mäder
Realisierung 1996–1998

Pfarrheim
Lochau
Realisierung 1996–1998

Gewerbebau VGK
Bludenz
Realisierung 1996–1997

Umspannwerk VKW
Hörbranz
Realisierung 1996–1997

Pfarrheim
Satteins
Realisierung 1996

Einfamilienhaus Allgaier-Gaugg
Bregenz
Realisierung 1996–1998

Wohnanlage Mozartstraße
Dornbirn
Realisierung 1996–1997

Umbau Baschnegger
Dornbirn
Realisierung 1997–1998

Wohnanlage Rohrbach II
Dornbirn
Realisierung 1996–1997

**HTL Bregenz
Sanierung und Erweiterung**
Bregenz
Realisierung 1995–1998

Einfamilienhaus Kern
Lochau
Realisierung 1995–1996

Einfamilienhaus Büchel
Vaduz (FL)
Realisierung 1995–1996

Raiffeisen-Bankgebäude
Bregenz
Realisierung 1995–1996

Wettbewerbe
Competitions

2002
Cornloft
Prag (CZ)
Platz 1

Altana Pharma
Konstanz (D)
Platz 3

AUA
Wien
Platz 3

ETH Zürich HIT
Zürich (CH)
Platz 1

WIFI
Dornbirn
Ankauf

2001
Bahnhofsareal
Basel (CH)

Fachhochschule
Dornbirn
Anerkennung

Flughafen
Antwerpen (B)
Platz 1

Haus Witt am Wellingsbüttel
Hamburg (D)
Platz 1

WHO/UNAIDS
Genf (CH)
Platz 1

Parkstadt Schwabing
München (D)

Porta Susa
Turin (I)

Räffel Park
Zürich (CH)
Platz 1

Rieden West
Bregenz
Platz 1

Rosenbüchel
St. Gallen (CH)
Platz 1

Schulzentrum Messestadt Ost
München (D)
Ankauf

Krankenhaus
Kortrijk (B)
Platz 1

Städtebau
Urban Design Prag (CZ)

Verwaltungsgebäude Marstall
München (D)
Platz 1

Studentenwohnheim
Krems-Wieden
Platz 1

2000
CSCC 1/2
Horgen (CH)

Flughafen
Wien-Schwechat
Platz 1

La Roche Forum
Buonas (CH)
Ankauf

Rathaus
Dornbirn
Platz 3

Steiner Areal
Zürich (CH)

TIC Steyr
Steyr

Tivoli
Innsbruck

Uni Klinikum
Freiburg (D)
Ankauf

Wienerberg City
Wien
Platz 2

Stellwerke ÖBB
Österreich

1999
Deutsche Schule
Peking (China)

Krems Wieden
Krems
Platz 1

Städtebau Falkenried/Lehmweg
Hamburg (D)
Platz 2

1998
Confida Vaduz
Vaduz (FL)
Platz 2

Peterstor
Regensburg (D)
Platz 1

Rum
Innsbruck
Platz 2

Salzmagazin
Zürich (CH)
Ankauf

VB Bank
Triesen (FL)
Platz 3

1997
Deutsche Post AG
Bonn (D)

Klosterwiesenweg
Schwarzach
Platz 1

Lohbach (Hötting West)
Innsbruck
Platz 1

Münchener Rück Versicherung
München (D)
Platz 1

Neu Hötting
Innsbruck
Platz 1

Öko-Hauptschule
Mäder
Platz 1

Pfarrheim
Lochau
Platz 1

1996
Bayerische Spielbank
Lindau (D)
Platz 1

Gartenstadt Hellerau Erweiterung
Hellerau (D)

Kraftwerk
Schruns

Mitterweg
Innsbruck
Platz 1

Österreichische Botschaft
Berlin (D)

Pester
Baden-Württemberg (D)
Platz 2

Stadion
Sapporo (Japan)
Platz 4

Volksschule
Wien
Ankauf

Zubau Gymnasium
Feldkirch
Platz 2

Biographie
Biography

Foto | photo Helene Waldner

Carlo Baumschlager

1956
geboren in Bregenz, Vorarlberg
born in Bregenz, Vorarlberg

1974-1975
Design-Volontariat bei BBC Bregenz
design-trainee at BBC Bregenz

1975-1982
Studium an der Hochschule für angewandte Kunst in Wien
Studied at the University of Applied Arts in Vienna,
Industrie-Design (Prof. Hans Hollein)
Industrial Design (Prof. Hans Hollein)
Architektur (Prof. Wilhelm Holzbauer, Prof. Oswald M. Ungers)
Architecture (Prof. Wilhelm Holzbauer, Prof. Oswald M. Ungers)

1982
Diplomabschluß bei Prof. Wilhelm Holzbauer
Diploma Prof. Wilhelm Holzbauer

1982-1984
Selbständiger Baukünstler
Freelance "Baukünstler"

1984-1985
Arbeitsgemeinschaft Baumschlager-Eberle-Egger
Collaboration Baumschlager-Eberle-Egger

ab | since 1985
Arbeitsgemeinschaft und Büro mit Dietmar Eberle
Collaboration and office with Dietmar Eberle

Lehrtätigkeit | Teaching Engagements:

1994
Syracuse University, New York, USA
Syracuse University, New York, USA

1997
FH Stuttgart
University of Applied Sciences Stuttgart, Germany

Dietmar Eberle

1952
geboren in Hittisau, Bregenzerwald, Vorarlberg
born in Hittisau, Bregenzerwald, Vorarlberg

1973-1978
Studium an der Technischen Hochschule in Wien
(Diplomabschluß bei Prof. Anton Schweighofer)
*Studied at the Technical University of Vienna
(Diploma Prof. Anton Schweighofer)*

1976-1977
Arbeitsaufenthalt im Iran, Städtebaustudie
Iran, worked on urban development

1979-1982
Arbeitsgemeinschaft Cooperative Bau- und Planungsges.m.b.H.
mit Markus Koch, Norbert Mittersteiner und Wolfgang Juen
*Collaboration Cooperative Bau- und Planungsges.m.b.H.
with Markus Koch, Norbert Mittersteiner und Wolfgang Juen*

1982-1984 (ab 1984 mit Carlo Baumschlager)
Arbeitsgemeinschaft Eberle-Egger
Collaboration Eberle-Egger

ab | since 1985
Arbeitsgemeinschaft und Büro mit Carlo Baumschlager
Collaboration and office with Carlo Baumschlager

Lehrtätigkeit | Teaching Engagements:

1983-1988
Technische Universität Hannover
Technical University in Hannover, Germany

1987-1989
Technische Universität Wien, Institut für Wohnbau
Technical University in Vienna, Austria

1989-1990
Hochschule für künstlerische und industrielle Gestaltung, Linz
University for Art and Industrial Design, Linz, Austria

1991-1993
ETH Zürich, Schweiz
Technical University in Zurich, Suisse

1994
Syracuse University, New York, USA
Syracuse University, New York, USA

1996-1999
TU Darmstadt
Technical University in Darmstadt, Germany

ab | since 1999
ETH-Zürich, Schweiz
Professur für Architektur und Entwerfen
*Technical University in Zurich, Suisse
professorship faculty of architecture*

Leiter des ETH Wohnforums
*head of the center for housing and
sustainable urban development*

Firmengeschichte
Company History

Büro Lochau

seit | since 1985	Baumschlager – Eberle GesbR
seit | since 1996	Architekturbüro B&E Ziviltechniker GmbH
seit | since 2001	B&E Baumschlager-Eberle GmbH
Gesellschafter	Carlo Baumschlager
	Dietmar Eberle
Geschäftsführer	Hans Ullrich Grassmann
	Elmar Hasler

Büro Vaduz

seit | since 1999	Baumschlager-Eberle Architekturbüro
Gründerrechtsinhaber	Carlo Baumschlager
	Dietmar Eberle
Geschäftsführer	Christian Tabernigg
seit | since 2001	Baumschlager Eberle Anstalt

Büro Wien

seit | since 2001	P.ARC Baumschlager Eberle Gartenmann Raab GmbH
Gesellschafter	Carlo Baumschlager
	Dietmar Eberle
	Nick Gartenmann
	Peter Raab
Geschäftsführer	Jost Kutter
	Peter Raab

Mitarbeiter/innen
Assistants

Büro
Lochau Wien Vaduz

Oliver Baldauf
Michael Barth
Martina Barth-Sedelmayer
Susanne Bärtsch
Luzia Baumschlager
René Bechter
Stefan Beck
Kai-Uwe Bergmann
Sonja Berthold
Gabriele Bischof
Anita Boch
Roman Bönsch
Christian Bollmann
Heike Braungardt
Willem Bruijn
Frank Brunhard
Sabrina Contratto
Philipp v. Dalvig
Martin Deutenhauser
Reinhard Drexel
Christian Dürr
Konstantin Eleftheriadis
Christine Falkner
Gregor Fasching
Sascha Fässler
Christoph Feurstein
Marc Fisler
Bernhard Flühler
Robert Fritz
Sonja Funk
Karin Geisberger
Cordula Good
Sead Grcic
Doris Gruber
Torsten Guder
Ulrike Hahn
Christian Hallweger
Otto Höller
Rainer Huchler
Romeo Hutter
Sebastian Illchmann

Joanna Janiec
Oliver Kaps
Claudia Kees
Robert Keiser
Thomas Keller
Iris Kellner
Gerhard Klocker
Christian Kronaus
Mateusz Kropop
Martin Ladinger
Brigitte Löcker
Eckehart Loidolt
Marika Marte
Gerhard Matt
Christine Mayr
Alexia Monauni
Julia Nägele-Küng
Michael Ohneberg
Verena Pankoke
Renate Pflügl
Nicolas Prikatzky
Erika Ratvay
Philipp Raupach
Konrad Rautter
Tobias Reichart
Astrid Reiter
Brigitte Reith
Christof Ruegg
Werner Silbermayr
Marlies Sofia
Matt Sofroniou
Alexander Spauwen
Antje Stender
Andreas Stickel
Bernhard Stöhr
Mattheus Wagner
René Weber
Guido Welzl
Clemens Werb
Judith Wirthensohn
Nici Wohlwend
Stefan Zürcher
Stephan Zwahlen
Gerhard Zweier

Bibliographie
Bibliography

Zeitschriften ab 1996
Periodicals since 1996

A + T (E) 1997-09
Elektro Graf Dornbirn p. 48-59

A + T (E) 1997-09
Kraftwerk Alberschwende p. 48-59

A + T (E) 1997-09
Reithalle Fischer Breitbrunn, OÖ p. 48-59

A + U 1998-05 332
Kern EFH Lochau p. 36-45

A + U 1998-05 332
Nüziders WA p. 26-35

A + U 2000-01 352
HS Mäder p. 84-99

A + U Architecture and Urbanism (Japan)
2001-05 373
Gemeindezentrum Lochau p. 118-125

A + U Arquitetura & Urbanismo
2001-08/09 97
Lohbach WA Innsbruck p. 60-65

A+D (D) 1996-06
GBS Bregenz p. 28-31

A+D (D) 1996-06
Nofels WA p. 32-35

AAR Arkitekten 2000-02
B. Burger EFH Bregenz p. 26-33

ab (architektov bilten – architect's bulletin)
1998-11 141-142
Holz Altenried Hergatz p. 34-47

ab (architektov bilten – architect's bulletin)
1998-11 141-142
GBS Bregenz p. 34-47

ab (architektov bilten – architect's bulletin)
1998-11 141-142
Kern EFH Lochau p. 34-47

ab (architektov bilten – architect's bulletin)
1998-11 141-142
Mozartstraße WA Dornbirn p. 34-47

ab (architektov bilten – architect's bulletin)
1998-11 141-142
Rohrbach 2 WA Dornbirn p. 34-47

AIT (D) 1996-04
LTW Wolfurt p. 45-51

AIT (D) 1997-05
Holz Altenried Hergatz p. 42-43

AIT (D) 1997-05
Burger EFH Bregenz p. 42-43

AIT (D) 1999-01
Kapellenweg WA Feldkirch p. 56-63

AIT (D) 1999-01
LTW Wolfurt p. 45

AIT (D) 1999-03
Kern EFH Lochau p. 42-43

AIT (D) 1999-03
Lindenweg WA Lauterach p. 44-45

AIT (D) 1999-03
Hotel Martinspark Dornbirn p. 40-41

AIT (D) 1999-03
Mitterweg WA Innsbruck p. 36-39

AIT (D) 1999-03
Rohrbach 2 WA Dornbirn p. 44-45

AIT (D) 2000-01
HS Mäder p. 25-33

AIT (D) 2000-06
Achslengut WA St. Gallen p. 16

AIT (D) 2001-04 9607
Hafengebäude Rohner Fussach p. 122-127

AIT (D) 2002-06
Dietmar Eberle Lochau p. 14

AIT (D) 2002-06
Münchener Rück München p.10

Aktuelle Wettbewerbs Scene 1997-06
Salzmagazin Wettbewerb Zürich p. 28

Allgäuer Zeitung (Holzbaupreis 2002)
2002-07 167
Sirch Böhen p. 27

AMC 1996-09 73
LTW Wolfurt p. 86-89

AMC 1998-11
Raiffeisenbank Bregenz p. 51

AMC 1999-6/7 99
Sirch Böhen p. 110

AMC 2000-12
Hotel Martinspark Dornbirn p.104-105

AMC 2001-05 116
Hafengebäude Rohner Fussach p. 96-97

AMC 2002-09 127
BTV Wolfurt p. 114-115

Arc Design 1999-11 11
Holz Altenried Hergatz p. 24-29

Arc Design 1999-11 11
Häusler EFH Hard p. 24-29

Arch+ 1998-12
Kern EFH Lochau p. 66-69

Architécti 2001-01/03
Flatz EFH Schaan p. 74-79

Architécti 2001-01/03
Lohbach WA Innsbruck p. 66-73

Architécti 2001-01/03
HS Mäder p. 58-65

Architects in the World 1996
Alcatel Lustenau p. 142

Architects in the World 1996
LTW Wolfurt p. 142

Architects in the World 1996
Hotel Martinspark Dornbirn p. 142

Architects in the World 1996
Reithalle Fischer Breitbrunn, OÖ p. 142

Architectura viva (E) 1999 64
Nüziders WA p. 22-25

Architectura viva (H) 1996-05/06
Holz Altenried Hergatz p. 34-37

Architectura viva (H) 1998-05/06
Elektro Graf Dornbirn p. 80-83

Architectural design (LINKS)
„New apartment buildings" 2001-04
Mozartstraße WA Dornbirn p. 32-37
Nüziders WA p. 209-217

Architectural Record 2002-02
Lohbach WA Innsbruck p. 164-166

Architectural Review 2000-01 1235
HS Mäder p. 42-45

Architectural Review 2001-06 1252
Lohbach WA Innsbruck p. 70-74

architecture 1997-10
Holz Altenried Hergatz p. 87

architecture 1997-10
Büchel EFH Vaduz p. 85

architecture 1997-10
Elektro Graf Dornbirn p. 88-89

architecture 1997-10
Kern EFH Lochau p. 84-89

Architecture + Techniques 1998 440
Kern EFH Lochau p. 41-43

architecture today 2002-09 131
Flatz EFH Schaan p. 15-18

Architekten heute 1998-10/11/12
Mozartstraße WA Dornbirn p. 58-61

Architektonische Akzente 2001
LTW Wolfurt p. 14-15

Architektonische Akzente 2001
Mildenberg WA Bregenz p. 36-37

architektur 1996-09 5
Zellgasse WA Lustenau p. 24

architektur 1996-11 7
St. Pölten WA p. 50-52

Architektur 1998-04
Mitterweg WA Innsbruck p. 38-41

Architektur 1998-09 6
Mozartstraße WA Dornbirn p. 30-33

Architektur 2000-09
Lohbach WA Innsbruck p. 60-64

Architektur & Bauforum 2002-07/08 219
Fang WA Höchst p. 132

Architektur & Technik 1996-11
Hotel Martinspark Dornbirn p. 20-24

Architektur + Farbe 1996
Saal Mäder p. 8-11

Architektur + Wettbewerbe (A) 1997-12
GBS Bregenz p. 16-19

Architektur + Wettbewerbe (A) 1998-09
Kern EFH Lochau p. 24-27

Architektur + Wettbewerbe (A) 1998-09
Mitterweg WA Innsbruck p. 2-5

Architektur + Wettbewerbe (A) 1998-09
Mozartstraße WA Dornbirn p. 30-33

Architektur + Wettbewerbe (A) 2000-09
Lohbach WA Innsbruck p. 60-64

Architektur Aktuell (A) 1996-02
Elektro Graf Dornbirn p. 106-117

Architektur Aktuell (A) 1996-10
Raiffeisenbank Bregenz p. 86-93

Architektur Aktuell (A) 1997-03
Pfarrheim Satteins p. 92-101

Architektur Aktuell (A) 1997-11
Kern EFH Lochau p. 122-127

Architektur Aktuell (A) 1997-11
Nüziders WA p. 114-121

Architektur Aktuell (A) 1998-05
Mitterweg WA Innsbruck p. 44-45

Architektur Aktuell (A) 1999-10 233/234
HS Mäder p. 140-149

Architektur Einfach Bauen (A) 1996-03
Eulentobel WA Wolfurt p. 58-61

Architektur und Bauforum (A)
2001-01/02 210
Lohbach WA Innsbruck p. 86-87

Architektur und Bauforum (A)
2002-03/04 217
Lohbach WA Innsbruck p. 119

Architektura & Biznes 1998-09 73
Mitterweg WA Innsbruck p. 15

Architektura & Biznes 1998-09 73
Mozartstraße WA Dornbirn p. 19

Architektura & Biznes 1998-09 73
Nüziders WA p. 16-17

Architektura & Biznes 1998-09 73
Rohrbach 2 WA Dornbirn p. 18

archithese 1996-04
Kapellenweg WA Bludenz
Lindenweg WA Lauterach p. 38-41

archithese 1996-06
LTW Wolfurt p. 34

archithese 1998-04
Mitterweg WA Innsbruck p. 38-41

AV 1998 72
Kern EFH Lochau p. 60-63

AV 2000 86
Lohbach WA Innsbruck p. 42-45

AV 2000 86
Residential Rules Nüziders, Dornbirn p. 4-9

AW Architektur + Wettbewerbe
2002-03 189
Flatz EFH Schaan p. 12-15

AW Architektur + Wettbewerbe
2002-03 189
Witt Hamburg p. 68-69

AW Architektur + Wettbewerbe
2002-06 190
Sirch Böhen p. 2-5

Baudoc-Bulletin 2001-01
Flatz EFH Schaan p. 8

Bauen in Beton 2000-01
Häusler EFH Hard p. 6-7

Bauen in Beton 2000-01
LTW Wolfurt

Bauen mit Holz (D) 1997-06
Holz Altenried Hergatz p. 404-408

Bauen mit Holz (D) 2002-05 5
Sirch Böhen p. 6-9

Baumeister (D) 1996-01
Eulentobel WA Wolfurt p. 25

Baumeister (D) 1996-01
Häusler EFH Hard p. 32-35

Baumeister (D) 1996-01
Hotel Martinspark Dornbirn p. 14-18

Baumeister (D) 1996-01
Saal Mäder p. 32-35

Baumeister (D) 1996-03
Rohrbach 1 WA Dornbirn p. 41-43

Baumeister (D) 1996-05
Elektro Graf Dornbirn p. 43-47

Baumeister (D) 1997-03
Raiffeisenbank Bregenz p. 16-21

Baumeister (D) 1998-01
Kern EFH Lochau p. 46-49

Baumeister (D) 1998-06
Nüziders WA p. 34-39

Baumeister (D) 2000-02
HS Mäder p. 32-38

Baumeister (D) 2002-07 99
B. Burger EFH Bregenz p. 10

Baumeister (D) 2002-07 99
Münchener Rück München p. 48-55

Bauwelt 2002-05 17/02
Bahnhof Bern p. 8

Bauwelt (D) 1999-04
Sirch Böhen p. 874-877

Bauwelt (D) 2001-16
Lohbach WA Innsbruck p. 28-32

Bauzeitung 2002-03
Flatz EFH Schaan p. 20-23

Bauzeitung 2002-10
Münchener Rück München p. 32-38

Betonzement 1997
Häusler EFH Hard p. 22-24

Betonzement 2001
Hafengebäude Rohner Fussach p. 46

Betonzement (A) 1998-08
Häusler EFH Hard p. 22-24

Betonzement (A) 1999-02
HS Mäder p. 49

Bolero 1999-10
Holz Altenried Hergatz p. 142

Brutus Magazine, Japan 2001-
Hotel Martinspark Dornbirn p. 111

Casabella (I) 1998-06
Holz Altenried Hergatz p. 68

Casabella (I) 1998-06
Burger B. EFH Bregenz p. 70-73

Casabella (I) 1998-06
Häusler EFH Hard p. 67

Casabella (I) 1998-06
Hölbl EFH Lauterach p. 64

Casabella (I) 1998-06
Hopfengarten WA p. 68

Casabella (I) 1998-06
Kern EFH Lochau p. 78-81

Casabella (I) 1998-06
LTW Wolfurt p. 66

Casabella (I) 1998-06
Negrellistraße WA Lustenau p. 64

Casabella (I) 1998-06
Nüziders WA p. 82-85

Casabella (I) 1998-06
Pfarrheim Satteins p. 74-77

Casabella (I) 1998-06
Raiffeisenbank Bregenz p. 66

Casabella (I) 1998-06
Saal Mäder p. 65

Casabella (I) 2000-08
Sirch Böhen p. 12-15

Casabella (I) 2002-03 698
Lohbach WA Innsbruck p. 54-61

CNDB-Frankreich 2000
HS Mäder p.18-19

Commercial Space (GB) 1996
Hotel Martinspark Dornbirn p. 126-135

Costruire 2002-02 225
Lohbach WA Innsbruck p. 56-61

D'Architectures 2000-04 101
HS Mäder p. 25-26

DAM-Architektur Jahrbuch 1996
Holz Altenried Hergatz p. 52-57

db (D) 1997-02
Fang WA Höchst p. 78-82

db (D) 1998-12
Rohrbach 2 WA Dornbirn p. 70-80

db (Deutsche Bauzeitung) 2001-10 135
Lohbach WA Innsbruck p. 89-95

db (Deutsche Bauzeitung) 2001-12 135
Sagmeister Bregenz p. 88-93

db (deutsche Bauzeitung) 2002-07 136
Münchener Rück München p.17

DBZ 1997-12
Pfarrheim Satteins p. 30 - 36

DBZ 1998-09
HS Mäder p. 55-60

DBZ 1999-01
Mozartstraße WA Dornbirn p. 52-53

DBZ 2001-04
Hotel Martinspark Dornbirn p. 153-156

de Architect 1998-04
Nüziders WA p. 58-63

Detail (D) 1997-07/08
Unterfeld WA Lauterach p. 719-722

Detail (D) 1997-12
HTL Bregenz p. 1344-1347

Detail (D) 1998-10/11
Mitterweg WA Innsbruck p. 1143

Detail (D) (+ Titelbild!) 2002-10 2772
Münchener Rück München p. 1266-1275

Detail (Konzept) 2002-03 2772
Lohbach WA Innsbruck p. 230-253

Detail (Konzept) 2002-03 2772
McNair Berlin p. 344

Deutsches Architektenblatt 2001 - 05
Pfarrheim Satteins p. 15-17

Domus (I) 1996-04
Holz Altenried Hergatz p. 32-35

Domus (I) 2002-04
Flatz EFH Schaan p. 112-121

Domus (I) 2002-09 851
Münchener Rück München p.106-113

Domus, M (Türkei) 2001-04/05
HS Mäder p. 84-91

Einfamilienhäuser 1998-01
Kern EFH Lochau p. 24-29

*Espacios Comerciales Restaurantes
(arco Verlag)* 1996
Hotel Martinspark Dornbirn p. 124-135

Etagehuse of TRAE i Europa 1999-10
Holz Altenried Hergatz p. 100-103

Frankfurter Allgemeine Zeitung
2000-03 57
Nüziders WA p. 54

Gebäudetechnik 2002-01 1/02
Lohbach WA Innsbruck p. 6-12

Gebäudetechnik 2002-01 1/02
Münchener Rück München p. 6-12

GFF-Glas, Fenster, Fassade 1999-02
Pfarrheim Lochau p. 56

Glas Architektur u. Technik (D) 1996-01
GBS Bregenz p. 25-32

Glas Architektur u. Technik (D)
2002-08/09 4/2002
Münchener Rück München p. 28-35

Häuser 1996-05
B. Burger EFH Bregenz p. 48-53

Häuser 1998-06
Kern EFH Lochau p. 46-51

Häuser 2001-02
Agip WA Bregenz p. 130-140

Häuser 2001-02
Holz Altenried Hergatz p. 130-140

Häuser 2001-02
Begle EFH Lochau p. 130-140

Häuser 2001-02
BTV Wolfurt p. 130-140

Häuser 2001-02
Flatz EFH Schaan p. 130-140

Häuser 2001-02 0703
Flughafen Wien-Schwechat p. 130-140

Häuser 2001-02
Häusler EFH Hard p. 130-140

Häuser 2001-02
Hohe Wies Hohenems p. 130-140

Häuser 2001-02
Kern EFH Lochau p. 130-140

Häuser 2001-02
Lohbach WA Innsbruck p. 130-140

Häuser 2001-02
LTW Wolfurt p. 130-140

Häuser 2001-02
HS Mäder p. 130-140

Häuser 2001-02
Messestand Zumtobel Hannover
p. 130-140

Häuser 2001-02
Mildenberg WA Bregenz p. 130-140

Häuser 2001-02
Mozartstraße WA Dornbirn p. 130-140

Häuser 2001-02
Münchener Rück München p. 130-140

Häuser 2001-02
Negrellistraße WA Lustenau p. 130-140

Häuser 2001-02
Nüziders WA p. 130-140

Häuser 2001-02
Reithalle Fischer Breitbrunn, OÖ
p. 130-140

Häuser 2001-02
Rohrbach 1 WA Dornbirn p. 130-140

Häuser 2001-02
Rohrbach 2 WA Dornbirn p. 130-140

Häuser 2001-02 9501
EFH in H p. 130-140

Häuser 2001-05
Hafengebäude Rohner Fussach p. 26

Häuser 2002-05
LTW Wolfurt p. 55

Hochparterre (CH) 2000-08
Flughafen Wien-Schwechat p. 10-17

Hochparterre.wettbewerbe (CH) 2002-03
Bahnhof Bern p. 34-39

Hochparterre.wettbewerbe (CH) 2002-03
ETH Zürich p. 3-5

Holzbau Handbuch 2001-12 1/8/3
Sirch Böhen p. 9

Holzbulletin 2002-09 64
Sirch Böhen p. 1082-1087

Home „The twentieth century house"
1999
Ulmer EFH Schwarzach p. 128-131

Hotel Journal Schweiz 1999
Hotel Martinspark Dornbirn p. 7-11

Ideales Heim 1997-07/08
Büchel EFH Vaduz p. 104-110

Intelligente Architekten 1998-05
Mitterweg WA Innsbruck p. 50-55

Intelligente Architektur 2000-01
HS Mäder p. 25-33

Intelligente Architektur 2001-06/07
Lohbach WA Innsbruck p. 12

Katholische Kirche Vorarlberg 2002 7
Pfarrheim Lochau p. 7

Krems 1999
Stadt im Aufbruch p. 56-58

Kunst aus Österreich 1896-1996 1996
Holz Altenried Hergatz, D p. 292

L'architecture d'aujourd'hui 1999-06
Rohrbach 2 WA Dornbirn p. 38-39

L'architettura Naturale 2000-9
HS Mäder p. 6-13

Le Compagnonnage du Bois 2001
Fang Höchst p. 47

light-live (Das Lichtmagazin) 2000-02
Hotel Martinspark Dornbirn p. 56-59

light-live (Das Lichtmagazin) 2000-02
Saeco Lustenau p. 60-61

Lotus 2000 105
BTV Wolfurt p. 64-65

Materia 2000 31
Kern EFH Lochau p. 56-65

Mauerwerk Atlas (Edition Detail) 2001
Pfarrheim Lochau p. 346-351

Mauerwerk, Das (D) 1997-04
Kapellenweg WA p. 220-227

Mohutop (= Monitor auf russisch)
2002-07 14
Hafengebäude Rohner Fussach p. 106-108

mosaik 1998-02
Stadthaus Hohenems p. 20

Mountain Houses (LOFT) 2000
Büchel EFH Vaduz p. 48-53

Münchner Rück – Perspektiven 2000
Münchener Rück München p. 34-39

Neues Wohnen (D) 1996-05
Rohner EFH p. 88-91

news 1997-03 11
B. Burger EFH Bregenz p. 108

NZZ FOLIO (CH) 1996-08
Holz Altenried Hergatz p. 7

NZZ FOLIO (CH) 2002-04 4
Achslengut St. Gallen p. 74-75

ÖISS 2001-6/00
Schule & Sportstätte p. 13-14

Plannenmap Voor De Basis 1999
Rohrbach 2 WA Dornbirn p. 154-157

Presse 2002-07-27 Spektrum
Münchener Rück München p. 7

Profil 2000-06
Flughafen Wien-Schwechat p. 56

Quaderns 1999
LTW Wolfurt p. 6-15

Quadriga (D) 1999-05
Sirch Böhen p. 20-22

Raum und Wohnen (CH) 1997-04
Häusler EFH Hard p. 66-77

Raum und Wohnen (CH) 1999-05
Büchel EFH Vaduz p. 80-89

Raum und Wohnen (CH) 2002-02
Flatz EFH Schaan p. 30-46

Schulbau in Österreich 1996
GBS Bregenz p. 148-153

SD (Space Design) 1997-02 9702
LTW Wolfurt p. 20

Séquences Bois 1999-04
Holz Altenried Hergatz p. 16

Séquences Bois 2000-01
Kern EFH Lochau p. 12-13

Séquences Bois 2000-02
HS Mäder p. 18-19

Sonnen Energie 2000-02
Lohbach WA Innsbruck p. 33-34

SonntagsZeitung 1999-11 137
Hotel Martinspark Dornbirn

Stammtisch 1998-06
Hotel Martinspark Dornbirn p. 10-11

Standard 2000-09
Büro Zumtobel Dornbirn p. 14

Standard 2001-06
Flughafen Wien-Schwechat p. 11

Stern 2000-10
Nüziders WA p. 142-150

Stern 2002-04 15
Dietmar Eberle Jury Sternstadt p. 98

Süddeutsche Zeitung 2002 108
Münchener Rück München p. 42

Techniques & Architecture 1999-00 446
HS Mäder p. 130

Techniques & Architecture 2001-06/07 454
Lohbach WA Innsbruck p. 92-95

Techniques & Architecture 2002-08/09 461
Münchener Rück München p. 42-45

Trend 2002-06
Hafengebäude Rohner Fussach p. 122

trend spezial 1997-01
Kern EFH Lochau p. 74

Umbauen und renovieren 1998-03/04
Kern EFH Lochau p. 48-49

Ville Giardini 1998-09 339
Kern EFH Lochau p. 3-9

Vivienda nuevas ideas urbanas (H) 1996 211
LTW Wolfurt p. 6-15

Vorarlberger Wirtschaftsblatt 1998-08
LTW Wolfurt p. 10

Werk, Bauen + Wohnen 1998-11
Head Wolfurt p. 8-9

Wettbewerbe (A) 1996-04/05
Bundesgymnasium Feldkirch p. 170

Wettbewerbe (A) 1997-10/11
Lohbach Wettbewerb WA Innsbruck p. 152-153

Wettbewerbe (A) 2000-04/5/6
Flughafen Wien-Schwechat p. 51-88

Wettbewerbe (A) 2000-10/11 198/199
Lohbach WA Innsbruck p. 148

Wettbewerbe (A) 2002-04/5/6 26
ETH Zürich p. 192-193

Wettbewerbe (A) 2002-04/5/6
ETH Zürich p. 192

Wettbewerbe (A) 2002-04/5/6 26
FH Dornbirn p. 70

Wettbewerbe (A) 2002-04/5/6
FH Dornbirn p. 70

Wettbewerbe (A) 2000-10/11 198/199
Mitterweg WA Innsbruck p. 152

Wohnen plus 2001-5 5
Lohbach WA Innsbruck p. 10-12

Wohntex (A) 1997 50
Hotel Martinspark Dornbirn p. 8-9

World Architecture 2001 - 07/08
Lohbach WA Innsbruck p. 83

Zeit 1999-06
Ulmer EFH Schwarzach p. 92

Zement + Beton (A) 1996-02
Rohner EFH Fussach p. 28-31

Zement + Beton (A) 1998-04
Rohrbach 2 WA Dornbirn p. 38-39

Ziegel Presse 2000-11 12
Mildenberg WA Bregenz p. 11

Zlatý rez 1997 14
Saal Mäder p. 20-23

Zuhause Wohnen (D) 1996 Sonderheft
Begle EFH Lochau

Zuschnitt 6 (pro:Holz) 2002-06 2
Sirch Böhen p. 2

EFH Einfamilienhaus | One-Family House
WA   Wohnanlage | Residential Project
FH   Fachhochschule | College
HS   Hauptschule | Secondary School

Bücher und Katloge ab 1996
Books and Catalogues since 1996

Architecture in Austria
(a survey of the 20th century)
Actar Birkhäuser Publishers, Basel 1996
B&E

*Die Stadt über die Stadt bauen –
Städtebauliche Projekte*
European Suisse Verlag, Zürich 1996
B&E

Neue Architektur in Vorarlberg
Sayah Amber
Callwey Verlag, München 1996
B. Burger EFH Bregenz p. 88-89
M. Burger EFH Bregenz/Fluh p. 91-92
Elektro Graf Dornbirn p. 46-47
Eulentobel WA Wolfurt p. 34-35
GBS Bregenz p.16-19
Häusler EFH Hard p. 90-91
LTW Wolfurt p. 44-45
Hotel Martinspark Dornbirn p. 84-87
Negrellistraße WA Lustenau p. 32-33
Pfarrheim Satteins p. 136-139
Raiffeisenbank Bregenz p. 118-121
Saal Mäder p. 132-135

Neue Eingänge
Thomas Drexel
Callwey Verlag, München 1996

Carlo Baumschlager – Dietmar Eberle
Monographie
Liesbeth Waechter-Böhm (Hg.)
Springer Verlag, Wien 1996

Der ideale Grundriß
Thomas Drexel
Callwey Verlag, München 1997

*Editorial Manager – The Architecture
of Minimalism*
F. A. Cerver
Hearst Books International 1997
LTW Wolfurt p.120-129

Bauen in Europa Detail
Edition Springer Verlag, Wien 1998

Dumont – Kunstführer Bodensee
Eva Moser
Dumont Verlag 1998
B. Burger EFH Bregenz p. 259

Individuelle Doppelhäuser+Reihenhäuser
Stephan Isphording , H. Reiners
Callwey Verlag, München 1998
Nofels AH Nofels p. 148-151

Baukunst in Vorarlberg seit 1980
Otto Kapfinger
Kunsthaus Bregenz, VAI, Hatje 1998
HTL Bregenz p. 1.2
Raiffeisenbank Bregenz p. 1.3
Burger B. EFH Bregenz p. 1.10
GBS Bregenz p. 1.18
Burger M. EFH Bregenz p. 1.27
Agip WA Lochau p. 1.29
Pfarrheim Lochau p. 1.33
Burger B. EFH Lochau p. 1.34
Haus H. EFH Hard p. 2.10
Achpark Lauterach p. 2.12
Haus H. EFH Lauterach p. 2.13
LTW Wolfurt p. 2.23
Eulentobel WA Wolfurt p. 2.27
Negrellistraße WA Lustenau p. 3.18
Hotel Martinspark Dornbirn p. 4.4
Pongartstraße WA Dornbirn p. 4.7
Kehlerstraße WA Dornbirn p. 4.8
Rohrbach WA Dornbirn p. 4.11
Elektro Graf Dornbirn p. 4.15
Haus G. EFH Dornbirn p. 4.24
Hohe Wies WA Hohenems p. 5.5
Pfarrheim Mäder, p. 5.9
Pfarrsaal Mäder p. 5.10
Götzis WA Götzis, p. 5.13
Nofels WA Feldkirch p. 7.7
Pfarrheim Satteins p. 8.3
Wohn- u. Geschäftshaus Bludenz, p. 9.7

Eingang – Weg+Raum
Jürgen Knirsch
Alexander Koch Verlagsanstalt 1998
Pfarrheim Satteins p. 55

AA20
Birkhäuser Actar, Barcelona 1999

European House Now
Susan Doubilet, Daralice Boles
Universe Publishing 1999

Home – The Twentieth Century House
Deyan King Sudjic
Laurence Publishers 1999
Baumschlager & Eberle 1992-1999

Lee Uje C3 Design Group
Korea 1999
Büroprojekte Lochau

Baumschlager & Eberle
Giacinto Cerviere
Liberia Edizioni, Melfi (I) 1999

Casas Corprendentes
Paco Asensio
Loft Publications, Barcelona 1999
Kern EFH Lochau p. 134-139

Architektur Szene Österreich
Otto Kapfinger, Walter Zschokke
Anton Pustet Verlag 1999
HS Mäder p. 54-55

Holzfassaden
Ursula Baus, Klaus Siegele
db das buch, dva Stuttgart 1999
Kern EFH Lochau p. 62-65

Metarmorphosen
Christine Weiske, Jürgen Schmitt
Werner Verlag 1999
Kern EFH Lochau p. 52-57

Baumschlager & Eberle
Guim Costa, Moisés Puente
Gustavo Gili SA Editorial, Barcelona 1999

Neue Treppen
Thomas Drexel
Callwey Verlag, München 2000
Kern EFH Lochau p. 88-89

*A Tecnologia na Arquitectura
Contemporanea* Cannatà Michele /
Fernandes Fátima Estar Editoria,
Lisboa 2000
LTW Wolfurt p. 64-77
Lohbach WA Innsbruck p. 78-89

Bauen in Liechtenstein
Patrik Birrer
Patrik Birrer Verlag 2000
Büchel EFH Vaduz p. 342

Design Hotels
Martin M. Kunz
Deutsche Verlags-Anstalt 2000

Carlos Brotos, Josep Miminguez
Links international 2000
Hotel Martinspark Dornbirn p. 56-65

Häuser am Hang
Alfred Steiner
Callwey Verlag, München 2000
B. Burger EFH Bregenz p. 76-79
Büchel EFH Vaduz p. 44-47
M. Burger EFH Bregenz/Fluh p. 158-161

Design Hotels and Destinations
David Kaufman
Lebensart Media Design 2000
Hotel Martinspark Dornbirn

House-ing – Über Wohnbau
Carlo Baumschlager, Dietmar Eberle
Liesbeth Waechter-Böhm (Hg.)
Springer Verlag, Wien 2000

10 x 10
Jaime Salazar
Phaidon Press, New York 2000
GBS Bregenz p. 76
BTV Wolfurt p. 77
Nüziders WA p. 78-79

Interiores Minimalistas
Loft Publications, Barcelona 2001
Elektro Graf Dornbirn p. 82-89

Holztreppen
Ursula Baus, Klaus Siegele
db das buch, DVA Stuttgart 2001
LTW Wolfurt p. 104-105

L'architecture écologique
Dominique Gauzin-Müller
Le Moniteur 2001
Kern EFH Lochau p. 19
HS Mäder p. 60-62
HS Mäder p. 190-195

New Working Spaces
Arian Mostaedi
Broto & Josep, Barcelona 2001
Elektro Graf Dornbirn p. 36

International Architecture
Image Publishing Group Australia, 2002
Lohbach WA Innsbruck p. 187

Architectdocuments – KAZimKuba
Bettina Fraschke
Kasseler Architekturzentrum 2002 Katalog
Rohner EFH Hard p. 7

Atriumhäuser Hofhäuser Wohnhöfe
Hans Weidinger
Deutsche Verlags-Anstalt 2002
Häusler EFH Hard p. 42-45

Bauen in Tirol seit 1980
Otto Kapfinger
Anton Pustet Verlag 2002
Lohbach WA Innsbruck p. 54

Contemporary Doorways
Catherine Slessor
Beazley Mitchell 2002
Sirch Böhen p. 164-167

Licht
H. Kramer / W. von Lom
Rudolf Müller Verlag, Köln 2002
Sirch Böhen p. 200-201

Münchener Rück Umweltmagazin
Oliver Herwig
Münchener Rückversicherung 2002
Sonderdruck